Overcoming Anxiety For Dummies®

Cheat Sheet

Do You Have Anxiety? Check Your Symptoms

Anxiety appears in different forms for different folks. You may find that anxiety affects your thoughts, behaviors, and feelings. Some of the more common symptoms are listed as follows:

You're *thinking* anxiously if you're . . .

- Making dire predictions about the future.
- Thinking you can't cope.
- Frequently worrying about pleasing people.
- Thinking that you need to be perfect.
- Have excessive concerns about not being in control.

You're *behaving* anxiously if you're . . .

- Avoiding many social events.
- Leaving situations that make you anxious.
- Never taking reasonable risks.
- Staying away from feared objects or events, such as flying or spiders.

You're *feeling* anxious if you have . . .

- Butterflies in your stomach
- Dizziness
- Muscle tension
- A racing heart
- A shaky feeling
- Sweaty palms

Warning: The physical symptoms of anxiety may result from medical problems. If you have a number of these symptoms, please see a physician for a checkup.

Quelling Your Anxious Thoughts

When your mind fills with worries and concerns, try asking yourself these questions:

- How will I look at this concern six months from now?
- Have I had this worry before only to discover that what I worried about never actually occurred?
- What evidence truly supports or refutes my worry?
- If a friend of mine had this thought, what advice would I give?
- If the worst happens, could I find a way to cope with it?

See Chapter 5 for sensible answers.

For Dummies: Bestselling Book Series for Beginners

Overcoming Anxiety For Dummies®

Three Quick Ways to Reduce Anxiety

- Engaging in 20 minutes of aerobic exercise.
- Taking a walk with a friend.
- Soaking in a warm bath.

See Chapter 10 for more suggestions.

Calming Your Anxious Feelings

When your body trembles with anxious sensations like sweaty hands, a shaky voice, a racing heart, or an upset stomach, try a few relaxing breaths:

1. Put your hand on your abdomen.
2. Take a slow, deep breath and notice your abdomen expanding.
3. Hold that breath for 5 or 6 seconds.
4. Slowly breathe out and let your shoulders droop.
5. As you exhale, say the word "relax" to yourself.
6. Repeat this type of breath ten times.

See Chapter 12 for more relaxation techniques.

Conquering Your Anxious Behavior

When you find that you're avoiding important life events or opportunities, it's time to take action. To begin, try out the following:

1. **Analyze what you're avoiding.**

   For example, if you're afraid of social gatherings, think about every component of what you fear — talking, eating in front of others, the size of the crowd, losing control, and/or approaching other people.

2. **Break your avoidance into little pieces.**

   For example, social gatherings come in all sizes and degree of difficulty.

3. **Rank those little pieces from least to most distressing.**

   You may not feel anxious about family gatherings, but the company picnic arouses a little more anxiety, and a party with people that you don't know well terrifies you.

4. **Take small steps and conquer each one of the steps before moving on.**

See Chapter 8 for details on coming to terms with your fears.

For Dummies: Bestselling Book Series for Beginners

Praise for Overcoming Anxiety For Dummies

"In *Overcoming Anxiety For Dummies,* Elliott and Smith have provided a timely and informative description of the reasons why people become anxious and what they can do about it. Clinical science has made great strides in the last several decades in the treatment of anxiety, and Elliott and Smith have done a marvelous job of describing those advances in a clear and simple fashion that can be used by anyone. This is an excellent self-help manual — clear, concise, and comprehensive. I recommend it for anyone who has ever been troubled by anxiety in all its many forms."

> — Steven D. Hollon, PhD, Former President, Association for the Advancement of Behavior Therapy, Professor of Psychology, Vanderbilt University, Nashville, Tennessee

"Elliott and Smith have captured the essence of anxiety management. They have the wise clinician's perspective that confronting fear and challenging the sources of fear is a job of a lifetime. Their guide will be consumed by everyone dealing with the vagaries of life."

> — Dr. Brian F. Shaw, Chief, Community Health and Knowledge Transfer, Community Health Systems Resource Group, The Hospital for Sick Children, Toronto, Ontario, Canada

"*Overcoming Anxiety For Dummies* offers a comprehensive and up-to-date review of adaptive ways to think about and possibly overcome anxiety. It offers practical methods to understand and cope with anxiety, based on recent and well-researched psychological and medical knowledge. A particular strength of this book is that it recognizes that some degree of anxiety is a normal and healthy part of living. There is wisdom here about learning from the tension and anxiety in our lives, rather than simply trying to eliminate it from our experience."

> — Keith S. Dobson, PhD, Professor of Clinical Psychology, Department of Psychology, University of Calgary, Calgary, Alberta, Canada

"This is an excellent blend of the latest scientific evidence and a wealth of clinical experience by the authors on how to deal with the stresses and anxieties of life. It is a book that offers hope to those who struggle, for there is much that can be done to relieve the pain that many experience from anxiety and related problems. This book should be of use to those who seek relief and to those who want to live life to the fullest. The authors have performed a real service for us all."

— C. Eugene Walker, PhD, University of Oklahoma
Medical School, Edmond, Oklahoma

Overcoming
Anxiety
FOR

DUMMIES®

Overcoming Anxiety FOR DUMMIES®

by Charles H. Elliott, PhD
and Laura L. Smith, PhD

Wiley Publishing, Inc.

Overcoming Anxiety For Dummies®

Published by
Wiley Publishing, Inc.
909 Third Avenue
New York, NY 10022
www.wiley.com

Copyright © 2003 by Wiley Publishing, Inc., Indianapolis, Indiana

Published by Wiley Publishing, Inc., Indianapolis, Indiana

Published simultaneously in Canada

For general information on our other products and services or to obtain technical support, please contact our Customer Care Department within the U.S. at 800-762-2974, outside the U.S. at 317-572-3993, or fax 317-572-4002.

Wiley also publishes its books in a variety of electronic formats. Some content that appears in print may not be available in electronic books.

Library of Congress Control Number: 2002110284

ISBN: 0-7645-5447-6

Manufactured in the United States of America

10 9 8 7 6 5 4

1B/RQ/RQ/QS/IN

About the Authors

Charles H. Elliott, PhD, is a clinical psychologist and a member of the faculty at the Fielding Graduate Institute. He is a Founding Fellow in the Academy of Cognitive Therapy, an internationally recognized organization that certifies cognitive therapists for treating anxiety, panic attacks, and other emotional disorders. In his private clinical practice, he specializes in the treatment of anxiety and mood disorders. Elliott is the former president of the New Mexico Society of Biofeedback and Behavioral Medicine. He previously served as Director of Mental Health Consultation-Liaison Service at the University of Oklahoma Health Sciences Center. He later was an Associate Professor in the psychiatry department at the University of New Mexico School of Medicine. In addition, he has written many articles and book chapters in the area of cognitive behavior therapies. He has made numerous presentations nationally and internationally on new developments in assessment and therapy of emotional disorders. He is coauthor of *Why Can't I Get What I Want?* (Davies-Black, 1998; A Behavioral Science Book Club Selection), *Why Can't I Be the Parent I Want to Be?* (New Harbinger Publications, 1999), and *Hollow Kids: Recapturing the Soul of a Generation Lost to the Self-Esteem Myth* (Prima, 2001).

Laura L. Smith, PhD, is a clinical psychologist at Presbyterian Medical Group, Albuquerque, New Mexico. At the Presbyterian Behavioral Medicine Clinic, she specializes in the assessment and treatment of both adults and children with anxiety and other mood disorders. She is an adjunct faculty member at the Fielding Graduate Institute. Formerly, she was the clinical supervisor for a regional educational cooperative. In addition, she has presented on new developments in cognitive therapy to both national and international audiences. Dr Smith is coauthor of *Hollow Kids* (Prima, 2001) and *Why Can't I Be the Parent I Want to Be?* (New Harbinger Publications, 1999).

Dedication

We dedicate this book to our children: Alli, Brian, Sara, and Trevor. And to our parents: William Thomas Smith (1914–1999), Edna Louise Smith, Joe Bond Elliott, and Suzanne Wieder Elliott.

Authors' Acknowledgments

We would like to thank, as usual, our families and friends, once again neglected. We promise: This really is the last book for a while, although we realize you don't believe us.

Thanks also to our enthusiastic agents, Ed and Elizabeth Knappman, who have shown consistent faith in our writing. We appreciate the expertise and professionalism of our editors at John Wiley & Sons, Inc.; special thanks to Norm Crampton, Esmeralda St. Clair, and Natasha Graf.

Thanks to Tracie Antonuk for expert library and research assistance, Audrey Hite for keeping the house in order, Scott Love for designing our Web site and keeping our computers up and running, Diana Montoya-Boyer for keeping us organized and gathering materials, and Karen Villanueva, our personal publicist.

We took our own advice from Chapter 9 and simplified our lives. Although we love our dogs Joey and Quinton, they sometimes create work for us. So we hired Poop Busters for, well, let's just say useful help. And we streamlined our time and upgraded our diets from the usual takeout disasters by signing up a personal chef, The Dancing Chef. Thanks to both of these wonderful services!

Finally, we appreciate all that we've learned from our many clients over the years. They have provided us with a greater understanding of the problems those with anxiety face, as well as the brave struggle involved in overcoming anxiety.

Drs. Elliott and Smith are available for speaking engagements and workshops. You may visit our Web site at www.PsychAuthors.com. Interested readers also can find a list of background literature relevant to *Overcoming Anxiety For Dummies* at our Web site.

Publisher's Acknowledgments

We're proud of this book; please send us your comments through our Dummies online registration form located at www.dummies.com/register/.

Some of the people who helped bring this book to market include the following:

Acquisitions, Editorial, and Media Development

Project Editor: Norm Crampton

Acquisitions Editor: Natasha Graf

Copy Editor: Esmeralda St. Clair

Technical Editor: Susan Ball, PhD

Editorial Manager: Christine Beck

Editorial Assistant: Carol Strickland

Cover Photo: © The Image Bank/Alain Daussin

Author Photo: Matt Foster

Cartoons: Rich Tennant, www.the5thwave.com

Production

Project Coordinator: Nancee Reeves

Layout and Graphics: Amanda Carter, Joyce Haughey, LeAndra Johnson, Stephanie D. Jumper, Barry Offringa, Julie Trippetti, Jeremey Unger

Special Art: Kathryn Born

Proofreader: TECHBOOKS Production Services

Indexer: TECHBOOKS Production Services

Publishing and Editorial for Consumer Dummies

> **Diane Graves Steele,** Vice President and Publisher, Consumer Dummies

> **Joyce Pepple,** Acquisitions Director, Consumer Dummies

> **Kristin A. Cocks,** Product Development Director, Consumer Dummies

> **Michael Spring,** Vice President and Publisher, Travel

> **Brice Gosnell,** Publishing Director, Travel

> **Suzanne Jannetta,** Editorial Director, Travel

Publishing for Technology Dummies

> **Andy Cummings,** Acquisitions Director

Composition Services

> **Gerry Fahey,** Vice President of Production Services

> **Debbie Stailey,** Director of Composition Services

Contents at a Glance

Table of Contents

Introduction

● ●

*W*e were grade-school children in the '50s and '60s. We both recall school alarm bells ringing and teachers ordering us to crouch under wooden school desks with hands covering our heads. Somehow, this was to protect us from an imminent nuclear attack. Most kids begged their parents to dig deep and build bomb shelters. We all knew the futility of crouching under our desks. We worried.

Grade-school children today worry as well. They worry about school shooters and terrorist attacks. Our kids beg us to keep them safe. Like us, our children worry about the futility of huddling in closets during school-safety drills and their parents buying gas masks. We all worry.

So today's world gives us plenty to worry about, and it always has. But just as we don't want to become victims of terror, we can't let ourselves become victims of anxiety. Anxiety clouds our thinking and weakens our resolve to live life to the fullest. We realize that some anxiety is realistic and inescapable; yet we can keep it from dominating our lives. Even under duress, we can preserve a degree of serenity; we can hold on to our humanity, vigor, and zest for life. We can love and laugh.

Because we believe in our collective resilience, we take a humorous and at times irreverent approach to conquering anxiety. Our message is based on sound, scientifically proven methods. But we won't bore you with the scientific details. Instead, we present a clear, rapid-fire set of strategies for beating back anxiety and winning the war against worry.

About This Book

We have three goals in writing this book. First, we want you to understand just what anxiety is and its different forms. Second, we think that knowing what's good about anxiety and what's bad about it is good for you. Finally, we cover what you're probably most interested in — discovering how to overcome your anxiety or how to help someone else who has anxiety.

Unlike most books, you don't have to start on page one and read straight through. Use the extensive Table of Contents to pick and choose what you want to read. Don't worry about reading parts in any particular order. For example, if you really don't want much information about the who, what, when, where, and why's of anxiety, and whether you have it, go ahead and skip Part I. However, we encourage you to at least skim Part I because it contains fascinating facts and information as well as ideas for getting started.

What Not to Read

Not only do you not have to read each and every chapter in order or at all, you don't have to read each and every icon or aside. We try to give you plenty of current information and facts about anxiety. Some may not interest you — so don't get too anxious about skipping around.

Foolish Assumptions

Who might pick up this book? We assume, probably foolishly, that you or someone you love suffers from some type of problem with anxiety or worry. We also hope that you want information to help tame tension and overcome anxiety. Finally, we imagine that you're curious about a variety of helpful strategies to choose from that can fit your lifestyle and personality.

How This Book Is Organized

Overcoming Anxiety For Dummies is organized into six parts and 22 chapters. Right now, we tell you a little about each part.

Part I: Detecting and Exposing Anxiety

In these first two chapters, you find out a great deal about anxiety — from who gets it to why people become anxious. We explain the different kinds of anxiety disorders; they're not all the same, and we tell you who is most susceptible and why.

In Chapter 3, we help you to clear the roadblocks to change. You discover the most common reasons that people resist working on their anxiety and what to do about it if you find yourself stuck. Chapter 4 gives you ways to track your progress.

Part II: The Thought Remedies

In Part II, you see how thinking contributes to anxious feelings. We show you a variety of proven strategies on how to transform anxious thoughts into calm thoughts. And you discover how the words that you use can increase anxiety and how simply changing your vocabulary decreases anxiety.

Part III: Anti-Anxiety Actions

One of the best ways to tackle anxiety is by taking action. No wimps here. We show you how to stare your fears in the face and conquer them. We also explore other anti-anxiety actions, such as changing your lifestyle.

Part IV: Focusing on Feeling

In this part, we offer a cornucopia of ideas for quelling anxious feelings. These ideas range from special breathing techniques to imaginary journeys to using various potions to relax your body and mind. We give you the latest research findings on what works and what doesn't among herbs, supplements, and medications.

Part V: Helping Others with Anxiety

What do you do when someone you love worries too much? We give you the tools to understand the differences between normal fear and anxiety in children. We also provide some simple guidelines to help out anxious kids. Next, we look at how you can help a significant adult in your life with anxiety. As a coach or simply a cheerleader, you can help your friend or family member conquer anxiety.

Part VI: The Part of Tens

If you're looking for a quick fix or a simple review, take a look at these helpful lists. You can read about Ten Ways to Stop Anxiety Quickly, Ten Anxiety Busters That Just Don't Work, Ten Ways to Deal With Relapse, and Ten Signs That You Need Professional Help.

Icons Used in This Book

 This icon represents a particular tip for getting rid of anxiety.

 The Anxiety Quiz icon lets you know when it's time to take a quiz. (Don't worry; the quizzes aren't graded.)

 This icon appears when we want your attention. Please read for critical information.

 The Tip icon alerts you to important insights or clarifications.

 These icons appear when you need to be careful or seek professional help.

Where to Go from Here

Overcoming Anxiety For Dummies offers you the best advice based on scientific research in the area of anxiety disorders. We know that if you practice the techniques and strategies provided throughout, you're pretty likely to feel calmer. For most people, this book should be a complete guide to fighting frenzy and fear.

However, some stubborn forms of anxiety need more care and attention. For those whose anxiety and worry significantly gets in the way of work or play, get help. Start with your family doctor. Anxiety can be conquered; don't give up.

Part I
Detecting and Exposing Anxiety

The 5th Wave   By Rich Tennant

"Sudden perspiration, shallow breathing, and a rapid heart rate are all signs of anxiety. The fact that these symptoms only occur when the pool boy is working in your backyard, however, raises some questions."

In this part . . .

Exploring the ins and outs of anxiety, we discuss the anxiety epidemic that's going around and show how anxiety affects the entire body. In this part, you can find all the major categories of anxiety disorders and overview some of what you can do to reduce anxiety. You'll discover how you can easily get stuck tackling your anxiety, and we tell you how to keep that from happening. Finally, we give you ways to track your anxiety, and you can look forward to the progress that you'll surely make toward reducing your anxiety.

Chapter 1

Analyzing and Attacking Anxiety

• •

• •

Anxiety, stress, and worries. Everyone has these experiences sometimes. But for a surprising number of people, anxiety causes pain. Anxiety creates havoc in the home, destroys relationships, causes employees to lose time from work, and prevents people from living full, productive lives.

When people talk about their anxiety, you may hear any one or all of the following descriptions:

✔ I can't come up with the right words to describe my feelings. It's like dread and doom but a thousand times worse. I want to scream, cry for help, but I'm paralyzed. It's the worst feeling in the world.

✔ When my panic attacks begin, I feel tightness in my chest. It's as though I'm drowning, suffocating, and I begin to sweat; the fear is overwhelming. I feel like I'm going to die, and I have to sit down because I might faint.

✔ I'm lonely. I've always been painfully shy. I want friends, but I'm too embarrassed to call anyone. I guess I feel like anyone I call will think I'm not worth talking to.

> ✔ I wake with worry every day, even on the weekends. I never feel like I'm done — there's always a list — always responsibility. I worry all the time. Sometimes, when it's really bad, I think about going to sleep and never waking up.

In this chapter, you find out how to recognize the symptoms of anxiety. We clarify the costs of anxiety — both personal and societal. We briefly overview the treatments presented in greater detail in later chapters and give you a tool for choosing the one that may fit your personality best as a way to begin overcoming anxiety. You also get a glimpse of how to help if someone you care about has anxiety.

Anxiety: Everybody's Doing It

Anxiety is the most common of all the so-called mental disorders. Estimates suggest that somewhere around 25,000,000 Americans suffer from an anxiety disorder in any given year, and some calculate that as many as 25 percent of Americans may suffer from an anxiety disorder at one point or another over a lifetime. Statistics around the world vary somewhat from country to country, but anxiety is the most common mental disorder worldwide. And even if you don't have an actual anxiety disorder, you may experience more anxiety than you wish.

In other words, you definitely aren't alone if you have unwanted anxiety. And the numbers have grown over the years. There's never been a time in history in which anxiety tormented more people than it does today. Why?

Life has never been as complicated as it is today. The workweek has grown longer rather than shorter. Broken and blended families create increased stresses to manage. Television news blares the latest horrors into your living room. Newspapers and magazines chronicle crime, war, and corruption. Terrorism has crossed the oceans, landed full force on our shores, and escalated to new heights. The media's portrayal of these modern plagues includes full-color images with unprecedented, graphic detail.

Unfortunately, as stressful and anxiety arousing as the world is today, only a minority of those suffering from anxiety seek treatment. That's a problem because anxiety causes not only emotional pain and distress, but also even death — given that anxiety sometimes contributes to suicide. Furthermore, anxiety costs society as a whole, billions of dollars.

The lingering effects of 9-11

How many hundreds of times did you witness the destruction of the World Trade Center on television? A survey taken almost a half-year following the September 2001 attack indicated nearly one quarter of Americans reported feeling more anxious or depressed than at any previous time in their lives. Furthermore, about 16 percent attribute their worsened mood directly to the events of September 11. Not surprisingly, New Yorkers report similar feelings but in larger numbers and with greater intensity.

The good survey news is that about three quarters of Americans have since attempted to simplify their lives, gain perspective, and focus on reprioritizing their goals. Perhaps out of tragedy, it's possible to reclaim new purpose and meaning.

Tabulating the Costs of Anxiety

Anxiety costs. It costs the sufferer in emotional, physical, and financial terms. But it doesn't stop there. Anxiety also incurs a financial burden for everyone. Stress, worry, and anxiety disrupt relationships, work, and family.

What does anxiety cost you?

Obviously, if you have a problem with anxiety, you experience the cost of distressed, anxious feelings. Anxiety feels lousy. You don't need to read a book to know that. But did you know that untreated anxiety runs up a tab in other ways as well? These costs include

- **A physical toll:** Higher blood pressure, tension headaches, and gastrointestinal symptoms can affect your body. In fact, recent research found that certain types of chronic anxiety disorders change the makeup of your brain's structures.

- **A toll on your kids:** Parents with anxiety more often have anxious children. This is due in part to genetics, but it's also because kids learn from observation.

- **FAT!** Anxiety and stress increase the stress hormone cortisol. *Cortisol* causes fat storage in the abdominal area, thus increasing the risk of heart disease and stroke. Stress also leads to increased eating.

✔ **More trips to the doctor:** That's because those with anxiety frequently experience worrisome physical symptoms. In addition, anxious people often worry a great deal about their health.

✔ **Relationship problems:** People with anxiety frequently feel irritable. Sometimes, they withdraw emotionally or do the opposite and dependently cling to their partners.

✔ **Downtime:** Those with anxiety disorders miss work more often than other people, usually as an effort to temporarily quell their distress.

Adding up the cost to society

Anxiety costs many billions of dollars worldwide. A U.S. government report says that anxiety costs more than depression, schizophrenia, or any other emotional problem. The annual tab is estimated at more than 65 billion dollars. The United Kingdom spent 32 billion pounds (approximately 47 billion U.S. dollars) on mental health care in 2002, a huge portion of which was spent on anxiety related problems. Even countries that spend little on mental health care incur substantial costs from anxiety disorders. These costs include

✔ Decreased productivity

✔ Healthcare costs

✔ Medications

Decreased productivity is sometimes due to suicide or the other adverse effects of anxiety on a person's health. But the financial loss from downtime and healthcare costs doesn't include the dollars lost to substance abuse, which many of those with anxiety disorders turn to in order to deal with their anxiety. Thus, directly and indirectly, anxiety extracts a colossal toll on both the person who experiences it, as well as society at large.

The heartbreak of anxiety

Two recent studies have found a critical relationship between anxiety and heart disease. One investigation at Duke University divided cardiac patients into three groups: an exercise group, a stress management group, and a care-as-usual group. After five years, the stress management group had fewer additional heart-related problems than the other two groups. Although this was a small study, one researcher concluded that managing stress and anxiety is one of the most powerful tools in fighting heart disease. The other study, published in the January 2002 issue of the journal *Stroke*, found that men who suffer from anxiety and depression are much more likely to die from strokes than those without these psychological problems.

Recognizing the Symptoms of Anxiety

You may not know if you suffer from anxiety or an anxiety disorder. That's because anxiety involves a rather wide range of symptoms. Each person experiences a slightly different constellation of these symptoms. And your specific constellation determines what kind of anxiety disorder you may have. We discuss the various types of anxiety disorders in detail in Chapter 2.

For now, you should know that some signs of anxiety appear in the form of *thoughts or beliefs*. Other indications of anxiety manifest themselves in *bodily sensations*. Still other symptoms show up in various kinds of anxious *behaviors*. Some people experience anxiety signs in all three ways, while others only perceive their anxiety in one or two areas.

Thinking anxiously

In Part II, we discuss anxious thinking in great detail. For starters, folks with anxiety generally think in ways that differ from the way that other people think. You're probably thinking anxiously if you experience:

- **Approval addiction:** If you're an approval addict, you worry a great deal about what other people think about you.

- **Living in the future and predicting the worst:** When you do this, you think about everything that lies ahead and assume the worst possible outcome.

- **Magnification:** People who magnify the importance of negative events usually feel more anxious than other people do.

- **Perfectionism:** If you're a perfectionist, you assume that any mistake means total failure.

- **Poor concentration:** Anxious people routinely report that they struggle with focusing their thoughts. Short-term memory sometimes suffers as well.

- **Racing thoughts:** Thoughts that zip through your mind in a stream of almost uncontrollable worry and concern.

Finding anxiety in your body

Almost all people with severe anxiety experience a range of physical effects. These sensations don't simply occur in your head; they're as real as this

TIP

book you're holding. The responses to anxiety vary considerably from person to person and include:

- Accelerated heart beat
- A spike in blood pressure
- Dizziness
- Fatigue
- Gastrointestinal upset
- General aches and pains
- Muscle tension or spasms
- Sweating

These are simply the temporary effects that anxiety exerts on your body. Chronic anxiety left untreated poses serious risks to your health as well. We discuss the general health effects in greater detail in Chapter 2.

Behaving anxiously

We have three words to describe anxious behavior — avoidance, avoidance, and avoidance. Anxious people inevitably attempt to stay away from the things that make them anxious. Whether it's snakes, heights, crowds, freeways, parties, paying bills, reminders of bad times, or public speaking, anxious people search for ways out.

In the short run, avoidance lowers anxiety. It can make you feel a little better. However, in the long run, avoidance actually maintains and heightens anxiety. We discuss the role that avoidance plays to increase your anxiety in the "Avoiding only worsens anxiety" sidebar in Chapter 2. We give you ways of dismantling avoidance in Chapter 8.

One of the most common and obvious examples of anxiety-induced avoidance is how people react to their phobias. Have you ever seen the response of a spider phobic when confronting one of the critters? Usually, such folks hastily retreat.

Name that phobia!

Phobias are one of the most common types of anxiety disorder, and we discuss them in detail in Chapter 2. A phobia is an excessive, disproportionate fear of a relatively harmless situation or thing. Sometimes, the phobia poses some risk, but the person's reaction clearly exceeds the danger. Do you know the technical names for phobias? Draw arrows from the common name of each phobia to the corresponding technical name. See how many you get right. The answers are printed upside down at the bottom.

Be careful, if you have *triskaidekaphobia* (fear of the number thirteen) because we're giving you thirteen phobias to match!

Technical Name	Means a fear of _____
1. Ophidiophobia	A. Growing old
2. Zoophobia	B. Sleep
3. Gerascophobia	C. The mind
4. Acrophobia	D. Imperfection
5. Lachanophobia	E. Snakes
6. Hypnophobia	F. Fear
7. Atelophobia	G. New things
8. Phobophobia	H. Animals
9. Sesquipedalophobia	I. Small things
10. Neophobia	J. Mirrors
11. Psychophobia	K. Heights
12. Tapinophobia	L. Long words
13. Eisoptrophobia	M. Vegetables

Answers: 1-e, 2-h, 3-a, 4-k, 5-m, 6-b, 7-d, 8-f, 9-l, 10-g, 11-c, 12-i, 13-j.

Seeking Help for Your Anxiety

As we said earlier in this chapter, most people choose to simply live with anxiety rather than seek help. Some people worry that treatment won't work. Or they believe that the only effective treatment out there is medication, and they hate the possibility of side effects. Others fret about the costs of getting help. And still others have concerns that tackling their anxiety can cause their fears to increase so much that they couldn't stand it.

Well, stop adding worry to worry. You can significantly reduce your anxiety through a variety of interesting strategies. Many of these don't have to cost a single cent. And if one doesn't work, try another. Most people find that at least a couple of the approaches that we review work for them.

Untreated anxiety may cause long-term health problems. It doesn't make sense to avoid doing something about your anxiety.

Matching symptoms and therapies

Anxiety symptoms appear in three different spheres, as follows:

- ✔ Thinking symptoms: The thoughts that run through your mind.
- ✔ Behaving symptoms: The things you do in response to anxiety.
- ✔ Feeling symptoms: How your body reacts to anxiety.

Treatment corresponds to each of the following three areas.

Thinking therapies

One of the most effective treatments for a wide range of emotional problems, known as *cognitive therapy,* deals with the way you think about, perceive, and interpret everything that's important to you including

- ✔ Your views about yourself
- ✔ The events that happen to you in life
- ✔ Your future

When people feel unusually anxious and worried, they almost inevitably distort the way they think about these things. That distortion actually causes much of their anxiety.

For example, **Luann,** a junior in college, gets physically ill before every exam. She throws up, has diarrhea, and her heart races. She fantasizes that she will fail each and every test she takes and eventually the college will dismiss her. Yet, her lowest grade to date has been a B-. A cognitive approach would help her capture the negative predictions and catastrophic outcomes that run through her mind. Then it would guide her to search for evidence about her true performance and a more realistic appraisal of the chances of her actually failing.

As simple as this approach sounds, hundreds of studies have found that it works well to reduce anxiety. Part II of this book describes various cognitive or thinking therapy techniques.

Behaving therapies

Another highly effective type of therapy is known as *behavior therapy*. As the name suggests, this approach deals with actions that you can take and behaviors that you can incorporate to alleviate your anxiety. Some actions are fairly straightforward:

- ✔ Get more exercise (see Chapter 10)
- ✔ Simplify your life (see Chapter 9)
- ✔ Get more sleep (see Chapter 11)

On the other hand, one type of action that can feel a little scary is *exposure* — breaking your fears down into small steps and facing them one at a time. Exposure, however, involves a little more than this, as you can see in Chapter 8.

Feeling therapies — soothing the inner storm

Anxiety sets off a storm of distressing physical symptoms, such as a racing heartbeat, upset stomach, muscle tension, sweating, dizziness, and so on. We have a variety of suggestions for helping quell this turmoil. You may choose herbal remedies. If you want more information about herbs for anxiety, see Chapter 14. Some of these appear to work pretty well, while others are more hype than hope.

Do you have five minutes to spare in your daily schedule? If so, you can try a number of our five-minute strategies for relaxation. The key to all relaxation techniques is simple — if you're relaxed, it's pretty hard to feel anxious. See Chapter 12 for quick and easy ways to relax.

On the other hand, some folks choose to take medications. If that's your choice, Chapter 15 tells you about the available options. The decision to take medications involves a variety of costs and benefits that you should weigh carefully. We give you the tools for making this decision.

Choosing where to start

We organized this book so that you can pick anywhere to start that you want. But you might wonder whether one set of strategies would work better for you than another. While we can't really predict with certainty what will work best for you, we do have a guide for helping choose the approach that might feel most compatible for your initial efforts. On the other hand, if you just want to read the book from front to back, that's fine, too.

In the following anxiety quiz, check all the items that apply to you. If you check off more items in one category than the others, you may consider starting with the part of this book that applies to it. For example, Part II of this book is designed especially for thinkers and presents the thinking therapies, also known as cognitive therapy; Part III is aimed at doers and provides the essentials of behavior therapy and other direct actions that you can take against anxiety; Part IV focuses on feelers who may profit most by starting with strategies for quelling troubling bodily sensations and feelings. If you check an equal number of items for two or more categories, ask yourself which one seems most like you and start there.

Thinkers (see Part II for starting work on this problem)

__ I like to analyze problems.

__ I like to carefully consider pros and cons.

__ I enjoy dealing with facts.

__ I like to be logical.

__ I like to plan things in advance.

Doers (see Part III)

__ If I have a problem, I take action right away.

__ I love getting things done.

__ I'm energetic.

__ I'm an active person.

__ I hate sitting still with nothing to do.

Feelers (see Part IV)

__ I am always aware of every discomfort in my body.

__ I hate the feeling of anxiety.

__ I love to immerse myself in the arts.

__ Music speaks to me.

__ I love the feeling of a massage or a hot bath.

Finding the right help

So if you decide that you need help, where do you go? We suppose it's not too presumptuous to assume that because you're reading this book, either you or someone you know suffers from anxiety. And you'd probably like to tackle anxiety on your own. This *is* a self-help book after all.

The good news is that self-help does work. A number of studies support the idea that people can deal with important, difficult problems without seeking the services of a professional. People clearly benefit from self-help. They get better and stay better.

Then again, sometimes self-help efforts fall short. In the Part of Tens, Chapter 22 provides ten critical signs that indicate a likely need for professional help. And if you do need professional consultation, many qualified therapists will work with you on the ideas contained in this book.

Most mental health professionals will appreciate the comprehensive nature of the material and the fact that most of the strategies are based on well-proven methods. If research has yet to support the value of a particular approach, we take care to let you know that. At the same time, in Chapter 20, we review ten over-hyped techniques of dubious value. That's because we think you're much better off sticking with strategies known to work and avoiding those that don't.

Friends and family represent one more source of possible help. In Chapters 17 and 18, we discuss how to help a child or an adult who has anxiety. If you're asking a friend or family member to help, you both may want to read that section, and possibly more. Sometimes, friends and family can help you even if you're also working with a professional and making your own efforts.

Whichever sources, techniques, or strategies you select, overcoming anxiety will be one of the most rewarding challenges that you ever undertake. The endeavor could scare you at first, and the going may start slow and have its ups and downs, but stick with it, and we know that you'll find a way out of the quicksand of anxiety onto the solid ground of serenity.

Chapter 2

Examining Anxiety: What's Normal, What's Not

The physical symptoms of anxiety can be a part of normal, everyday experience. But sometimes they signal something more serious. How about you? Have you ever thought that you were suffering a nervous breakdown or worried that you were going crazy?

In this chapter, we help you figure out what's going on — whether you're suffering from an anxiety disorder — normal anxiety — or something else. You'll also see how your body responds to anxiety.

To demonstrate the difference between something so serious as an anxiety disorder and a normal reaction, read the following description and imagine ten minutes in the life of Tiffany.

At first, **Tiffany** feels restless and slightly bored. Standing, she shifts her weight from foot to foot. Walking forward a little, she notices a slight tightening of her chest. Her breathing quickens. She feels an odd mixture of excitement and mounting tension. She sits down and does her best to relax, but the anxiety continues to intensify. Her body suddenly jerks forward; she grips the sides of her seat and clenches her teeth to choke back a scream. Her stomach feels like it might come up through her throat. Then it settles down. She feels her heart race and her face flush. Her stomach seems to push up into her throat again. Tiffany's emotions run wild. Dizziness, fear, and a rushing sensation overtake her. It all comes in waves — one after the other.

You may wonder what's wrong with poor Tiffany. Maybe she has an anxiety disorder. Or possibly she's suffering a nervous breakdown. Perhaps she's going crazy.

But Tiffany spent those ten minutes plus many more at an amusement park. First, she waited in line to buy a ticket and felt bored. Then she handed her ticket to the attendant and buckled herself into a roller coaster. After that, we guess you understand the rest of her experience. Tiffany has no anxiety disorder; she isn't suffering a nervous breakdown, and she isn't going crazy. As her story illustrates, the symptoms of anxiety can be a normal reaction to life events.

Presenting the Seven Main Types of Anxiety

Anxiety comes in various forms. The word *anxious* is a derivative of the Latin word *angere,* meaning to strangle or choke. A sense of choking or tightening in the throat or chest is a common symptom of anxiety. However, anxiety also involves symptoms, such as sweating, trembling, nausea, and racing heartbeat; anxiety may also involve fears — fear of losing control and fear of illness or of dying. In addition, people with excessive anxiety avoid various situations, people, animals, or objects to an unnecessary degree. Psychologists and psychiatrists have compiled a list of seven major categories of anxiety disorders as follows:

- Generalized Anxiety Disorder (GAD)
- Social Phobia
- Panic Disorder
- Agoraphobia
- Specific Phobia
- Post-Traumatic Stress Disorder (PTSD)
- Obsessive-Compulsive Disorder (OCD)

In this chapter, we describe the signs and indications of each of the major types of anxiety disorders. Medical students are renowned for thinking they have developed every new disease they study. Readers of psychology books sometimes do the same thing. Don't freak out if you or someone you love experiences some of these symptoms. Almost everyone has a few.

You don't need a full-blown diagnosis to feel that you have some trouble with anxiety. Many people have more anxiety than they want but don't completely fit the category of having an official anxiety disorder.

Only a mental health professional can tell you for certain what type of anxiety you have because various other disorders can look similar, including medical problems discussed later in this chapter in the "Investigating medical anxiety imposters" section.

Although we provide the major signs and symptoms of each type of anxiety so that you can get a general idea of what category your anxiety may fall under, to really understand where your particular anxiety fits, you need to see a professional (see Chapter 22). If you do seek professional help, the ideas in this book can assist you in alleviating your problems with anxiety.

Generalized Anxiety Disorder: The common cold of anxiety

Some people refer to *Generalized Anxiety Disorder* as the common cold of the anxiety disorders. Generalized Anxiety Disorder, also known as GAD, afflicts more people throughout the world than any other anxiety disorder. So if you or a loved one has it, you're in good company. GAD involves a long-lasting, almost constant state of tension and worry. Realistic worries don't mean you have GAD. For example, if you worry about money and you just lost your job, that's not GAD — it's a real-life problem. But if you constantly worry about money and your name is Bill Gates, you just may have GAD!

You may have GAD if your anxiety has shown up almost everyday for the last six months. You try to stop worrying but you just can't. *And* you frequently experience a number of the following problems:

✔ You feel restless, often irritable, on edge, fidgety, or keyed up.

✔ You get tired easily.

✔ Your muscles feel tense, especially in your back, neck, or shoulders.

✔ You have difficulty concentrating, falling asleep, or staying asleep.

Not everyone experiences anxiety in exactly the same way. That's why only a professional can actually make a diagnosis. Some people complain about other problems, such as twitching, trembling, shortness of breath, sweating, dry mouth, stomach upset, feeling shaky, being easily startled, and having difficulty swallowing, and fail to realize that they actually suffer from GAD.

The following profile offers an example of what GAD is all about.

In a subway, **Brian** taps his foot nervously. He arches his back to stretch his tight shoulder muscles and checks his watch, fretting that he might arrive at work three or four minutes late. He hates showing up late. He didn't sleep much last night because his thoughts about presenting the design for the new Alaska resort project invaded his sleep; one preoccupation or another usually disturbs Brian's sleep. He struggles to concentrate on the newspaper that he's holding and realizes that he can't remember what he just read.

When Brian gets to work, he snaps at his new assistant. After he loses his temper at her, he feels immediate remorse and scolds himself, increasing his anxiety further. His office mates often tell him to chill out. His performance has always exceeded his employer's expectations, so he really has no reason to worry about his job. But he does. Brian suffers from *Generalized Anxiety Disorder.*

Social Phobia — avoiding people

Those with *Social Phobia* fear exposure to public scrutiny. They frequently dread performing, speaking, going to parties, meeting new people, entering groups, using the telephone, writing a check in front of others, eating in public, and/or interacting with those in authority. They see these situations as painful because they expect to receive humiliating or shameful judgments from others. Social phobics believe that they're somehow defective and inadequate; thus, they assume they'll bungle their lines, spill their drinks, shake hands with clammy palms, or commit any of a number of social *faux pas* and thus embarrass themselves.

Everyone feels uncomfortable or nervous from time to time, especially in new situations. For example, if you've been experiencing social fears for less than six months, you may not have a Social Phobia. A short-term fear of socializing may be a temporary reaction to a new stress — moving to a new neighborhood or getting a new job. However, you may have a Social Phobia if you experience the following symptoms for a prolonged period of time:

- ✔ You fear situations with unfamiliar people or where you might be observed or evaluated in some way.

- ✔ When forced into an uncomfortable social situation, your anxiety increases powerfully. For example, if you fear public speaking, your voice shakes, and your knees tremble the moment that you start your talk.

- ✔ You realize that your fear is greater than the situation really warrants. For example, if you fear meeting new people, logically you know nothing horrible will happen, but tidal waves of adrenaline and fearful anticipation course through your veins.

- ✔ You avoid fearful situations as much as you can or endure them only with great distress.

Check out the following prime example of a social phobic and see if any of it seems familiar.

The paradox of Social Phobia

Because of the expectation and fear of experiencing humiliation, those with Social Phobia withdraw and avoid social situations whenever possible. When forced into such encounters, they inhibit their actions in order to avoid saying or doing something that they believe will be seen as stupid. They often avoid eye contact, stand alone, add little to conversations, and generally look stiff.

Unfortunately, this fear of expressing themselves sometimes makes social phobics appear unfriendly, cold, distant, and/or self-centered.

Social phobics actually experience intense fear in these circumstances and react with surprise to feedback that they seem self-centered and unfriendly. Sometimes, they realize that others perceive them as unfriendly, which only fuels the phobia and convinces them that people won't like them and that they don't know how to interact successfully. In other words, a vicious cycle is created — the more that social phobics try to avoid negative reactions, the more that others react negatively.

Quinton, a 35-year-old eligible bachelor, wants a serious relationship. Women consider him fairly attractive, a good dresser, and they know he has a high-paying job. Quinton's friends invite him to parties and other social events in an effort to set him up. Unfortunately, he detests the idea of going; on the day after Christmas, he starts dreading the New Year's Eve party. In his mind, Quinton conjures up a number of good excuses for backing out. However, his desire to meet potential dates eventually wins. He runs scenes of meeting women over and over in his mind. Each time that he imagines one of these scenes, he feels intense, anxious anticipation. He berates himself, realizing that his fear is absurd but feeling powerless to do anything about it.

The afternoon of the party, he spends hours getting ready and has no appetite. When Quinton arrives, he immediately heads to the bar to quell his mounting anxiety. His hands shake as he picks up his first drink. Quickly downing the drink, he orders more in hopes of numbing his emotions. After an hour of non-stop drinking, he feels much braver. He interrupts a cluster of attractive women and spews out a string of jokes that he memorized for the occasion. Then he approaches various women throughout the night, sometimes making flirtatious, suggestive comments. He doesn't get far, but he feels good about his performance.

The next day, Quinton awakens in an unfamiliar bedroom, not remembering the end of the evening. His buddy pokes his head into the room and says, "You were so far gone last night that we took your keys and put you to bed. Do you remember what happened?" Quinton, shakes his head no, his face flush with embarrassment. His buddy continues, "Well, I hate to tell you this, but you were making some pretty on-the-edge come-on's to Brenda. She felt really turned off. Her brother almost lost it with you, and you were ready to fight. All in all, it wasn't a pretty sight."

Quinton has a Social Phobia. Drug and alcohol abuse often accompany social phobia. Perhaps you can see why.

Feeling panicky

Of course, everyone feels a little panicked from time to time. People often say they feel panicked about an upcoming deadline, an impending presentation, or planning a party. You're likely to hear the term used to describe concerns about rather mundane events such as these.

But people who suffer with Panic Disorders are talking about different phenomena entirely. They have periods of stunningly intense fear and anxiety. If you've never had a panic attack, we don't recommend it. The attacks usually last about ten minutes, and many people who have them fully believe that they will die during the attack. Not exactly the best ten minutes of their lives. Panic attacks normally include a range of robust, attention-grabbing symptoms, such as

- Irregular, rapid, or pounding heartbeat
- Perspiring
- A sense of choking, suffocation, or shortness of breath
- Vertigo or lightheadedness
- Pain or other discomfort in chest
- Feeling that events are unreal or a sense of detachment from yourself
- Numbness or tingling
- Hot or cold flashes
- Fearing that you will die, though without basis in fact
- Stomach nausea or upset
- Jitteriness or trembling
- Thoughts of going insane or completely losing control

Professionals generally agree that in order to have a full-blown Panic Disorder, panic attacks must occur more than once. People with Panic Disorder worry about when the next one will come and whether they'll lose control and embarrass themselves. Finally, they usually start changing their lives by avoiding certain places or activities.

Panic attacks begin with an event that triggers some kind of sensation, such as physical exertion or normal variations in physiological reactions. This triggering event induces physiological responses such as increased levels of adrenaline. No problem so far.

But the otherwise normal process goes awry at the next step — when the person who suffers from panic attacks misinterprets the meaning of the physical symptoms. Rather than viewing it as a normal event, the person with Panic Disorder sees it as a signal that something dangerous is happening, such as a heart attack or stroke. That interpretation causes escalating fear and thus more physical arousal. In other words, it becomes a vicious cycle. Fortunately, the body can sustain such heightened physical responses only for a while and it eventually calms down.

The good news: Many people have a single panic attack and never have another one. So don't panic if you have a panic attack.

Maria's story is a good example of a one-time panic attack.

Maria left the hospital after visiting her next-door neighbor. She still can't believe he had a heart attack at the age of 42. Maria, never one to worry about her health, ponders the fact that she just reached her 46th birthday. She resolves to lose that extra 20 pounds and to start exercising.

On her third visit to the gym, she sets the treadmill to a level 6. Almost immediately, her heart rate accelerates rapidly. Alarmed, she decreases the level to 3. She starts taking rapid, shallow breaths, but feels she can't get enough air. Reducing the level further doesn't seem to help. She stops the treadmill and goes to the locker room. Sweating profusely and feeling nauseous, she finds an empty dressing cubicle. She sits down and thinks maybe she just overdid the treadmill a little. But the symptoms intensify and her chest tightens. She wants to scream but can't get enough air. She's sure that she'll pass out and hopes someone will find her before she dies. She hears someone and weakly calls for help. An ambulance whisks her to a nearby emergency room while she prays that she'll live through her heart attack.

At the emergency room, Maria's symptoms subside, and the doctor comes in to explain the results of her examination. He says that she's apparently experienced a panic attack and inquires about what may have set it off. She explains that she was exercising due to concerns about her weight and health, and she mentions her neighbor's heart attack.

"Ah, that explains it," the doctor reassures, "Your concerns about health made you hypersensitive to any bodily symptom. When your heart rate naturally increased on the treadmill, you became alarmed. That fear caused your body to produce more adrenaline, which in turn created more symptoms. The more symptoms you had, the more that your fear and adrenaline increased. Knowing how this works may help you; hopefully, in the future, your body's normal physical variations won't frighten you. Your heart's in great shape. I recommend that you go back to exercising but just increase it slowly over time without sudden jumps in intensity. Also, you might try some simple relaxation techniques; I'll have the nurse come in and tell you about those. I have every reason to believe that you won't have another episode like this one. Finally, you may want to read *Overcoming Anxiety For Dummies* by Charles Elliott and Laura Smith (Wiley Publishing, Inc.); it's a great book!"

Maria doesn't have a diagnosis of Panic Disorder because she hasn't experienced more than one attack, and she may never have an attack again. If she believes the doctor and takes his advice, the next time that her heart races, she probably won't get so scared. She may even use the relaxation techniques that the nurse explained to her.

If you worry that you have a Panic Disorder, remember that it can be treated. This chapter gives you the knowledge that you need, and other chapters (see especially Chapters 8 and 10) tell you how to combine your understanding with actions.

The panic companion — Agoraphobia

Somewhere around half of those with a Panic Disorder have an accompanying problem: *Agoraphobia*. Unlike most fears or phobias, this strange disorder usually begins in adulthood. Individuals with Agoraphobia live in terror of being trapped. In addition, they worry about having a panic attack, throwing up, or having diarrhea in public. They desperately avoid situations from which they can't readily escape, and they also fear places where help might not be readily forthcoming should they need it. The agoraphobic may start with one fear, such as being in a crowd, but in many cases the feared situations multiply to the point that the person fears even leaving home.

When Agoraphobia combines with Panic Disorder, individuals fear any situation in which they might have an attack. As Agoraphobia teams up with panic, the double-barreled fears of not getting help and horror at the idea of feeling entombed with no way out, frequently lead to paralyzing isolation.

You or someone you love may have Agoraphobia if

- ✔ You worry about being somewhere where you can't get out or can't get help in case something bad happens, like a panic attack.
- ✔ You tremble over everyday things like leaving home, being in large groups of people, or travel.
- ✔ Because of your anxiety, you avoid the places that you fear so much that it takes over your life, and you become a prisoner of your fear.

You may have concerns about feeling trapped or have anxiety about crowds and leaving home. Many people do. But if your life goes on without major changes or constraints, you're probably not Agoraphobic.

Help! I'm dying!

Panic attack symptoms, such as chest pain, shortness of breath, nausea, and intense fear, often mimic heart attacks. Alarmed, those who experience these terrifying episodes take off in the direction of the nearest emergency room. Then after numerous tests come back negative, overworked doctors tell the victim of a panic attack in so many words, "It's all in your head." Unbelieving panic attack patients are sure that something was missed. The next time an attack occurs, panic attack victims are likely to return to the ER for another opinion again and again. The repeat visits frustrate people with panic attacks as well as ER staff. However, a simple 20- or 30-minute psychological intervention in the emergency room decreases the repeat visits dramatically. What is the intervention? It can be just providing education about what the disorder is all about and describing a few deep relaxation techniques to try out when panic hits. (You'll find many more ideas than that in this book; read on.)

Nevertheless, you could still have problems with your fears in this area or maybe not. For example, you may quake at the thought of entering large sports stadiums. You see images of stampeding crowds pushing and shoving, causing you to fall over the railings, landing below, only to be trampled by the mob as you cry out. If so, you could live an entire blissful life avoiding sports stadiums. Thus, your fears don't bother you much. But if you love watching live sports events, or you just got a job as a sports reporter, this fear could be *really bad.*

Patricia's story, which follows, demonstrates the overwhelming anxiety that often traps agoraphobics.

Patricia celebrates her 40th birthday without having experienced significant emotional problems. She'd gone through the usual bumps in the road of life like losing a parent, her child having a learning disability, and a divorce ten years earlier. She prides herself on being able to cope with whatever cards life deals her.

Lately, she notices that she stresses when she shops at the mall. She needs to pick up a birthday present and doesn't want to go because the mall is especially crowded on weekends. She finally finds a parking spot at the very end of a row. Her sweaty hands leave a smudge on the revolving glass door. She feels as though the crowd of shoppers is crushing in on her, and Patricia feels trapped. She's so scared that she can't bring herself to buy the present and flees the store.

Over the next few months, her fears spread. Although it started at the mall, fear and anxiety now overwhelm her in crowded grocery stores as well. Later, she can no longer cope when she's simply driving in traffic. Patricia suffers from agoraphobia. If not treated, Patricia could end up housebound.

Many times, panic, Agoraphobia, and anxiety strike people who are otherwise devoid of serious, deep-seated emotional problems. So if you suffer from anxiety, it doesn't necessarily mean you'll need years of psychotherapy. You may not like the anxiety, but you don't have to think you're nuts!

Specific Phobia — spiders, snakes, tornados, airplanes, and other scary things

Many fears appear to be hard-wired into the human brain. Cave men and women had good reasons to fear snakes, strangers, heights, darkness, open spaces, and the sight of blood — snakes could be poisonous, strangers could be enemies, a person could fall from a height, darkness could harbor unknown hazards, open spaces could leave a primitive tribe vulnerable to attack from all sides, and the sight of blood could signal a crisis, even potential death. Fear inspired caution and avoidance of harm. Those with these fears had a better chance of survival than the naively brave.

That's why many of the most common fears today reflect the dangers of the world thousands of years ago. Even today, it makes sense to cautiously identify a spider before you pick it up. However, sometimes fears rise to a disabling level. You may have a *Specific Phobia* if

- ✔ You have an exaggerated fear of a specific situation or object.

- ✔ When you're in fearful situations, you experience excessive anxiety immediately. Your anxiety *may* include sweating, rapid heartbeat, a desire to flee, tightness in the chest or throat, or images of something awful happening.

- ✔ Yet you know the fear is unreasonable. On the other hand, kids with Specific Phobias don't always know that their phobia is unreasonable. For example, they may really think that *all* dogs bite.

- ✔ You avoid your feared object or situation as much as you possibly can.

- ✔ Because your fear is so intense, you go so far as to change your day-to-day behavior at work, at home, or in relationships. Thus, your fear inconveniences you and perhaps others, and it restricts your life.

Almost two thirds of people fear one thing or another. For example, I, Laura Smith (one of the authors of this book), hate bugs. Whenever a cricket is in the house, I avoid it or get someone else to dispose of it. One year, I had an office in an old building. Every morning, dead roaches littered the floor. I devised ways of getting them out of my office using a huge wad of paper towels. If instead, I had quit my job because of the bugs, I would have had a diagnosis of Specific Phobia. But my fears don't significantly interfere with my life. You, like me, may have an excessive fear of something. That doesn't mean that you have a Specific Phobia in the diagnosable sense, as long as it doesn't disrupt your life in a major way. And you may or may not want to do something about it. In case you're wondering, I don't particularly mind the fact that bugs gross me out; I intend to live out my entire life in this manner and have no desire to work on this problem.

The following description of Ted's life is a prime picture of what someone with a Specific Phobia goes through.

Ted trudges up eight flights of stairs each morning to get to his office and tells everyone that he loves the exercise. When Ted passes the elevators on the way to the stairwell, his heart pounds, and he feels a sense of doom. Ted envisions being boxed inside the elevator, the doors slide shut, and there's no escape. In his mind, the elevator box rises on rusty cables, makes sudden jerks up and down, falls freely, and crashes into the basement.

Ted has never experienced anything like his fantasy, nor has anyone he knows had this experience. Ted never liked elevators, but he didn't start avoiding them until the past few years. It seems that the longer he stays away from riding them, the stronger his fear grows. He used to feel okay on escalators, but now he finds himself avoiding those as well. Several weeks ago at the airport, he had no alternative but to take the escalator. He managed to get on but became so frightened that he had to sit down for a while after he reached the second floor.

One afternoon, Ted rushes down the stairs after work, running late for an appointment. He slips and falls, breaking his leg. Now in a cast, Ted faces the challenge of his life. Ted has a Specific Phobia.

Post-Traumatic Stress Disorder: Feeling the aftermath

Tragically, war, rape, terror, crashes, brutality, torture, and natural disasters are a part of life. You or someone you know may have experienced one of life's traumas. No one knows why for sure, but some people seem to recover from these events without disabling symptoms. However, many others suffer considerably after their tragedy, sometimes for a lifetime.

More often than not, trauma causes at least a few uncomfortable emotional and/or physical reactions for a while. These responses can show up immediately after the disaster, or sometimes, they emerge years later. These symptoms are the way that the body and mind deal with and process what happened. If an extremely unfortunate event occurs, it's normal to react strongly.

Top ten fears

Various polls and surveys collect information about what people fear most. In the following list, we compiled the most common fears. Do you have any of these?

10 Dogs

9 Being alone at night

8 Thunder and lightning

7 Spiders and insects

6 Being trapped in a small space

5 Flying

4 Rodents

3 Heights

2 Giving a speech

And finally, the number one fear: Snakes

The diagnosis of Post-Traumatic Stress Disorder (PTSD) is complicated. If you suspect that you may have it, you should seek professional help. On the other hand, you may realize that you have a few of these symptoms but not the full diagnosis. If so, and if your problem feels mild and doesn't interfere with your life, you may want to try working on the difficulty on your own for a while. But seek help if you don't feel better.

You may have PTSD if you personally experienced or witnessed an event that you perceived as potentially life threatening or causing serious injury or you discovered that someone close to you experienced such an event. If your response included terror, horror, or helplessness, *three types of problems* also occur if you have PTSD:

✔ You *relive* the event in one or more ways:

- Having unwanted memories or flashbacks during the day or in your dreams.

- Feeling the trauma is happening again.

- Experiencing physical or emotional reactions when reminded of the event.

✔ You *avoid* anything that reminds you of the trauma and try to suppress or numb your feelings in several ways:

- Trying to block out thinking or talking about the event because you get upset when you remember what happened.

- Staying away from people or places that remind you of the trauma.

- Losing interest in life or feeling distant from people.

- Sensing somehow that you don't have a long future.

- Feeling numb or detached.

> ✔ You feel *on guard and stirred up* in several ways:
>
> - Becoming startled more easily.
> - Losing your temper quickly and feeling irritable.
> - Inability to concentrate as well as before.
> - Sleeping is fitful.

What's it like to live with PTSD? For Wayne, it's a constant struggle.

Wayne retired from the military at age 40 as a full colonel. Before retirement, the years following the Gulf War were a struggle for Wayne. He slept poorly, and nightmares frequently awakened him; he lost his temper easily, and he felt detached from life.

Wayne assumes his problems all stem from issues related to the military: his work hours, frequent separations from his family, numerous cross-country moves, and the intense pressure for promotions. He looks forward to retirement and a less stressful lifestyle. He promises his wife and children that his first goal is to spend more time with them.

But Wayne finds retirement less rewarding than he'd hoped. He continues to have trouble sleeping. He tries to fulfill his promise to his family but just can't muster any enthusiasm for their activities. He doesn't find anything to look forward to, and his distance from his family grows. He continues to feel irritable and jumpy. After six months of retirement, Wayne's wife insists they get marital counseling.

In taking their history, the psychologist asks Wayne about his Gulf War experience. Wayne says he doesn't want to talk about it; that's how he handles the disturbing memories of the war. That answer tipped the psychologist off to Wayne's problem. Wayne has PTSD.

Obsessive-Compulsive Disorder — over and over and over again

Obsessive-Compulsive Disorder (OCD) wreaks incredible havoc on people's lives because OCD frustrates and confuses not only the people afflicted with it but also their families and loved ones as well. If untreated, it's likely to last a lifetime. Even with treatment, symptoms often recur. That's the bad news. Thankfully, effective treatments are available.

A person with OCD may exhibit behaviors that include an obsession or a compulsion or both. (Table 2-1 lists common obsessions and compulsions.)

Obsessions are unwelcome repetitive images, impulses, or thoughts that jump into the mind. People find these thoughts and images disturbing and can't get rid of them. For example, a religious man may have a thought urging him to shout obscenities during a church service, or a caring mother may have intrusive thoughts of causing harm to her baby. Thankfully, people don't carry out these kinds of thoughts, but the obsessions haunt those who have them.

Compulsions are undesired repetitive actions or mental strategies carried out to temporarily reduce anxiety. From time to time, an obsessive thought causes the anxiety; at other times, the anxiety relates to some feared event or situation that triggers the compulsion.

For example, a woman may wash her hands literally hundreds of times each day in order to reduce her anxiety about germs, or a man may have an elaborate nighttime ritual of touching certain objects, lining up clothes in a specific way, arranging his wallet next to his keys in a special position, stacking his change, getting into bed in precisely the correct manner, and reading one section of the Bible before turning out the light. And if he performs any part of the ritual in less than the "perfect" way, he feels compelled to start all over until he gets it right.

You may have Obsessive-Compulsive Disorder (OCD) if you have obsessions, compulsions, or both. Regarding *obsessions,* the following applies:

✔ **Your obsessive thoughts do not involve real-life problems.**

   For example, if you worry about germs on your hands and you're a brain surgeon, we're glad about that, and you're being realistic. But if you constantly worry about many germs on your hands and you work in a library, you just may have an obsession.

✔ **When the thoughts occur, you try to get rid of them by thinking or doing something else.**

   For example, you may have a special prayer or saying that you repeat in your mind over and over again.

✔ **You know that your obsessive thoughts are coming from your own brain and not from some other source.**

   In other words, if you think an alien from another planet took over your mind, you have a kind of problem that this book doesn't cover, and you want to get help soon.

✔ **The thoughts bother you considerably.**

The following applies to *compulsions:*

✔ Compulsions are actions and behaviors or mental strategies that you feel compelled to repeat again and again in response to one of your obsessive thoughts or because you have a belief in some rigid rule that you feel can't be broken.

> ✔ You believe that your compulsive acts can in some way prevent a terrible event from happening or alleviate your anxiety, but what you do doesn't make much sense.

The OCD cycle

A pattern frequently develops in which obsessive thoughts create anxiety, which causes the person to engage in a compulsive act in order to reduce the anxiety and obtain relief. That temporary relief powerfully encourages the person to believe that the compulsive acts help. Unfortunately, the cycle begins again because the obsessive thoughts return.

Table 2-1	The Most Popular Obsessions and Compulsions
Obsessions	*Compulsions*
Worry about contamination, such as from dirt, germs, radiation, and chemicals.	Excessive hand washing or cleaning due to the obsessive fear of contamination.
Doubts about having remembered to turn the stove off, lock the doors, and so on.	Checking and rechecking to see that the stove is off, doors are locked, and so on.
Perverted sexual imagery that the person feels ashamed of.	Collecting an oversupply of objects that aren't collectibles and have little or no value, such as lint, piles of magazines, string, batteries, and so on.
Unwanted thoughts of harming someone you love.	Repeating rituals over and over again, often with a belief that something bad will happen if it isn't carried out.
Thoughts that would violate your own religious beliefs or code in some shameful way.	Arranging items in a rigid, precise way. Often, the person feels compelled to start over if it doesn't come out perfectly.
Thoughts urging you to behave in a socially strange and unacceptable way.	Counting stairs, ceiling tiles, steps walked, and so on ad nauseam.

Seeing OCD when it's not there

You may recall walking to school with your friends and avoiding cracks in the sidewalk. If you accidentally stepped on one, perhaps someone chided, "If you step on a crack, you'll break your mother's back!" And perhaps sometimes, you walked to school by yourself, and that same thought occurred to you, so you avoided stepping on the cracks. Obviously you knew that stepping on a crack wouldn't break your mother's back. So not stepping on cracks almost qualifies as a compulsion. That's because you may have done it repeatedly and known it wouldn't stop anything bad from happening. If you did it simply as a game and it didn't bother you that much, avoiding cracks was no big deal, and it wasn't. Besides, kids often have magical or superstitious thinking, which they usually outgrow.

On the other hand, if some part of you really worried that your mother might suffer if you stepped on a crack and if you couldn't even get to school because of your worry, you probably had a full-blown compulsion. Many people check the locks more than once, go back to make sure the coffee pot is turned off a couple of extra times, or count stairs or steps unnecessarily. It's only when doing these things starts taking too much time and interferes with relationships, work, or everyday life that you really have a problem.

Lisa's extreme preoccupation with hanging on to objects of no value that only serve to clutter up her home is an example of someone with OCD. Lisa is a collector, but you couldn't really call her a collector in the way most people think about collecting because what she accumulates never has any real value to anyone. She keeps every rubber band that holds her daily newspaper together; she never throws away a magazine; her garage holds nothing but a hodgepodge of batteries, string, pebbles, pieces of wire, nuts and bolts, and scraps of paper. Lisa simply can't get herself to throw anything away. Her house bursts at the seams with useless junk.

But Lisa thinks just maybe one day that she may need a few of these items. When she does think of what she might need, she can rarely find it through all the piles of rubble. As the years go by, Lisa becomes isolated. She can't invite anyone over out of embarrassment for the way her house looks. Lisa's obsession causes her to fret about not having something she needs. Thus, she has a compulsion to never throw anything out. Lisa suffers from OCD.

Sorting Out What's Normal from What's Not

Imagine a life with no anxiety at all. How wonderful. You awaken every morning anticipating nothing but pleasant experiences. You fear nothing. The future holds only sweet security and joy.

Think again. With no anxiety, when the guy in the car in front of you slams on the brakes, your response is slower, and you'll crash. With no worries about the future, your retirement may end up bleak. The total absence of anxiety may cause you to walk into a work presentation unprepared.

Avoiding anxiety only worsens anxiety

Avoidance underlies all the anxiety disorders. No one likes to feel anxious. People generally respond to anxiety by steering clear of the things that make them anxious. It makes sense, doesn't it?

Well, yes and no. At the moment of avoidance, anxiety decreases. The problem is that the momentary relief actually increases the desire to continue avoiding the situation. Furthermore, the range of feared events starts to increase. Check out the following example:

Nate doesn't like going to parties, especially weddings. He worries that someone may ask him to dance and that he'll look like a fool on the dance floor. He also worries about making conversations appropriately and not wearing the right thing. At first, he finds it fairly easy to avoid weddings. He simply turns down invitations with one excuse or another and sighs with relief each time he gets out of one.

His sense of relief encourages Nate to start avoiding more social situations, and he declines invitations to other types of parties, family gatherings, and after-work get-togethers. Each act of avoidance briefly soothes his anxiety.

However, Nate finds himself increasingly isolated, and his anxiety starts to show up in almost any situation with people around. Now he feels tense talking at work; he avoids using the telephone when he can, and he stays away from the break room at work. What started as a manageable fear, now consumes his life.

That's how avoidance works. Avoidance fertilizes your fears. With enough avoidance, anxiety grows out of control.

Everyone avoids a few things. You may avoid snakes, and it's no big deal because they're pretty easy to avoid. You may even avoid an occasional social gathering that makes you anxious. As long as you force yourself to go to at least some social gatherings, your anxiety won't likely blossom.

Anxiety is good for you! It prepares you to take action. It mobilizes your body for emergencies. It warns you about impending doom. Be glad you have some anxiety. Your anxiety helps you stay out of trouble.

Anxiety only poses a problem for you when

- ✔ Anxiety lasts uncomfortably long or occurs too often.
- ✔ It interferes with doing what you want to do.
- ✔ Anxiety greatly exceeds the level of actual danger or risk. In other words, when your body and mind feel like an avalanche is about to bury you, but all you have to do is take a test for school, your anxiety has gone too far.
- ✔ You struggle to control your worries, but they disturb you and never let up.

Knowing what anxiety isn't

Anxious symptoms may travel with other company. Thus, you may have anxiety along with other emotional disorders. In fact, about half of those with anxiety disorders develop depression, especially if their anxiety goes untreated. The treatment of other emotional problems differs somewhat from the treatment of anxiety. So knowing the difference between those problems and anxiety is important. Of course, people have both sometimes.

In addition, medications and medical conditions can mimic anxious symptoms. You may think that you're terribly anxious, but actually you may be ill or suffering from the side effects of a drug.

Other emotional disorders

Anxiety often accompanies other emotional problems. However, we want you to know that if you have anxiety, it means nothing about whether you have one of these other disorders. So realize that anxiety is not one of these other emotional disorders:

- ✔ **Depression:** Depression can feel like life in slow motion. You lose interest in activities that used to bring you pleasure. You feel sad. Most likely, you feel tired, and you sleep fitfully. Your appetite may wane, and your sex drive may droop. Similar to anxiety, you may find it difficult to concentrate or plan ahead. But unlike anxiety, depression saps your drive and motivation.

- ✔ **Bipolar Disorders:** These disorders seesaw between ups and downs. At times, you feel that you're on top of the world. You have grandiose ideas and need little sleep. You may invest in risky schemes, shop recklessly, engage in sexual escapades, or lose your good judgment in other nefarious ways. You may start working frantically on important projects or find ideas streaming through your mind. Then suddenly you crash and burn. Your mood turns sour and depression sets in.

- ✔ **Psychosis:** Psychosis may make you feel anxious, but the symptoms profoundly disrupt life. Psychosis weaves hallucinations into everyday life. For example, some people hear voices talking to them or see shadowy figures when no one is around. Delusions, another feature of psychosis, also distort reality. Common psychotic delusions include believing that the CIA or aliens are tracking your whereabouts. Other delusions involve grandiose beliefs, such as thinking you're Jesus Christ or that you have a special mission to save the world.

If you think that you hear the phone ringing when you're drying your hair or in the shower, only to discover that it wasn't, you're not psychotic. Most people occasionally hear or see trivial things that aren't there. It's only when these perceptions seriously depart from reality that you may worry about psychosis. Fortunately, anxiety disorders don't lead to psychosis.

✔ **Substance abuse:** When people develop a dependency on drugs or alcohol, withdrawal may create serious anxiety. The symptoms of drug or alcohol withdrawal include tremors, disrupted sleep, sweating, increased heartbeat, agitation, and tension. However, if these symptoms only come on in response to a recent cessation of substance use, it's not an anxiety disorder. On the other hand, those with anxiety disorders sometimes abuse substances in the misguided attempt to control their anxiety.

Mimicking Anxiety: Drugs and Diseases

As common as anxiety disorders are, believing that you're suffering from anxiety when you're not is all too easy. Prescription drugs may have a variety of side effects, some of which mimic some of the symptoms of anxiety. Various medical conditions also produce symptoms that imitate the signs of anxiety.

Exploring anxiety-mimicking drugs

The pharmaceutical industry reports on the most widely prescribed categories of medications every year. To show you how easily medication side effects can resemble the symptoms of anxiety, we list the top ten of the most widely prescribed drugs and their anxiety-mimicking side effects in Table 2-2. These medications have many other side effects that we don't list here.

Table 2-2		Angst in the Medicine Cabinet	
Popularity	*Drug name*	*Purpose*	*Anxiety-like Side Effects*
No. 1	Codeine	Alleviate pain and manage nonproductive cough	Agitation, dizziness, nausea, decreased appetite, palpitations, flushing, and restlessness
No. 2	Calcium channel blockers	Stabilize angina and reduce high blood pressure	Dizziness, flushing, palpitations, diarrhea, gastric upset, insomnia, anxiety, confusion, light-headedness, and fatigue

(continued)

Table 2-2 *(continued)*

Popularity	Drug name	Purpose	Anxiety-like Side Effects
No. 3	Anti-ulcerants	Treatment of ulcers	Dizziness, anxiety, confusion, headache, weakness, diarrhea, flushing, sweating, and tremors
No. 4	Angiotensin-converting enzyme (ACE) inhibitors	Reduce high blood pressure	Impotence, dizziness, insomnia, headaches, nausea, vomiting, and weakness
No. 5	Selective serotonin reuptake inhibitors (SSRIs)	Treatment of depression, anxiety, and bulimia	Headache, insomnia, anxiety, tremor, dizziness, nervousness, fatigue, poor concentration, agitation, nausea, diarrhea, decreased appetite, sweating, hot flashes, palpitations, twitching, and impotence
No. 6	Statins	Cholesterol reduction	Headache, dizziness, diarrhea, nausea, muscle cramps, and tremor
No. 7	Beta blockers	Reduce angina and high blood pressure, treat dysrhythmias	Dizziness, diarrhea, nausea, palpitations, impotence, and disorientation
No. 8	Hormone replacement medications	Reduce menopause symptoms, treat osteoporosis, and treat ovarian failure	Dizziness, headache, nausea, vomiting, diarrhea, and appetite changes
No. 9	Anti-arthritic and anti-inflammatory medications	Treat arthritis and pain	Fatigue, anxiety, dizziness, nervousness, insomnia, nausea, vomiting, sweating, tremors, confusion, and shortness of breath
No. 10	Benzodiazepines	Treat anxiety	Dizziness, headache, anxiety, tremors, stimulation, insomnia, nausea, and diarrhea

Angst from over the counter

One of the most common ingredients in over-the-counter cold medications is *pseudoephedrine,* a popular and effective decongestant. I, Charles Elliott (one of the two-author team that's writing this book), specialize in the treatment of panic and anxiety disorders. A couple of years ago, I had a bad cold and cough for longer than usual. I treated it with the strongest over-the-counter medications that I could find. Not only that, I took a little more than the label called for during the day, so I could see clients without coughing through the session. One day during that period, I noticed an unusually rapid heartbeat and considerable tightness in

breathing. I wondered for a while if I was having a panic attack. It didn't seem possible, but the symptoms stared me in the face. Could I possibly have caught a Panic Disorder from my clients?

Not exactly. Upon reflection, I realized that perhaps I'd taken more than just a little too much of the cold medication containing pseudoephedrine. I stopped taking the medication, and the symptoms disappeared, never to return.

So be careful with over-the-counter medications. Read the directions carefully. Don't try to be your own doctor like I did!

Interesting isn't it? Even medications for the treatment of anxiety can produce anxiety-like side effects. Of course, most people don't experience such side effects with these medications, but they do occur. If you're taking one or more of these commonly prescribed drugs and feel anxious, you may want to check with your doctor.

In addition, various over-the-counter medications may have anxiety-mimicking side effects. These include cold remedies, bronchodilators, and decongestants. Also, many types of aspirin contain caffeine, which can produce symptoms of anxiety if consumed excessively. These medications can cause restlessness, heart palpitations, tension, shortness of breath, and irritability.

Investigating medical anxiety imposters

More than a few types of diseases and medical conditions can create anxiety-like symptoms, too. That's why we strongly recommend, especially if you're experiencing significant anxiety for the first time, that you visit your doctor. Your doctor can help you sort out whether you have a physical problem, a reaction to a medication, an emotionally based anxiety problem, or some combination of these.

Table 2-3 lists some of the medical conditions that produce anxious symptoms. In addition, merely getting sick can cause anxiety about your illness. For example, if you receive a serious diagnosis of heart disease, certain cancers, or a chronic progressive disorder, you are likely to develop some anxiety about dealing with the consequence of what you've been told. The same techniques for dealing with anxiety throughout this book can help you with this type of anxiety as well.

Table 2-3	Medical Imposters	
Medical Condition	**What It Is**	**Anxiety-like Symptoms**
Hypoglycemia	Low blood sugar, sometimes associated with other disorders or can occur by itself. It is a common complication of diabetes.	Confusion, irritability, trembling, sweating, rapid heart beat, weakness, and a cold clammy feeling.
Hyperthyroidism	Excess amount of thyroid hormone. It has various causes.	Nervousness, restlessness, sweating, fatigue, sleep disturbance, nausea, tremor, and diarrhea.
Other hormonal imbalances	Various conditions associated with fluctuations in hormone levels such as premenstrual syndrome (PMS), menopause, or postpartum. Highly variable symptoms.	Tension, irritability, headaches, mood swings, compulsive behavior, fatigue, and panic.
Lupus	An autoimmune disease in which the patient's immune system attacks certain types of its own cells.	Anxiety, poor concentration, irritability, headaches, irregular heartbeat, and impaired memory.
Mitral valve prolapse	The mitral valve of the heart fails to close properly, allowing blood to flow back into the left atrium. Often confused with panic attacks in making the diagnosis.	Palpitations, shortness of breath, fatigue, chest pain, and difficulty breathing.
Ménière's syndrome	An inner ear disorder that includes vertigo, loss of hearing, and ringing or other noises in the ear.	Vertigo that includes abnormal sensations associated with movement, dizziness, nausea, vomiting, and sweating.

Preparing to Fight or Run

Your body responds to threats by preparing for action in three different ways: physically, mentally, and behaviorally. When danger presents itself, you reflexively prepare to stand and fight or run like you've never run before. Your body mobilizes for peril in complex and fantastic ways. Figure 2-1 gives you the picture.

First, the brain sends signals through your nervous system to go on high alert. It tells the adrenal glands to rev up production of adrenalin and noradrenalin. These hormones stimulate the body in various ways. Your heart pounds faster, and you start breathing more rapidly, sending increased oxygen to your lungs while blood flows to the large muscles, preparing them to fight or flee from danger.

Digestion slows to preserve energy for meeting the challenge and pupils dilate to improve vision. Blood flow decreases to hands and feet in order to prevent blood loss if injured and keep up the blood supply to the large muscles. Sweating increases in order to keep the body cool, and it makes you slippery, so aggressors can't grab hold of you. All your muscles tense to spring into action.

Mentally, you automatically scan your surroundings intensely. Your attention focuses on the threat and nothing else. In fact, you can't attend to much of anything else.

The chicken or the egg: Irritable bowel syndrome

Irritable bowel syndrome (IBS) is a common condition that involves a variety of related problems, usually including cramps or pain in the abdomen, diarrhea, and/or constipation. These occur in people with no known physical problems in their digestive systems. For many years, doctors told most of their patients that irritable bowel syndrome (IBS) was caused exclusively by stress, worry, and anxiety.

In 1999, Catherine Woodman, MD, and colleagues discovered a mutated gene in patients with irritable bowel syndrome more often than in those without it. Interestingly, that same rogue gene also occurs more often in those with Panic Disorders. Other possible physical causes of IBS may have to do with poor communication between muscles and nerves in the colon.

Various medications have been found to decrease some of the worst symptoms of IBS. In addition, psychotherapy that teaches relaxation techniques, biofeedback, and techniques for coping with anxiety and stress, also improve IBS symptoms. So at this point, no one really knows how much of IBS is due to physical causes, anxiety, or stress. It's more likely, however, that the mind and body interact in important ways that can't always be separated.

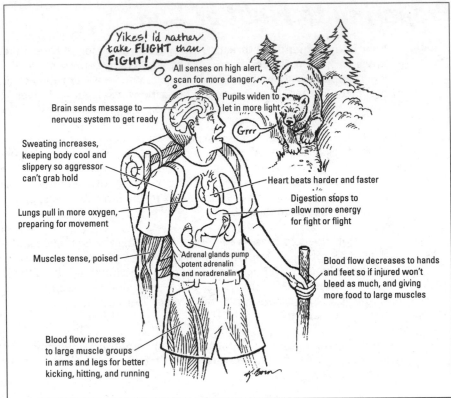

Figure 2-1:
Choices,
choices!

Behaviorally, you're now ready to run or fight. You need that preparation in the face of danger. When you have to take on a bear, a lion, or a warrior, you'd better have all your resources on high alert.

Just one problem — in today's world, most people don't encounter lions and bears. Unfortunately, your body reacts too easily with the same preparation to fight traffic, meet deadlines, speak in public, and other everyday worries.

When human beings have nothing to fight or run from, all that energy has to get out somehow. So you may feel the urge to fidget by moving your feet and hands. You feel like jumping out of your skin. You may impulsively rant or rave with those around you.

Most experts believe that if you experience these physical effects of anxiety on a frequent, chronic basis, it can't be doing you any good. Various studies have suggested the possibility that chronic anxiety and stress could conceivably contribute to a variety of physical problems, such as abnormal heart rhythms, high blood pressure, irritable bowel syndrome, asthma, ulcers, stomach upset, acid reflux, chronic muscle spasms, tremors, chronic back pain, tension headaches, and a depressed immune system. Figure 2-2 illustrates the toll of chronic anxiety on the body.

However, before you get too anxious about your anxiety, please realize that hard, definitive evidence doesn't exist yet that shows that anxiety is a major cause of most of these problems. Nevertheless, enough studies have suggested that it can make these disorders worse and that you should probably take chronic anxiety seriously. In other words, have concern, but not panic.

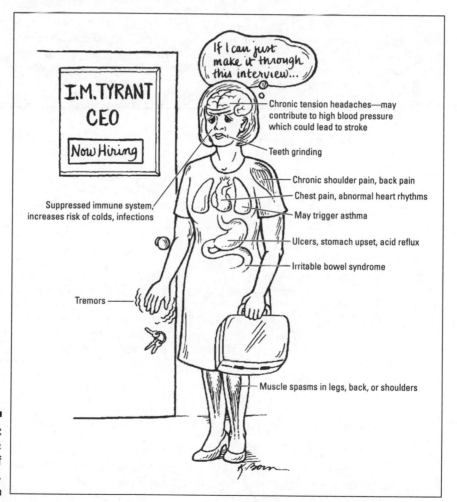

Figure 2-2:
The chronic effects of anxiety.

Defending against diabetes

If just the misery of chronic anxiety isn't enough, a couple more reasons to work on getting rid of excess stress are

✔ People with long-lasting stress are significantly more likely to develop type 2 diabetes.

✔ This isn't surprising, because stress increases the levels of glucose in the bloodstream.

Researchers at Duke University conducted a study with over 100 subjects and found that when stress management was added to the care of adults with diabetes, their blood sugar actually went down. These techniques weren't complex or time consuming. Many of these are the same techniques that you can read about in this book.

The amazing result of this study was that the glucose levels of those who found out how to calm down dropped as much as you would expect had the subjects been taking an extra diabetes-control drug. So if you don't have diabetes, protect yourself by overcoming anxiety, and if you do have diabetes, calm thoughts may help you and your doctor control the disease.

Chapter 3

Clearing the Roadblocks to Change

The odds are that if you're reading this book, you want to do something about your own anxiety or help someone that you love. If so, you should know that people start on the path to change with the best intentions, but as they move along, suddenly they encounter icy conditions and lose traction, spin their wheels, and slide off the road.

This chapter gives you ways to throw salt and sand on the ice and keep moving. First, we explain where anxiety comes from. When you understand the origins of anxiety, you can move from self-blame to self-acceptance, thus allowing yourself to direct your energy away from self-abuse and toward more productive activities. Next, we show you the other big barriers that tend to block the way to change. Finally, we give you effective strategies to keep you safely on the road to overcoming anxiety.

Digging Out the Roots of Anxiety

The three major causes of anxiety are

▶ **Genetics:** Your biological inheritance

▶ **Parenting:** The way that you were reared

▶ **Trauma:** The vexing events of everyday life

Studies show that when people experience an unanticipated trauma, only a minority ends up with severe anxiety. That's because anxiety usually stems from a combination of causes — perhaps genes and trauma or trauma and parenting or sometimes all three gang up to induce anxiety. At the same time, just one factor, if formidable enough, could possibly cause the entire problem.

For example, **Bonnie** manages to grow up in a drug war zone without developing terribly distressing symptoms. Bullets whiz through her bedroom window one night and one pierces her abdomen. She shows surprising resilience during her recovery. Surely, she must have some robust, anti-anxiety genes, and perhaps some pretty good parents as well in order to successfully endure such an experience. However, when she is raped at the age of sixteen, she develops serious problems with anxiety — she has sustained one trauma too many.

Thus, you can never ascertain the exact cause of anyone's anxiety with absolute certainty. However, if you examine someone's childhood relationship with his or her parents, family history, and the various events in one's life (such as accidents, war, disease, and so on), you can generally come up with some pretty good ideas as to why anxiety now causes problems. If you have anxiety, consider reviewing these fomenters of distress and think about which ones may have caused you the most trouble.

But what difference does it make where your anxiety comes from? Overcoming anxiety doesn't absolutely require knowledge of where it originated. The remedies change little whether you were born with anxiety or acquired it much later in your life.

Identifying the source of your anxiety lies can help you to realize that your anxiety isn't something that you brought on yourself. Anxiety develops for a number of good, solid reasons. The blame doesn't belong with the person who has anxiety.

Guilt and self-blame can only sap your energy. They drain resources and keep your focus away from the effort required for challenging your anxiety. By contrast, self-forgiveness and self-acceptance invigorate and vitalize your efforts.

Sleuthing your genetic villains

If you suffer from excessive worries and tension, look around at the rest of your family. Of those who have an anxiety disorder, typically about a quarter of their relatives suffer along with them. So your Uncle Ralph may not struggle with anxiety, but Aunt Melinda or your sister Charlene just might.

But you may argue that Uncle Ralph, Aunt Melinda, and your sister Charlene all had to live with Grandma who'd make anyone anxious. In other words, they lived in an anxiety-inducing environment. Maybe it has nothing to do with their genes.

Genetic goofs

Studies have shown a genetic mutation in people with anxiety disorders that affects the availability of the brain's neurotransmitter *serotonin,* which is believed to contribute to emotional well-being. If you don't have enough serotonin floating around in your brain, you're likely to fall prey to worries, anxiety, or the blues. Medications can increase the availability of serotonin in the brain (see Chapter 15).

Various researchers have studied siblings and twins who live together to verify that genes do play an important role as to how people experience and cope with anxiety. As predicted, identical twins were far more similar to each other in terms of anxiety than fraternal twins or other siblings. But even if you're born with a genetic predisposition toward anxiety, other factors such as environment, peers, and how your parents raised you, enter into the mix.

It's my parents' fault!

Parent-bashing is in. Blaming parents for almost anything that ails you is easy. Parents usually do the best they can. Raising children poses a formidable task. So in most cases, parents don't deserve to be vilified. However, they do hold responsibility for the way that you were brought up and thus may have contributed to your woes.

Three parenting styles appear to foster anxiety in children:

- **Overprotective:** These parents shield their kids from every imaginable stress or harm. If their kids stumble, they swoop them up before they even hit the ground. When their kids get upset, they fix the problem. Not surprisingly, their kids fail to find out how to tolerate fear, anxiety, or frustration.

- **Over-controlling:** These parents micro-manage all their children's activities. They direct every detail from how they should play to what they should wear to how they solve arithmetic problems. They discourage independence and fertilize dependency and anxiety.

- **Inconsistent:** The parents in this group provide their kids with erratic rules and limits. One day, they respond with understanding when their kids have trouble with their homework; the next day, they explode when their kids ask for help. These kids fail to discover the connection between their own efforts and a predictable outcome. Therefore, they feel that they have little control over what happens in life. It's no wonder that they feel anxious.

It's the world's fault!

The world today moves at a faster pace than ever, and the workweek has gradually inched upward rather than the other way around. Modern life is rife with both complexity and danger. Perhaps that's why mental health workers see more people with anxiety-related problems than ever before. Four specific types of vexing events can trigger a problem with anxiety even in someone who has never suffered from it much before:

- **Unanticipated threats:** Predictability and stability counteract anxiety and the opposite fuels it. For example, **Calvin** works long hours to make a decent living. Nevertheless, he lives from paycheck to paycheck with little left for savings. A freak slip on an icy patch of sidewalk disables him for six weeks, and he has insufficient sick leave to cover his absence. He now worries obsessively over his ability to pay bills. Even when he returns to work, he worries more than ever about the next financial booby trap that awaits him.

- **Escalating demands:** Nothing is better than a promotion. At least that's what **Jake** thinks when his supervisor hands him a once-in-a-lifetime opportunity to direct the new high-risk Research & Development division at work. Jake never expected such a lofty position this early in his career or the doubling of his salary. Of course, new duties, expectations, and responsibilities come along for the ride. Jake now begins to fret and worry. What if he fails to meet the challenge? Anxiety starts taking over his life.

- **Confidence killers: Tricia** is on top of the world. She has a good job and feels ecstatic about her upcoming wedding. However, she is stunned when her fiancé backs out of the proposal. Now, she worries incessantly that something is wrong with her; perhaps she'll never have the life she envisioned for herself.

- **Terrorizing trauma:** No one ever wants to experience a horrifying or even life-threatening experience. Unfortunately, these bitter pills do happen. Sexual abuse, horrific accidents, battlefield injuries, and rape have occurred for centuries, and we suspect that they always will. When they do, severe problems with anxiety often emerge. (See Chapter 2 for information about Post-Traumatic Stress Disorder.)

Moving from Self-Abuse to Self-Acceptance

Time and again, we see our worried, tense clients suffer from another needless source of pain. Their anxiety is bad enough, but they also pound on themselves *because* they have anxiety. If you do this to yourself, we suggest that you try Gary's approach to self-forgiveness.

Gary developed a panic disorder. His attacks of feeling nauseous, dizzy, out of breath, and thinking he's going crazy have increased recently. He feels deep shame and embarrassment that someone like him has this problem. When he starts having panic attacks at work, he finally caves in and seeks help. He tells his psychologist that a real man would never have this kind of problem. His psychologist helps Gary to be more self-forgiving. He asks Gary to write down the three major causes of his anxiety. He tells him to thoroughly review his life and come up with as many possible contributors to his worries as he can. Look at Table 3-1 in this chapter to see what Gary came up with.

Table 3-1	Gary's Anxiety Causes	
Possible Genetic Influence	*Parenting*	*Events: Old and New*
My Aunt Mary hardly ever leaves her house. Maybe she has something like I do.	Well, my father had quite an unpredictable temper. I never knew when he'd blow.	When I was 6 years old, we had a terrible car accident, and I spent three days in the hospital. I was scared.
My mother is high strung.	My mother's moods bounced all over the place. I could never tell how she'd react when I asked her for something.	My middle school was in a terrible neighborhood. Gangs ruled. I had to look over my shoulder at every turn.
My cousin Margarite seems shy. Maybe she has too much anxiety.		My first marriage ended when I caught my wife cheating. I couldn't believe she would do something like that. Even though I trust my new wife, I worry too much about her faithfulness.
My brother worries all the time. He seems totally stressed.		Two years ago, I was diagnosed with diabetes. I worry too much about my health now.

If you'd like to better understand the causes of your anxiety, write them down like Gary did in Table 3-1. Separate your paper into columns that are topped with the same headings, "Possible Genetic Influence," "Parenting," "Events: Old and New." Take your time; don't rush it. You may write several drafts before you come up with a definitive list. You may want to do this task over several days.

Anxiety among the rich and famous

So many of our clients seem to think that they're the only people in the world who struggle with anxiety. But we let them know that many millions of Americans suffer from anxiety. Perhaps you won't feel quite so alone if you consider some of the famous people through history who suffered from one or more of the various anxiety disorders discussed in this book.

Reportedly, Albert Einstein and Eleanor Roosevelt both suffered from fears of social situations. Further, Charles Darwin eventually became a virtual hermit because of his disabling Agoraphobia (see Chapter 2). Robert Frost also battled anxiety.

Billionaire Howard Hughes had many emotional problems, among them apparently, Obsessive-Compulsive Disorder (see Chapter 2). Hughes insisted on having three copies of a magazine delivered to him. When delivered, Hughes removed the middle magazine with his hands covered in tissue paper. Then he would instruct an assistant to burn the other two magazines. In addition, Hughes had a plethora of other bizarre compulsions involving preparation of his food, the handling of objects, and toileting. Finally, a quick search on the Internet shows you that hundreds of celebrities reputedly suffer from all kinds of severe problems with anxiety. Just use a major search engine and type in "famous people and anxiety." You'll be surprised by what you find.

After you list the likely culprits that led to your distress, ask yourself some questions like the ones that follow:

- ✔ Did I ask for my anxiety?

- ✔ Was there ever a time in my life that I actually wanted to feel anxious?

- ✔ Am I primarily to blame for my worries?

- ✔ What percentage of the blame can I realistically assign to myself as opposed to genes, parenting, and events, both old and new?

- ✔ If a couple of friends of mine had troubles with anxiety what would I say to them?

  - Would I think they were to blame?

  - Would I think as ill of them as I do myself?

- ✔ Does thinking badly about myself help me to get over my anxiety?

- ✔ If I decided to stop pummeling myself, would I have more energy for tackling my problems?

Hopefully, these questions can help you move toward self-acceptance. When you discover that having anxiety means nothing about your worth or value as a human being, you just might lighten up on yourself a little. We recommend it highly. If you find yourself completely unable to let go of self-abuse, you may want to seek professional help. Mind you, people get down on themselves at times. But, chronic, unrelenting self-abuse is another matter. You can read more about self-acceptance in a broader, deeper sense in Chapter 16.

Having Second Thoughts About Change

Clearly, no one likes feeling anxious, tense, and nervous, and anxiety may climb to such heights that it overwhelms personal resources and the capacity to cope. Chronic, severe anxiety frequently serves as a prelude to serious depression. Obviously, anyone experiencing this torment would jump at the chance to do something about it.

With good intentions, people buy self-help books, attend workshops, and even seek therapy. They fully intend to make meaningful changes in their lives. However, as the old proverb puts it, "Hell is paved with good intentions."

Have you ever gone to a health club in January? They're packed with new, enthusiastic members. By mid-March, health clubs return to normal. Like so many New Year's resolutions, the initial burst of resolve too often fades. What happens to all that determination?

When you bought this book, you may have vowed to do something about your anxiety once and for all. Like the January health club enthusiasts, you may still feel motivated and focused. If so, feel free to skip this section.

If you start losing your will power or your belief in your ability to do something about your anxiety, come back to this section! It can help you get back on track.

What happens to the folks at the health clubs in March? Usually, they think they've simply lost their willpower. Actually, interfering thoughts creep into their minds and steal away their motivation. They start to think that they don't have the time or the money or that they can get in shape later. Such thoughts seduce them into abandoning their goals.

Thoughts about abandoning your quest to overcome anxiety may disrupt your efforts at some point. If so, the first step involves identifying which one or ones stream through your mind. Then we give you strategies for fighting them off. So now, our top ten excuses for staying stuck:

10. Anxiety isn't really that big of a problem for me. I thought it was when I bought this book, but my anxiety isn't as bad as some of the people I've been reading about. Maybe it's not that big of a deal.

9. If I try and fail, I'll make a fool out of myself. My friends and family would think I was stupid to even try.

8. My anxiety feels too overwhelming to tackle. I just don't know if I could handle the additional stress of even thinking about it.

7. I'm afraid of trying and not getting anywhere. That would make me feel even worse than if I did nothing at all. I'd feel like a failure.

6. Feelings can't really be controlled. It's just fooling yourself to think otherwise. You feel the way you feel.

5. I'll do something about my anxiety when I feel the motivation. Right now, I don't really feel like it. I'm sure the motivation will come; I just have to wait for it.

4. Who would I be without my anxiety? That's just who I am. I'm an anxious person; it's just me.

3. I don't believe I can really change. After all, I've been this way my entire life. Books like these don't work anyway.

2. I'm too busy to do anything about my anxiety. These activities look like they take time. I could never work it into my hectic schedule.

1. The number one reason people stay stuck: I'm too anxious to do anything about my anxiety. Whenever I think about confronting my anxiety, it makes me feel worse.

Look over our preceding list several times. Mull over each excuse and circle any that seem familiar or reasonable to you. Any of these that you agree with will hinder your progress. Now, we have some ways for you to challenge these excuses, no matter how reasonable they may seem.

Deciding if You Really Want to Get the Show on the Road

If any of our top ten excuses for staying stuck resonate with you, then your decision to overcome anxiety is not stable. Those thoughts can sabotage your best intentions. Don't underestimate their power.

We have three types of strategies for helping you turn your intentions into actions:

✔ **Debate the decision with yourself.**

List your excuses for staying stuck and match them with reasons to move ahead.

✔ **Don't wait for a magical motivating moment.**

✔ **Kick-start your program.**

Half-hearted decisions lead to procrastination and avoidance of the task at hand. Anxiety hurts, but change is hard. The next section shows you how to push aside the fear of change.

Debating the decision

Pretend that you're judging a debate. One side favors the status quo, in other words, not changing. The other side takes the pro-change position. Ask which side makes the most sense; declare a victor.

Miguel worries about everything. He wakes up early in the morning with thoughts about what he must do that day for school. He dreams about going to class without his homework and being embarrassed by his teacher. He puts off applying for college out of fear that he won't get in, even though his grades and test scores pose no problem. He feels nervous, tense, and irritable much of the time. Lately, his worries disrupt his concentration to the extent that he spaces out during class lectures. His parents insist that he see a counselor for help with his anxiety, but Miguel doesn't believe it will help. The counselor, making up a chart like Table 3-2 in this chapter, works with him to debate his reluctance to work on overcoming his anxiety.

Table 3-2	Miguel's Great Debate
Excuses for Staying Stuck	*Reasons for Moving Forward*
If I try and fail, I'll make a fool out of myself. My friends and family would think I was stupid to even try.	Many of my friends have seen counselors, and I've never thought poorly of them, even if one or two of them didn't seem to get much better. At least they tried. Besides, I have a pretty good chance of succeeding; I usually do on most things I work at.
I'm afraid of trying and not getting anywhere. That would make me feel even worse than if I did nothing at all. I'd feel like a failure.	The only real failure would be to not do anything at all. This anxiety keeps me from doing the best I can in school. I run a bigger risk of failing in school if I stay stuck.
Feelings can't really be controlled. It's just fooling yourself to think otherwise. You feel the way you feel.	Just because I feel it's hopeless to do anything, doesn't mean it's true. Many people go to therapy for some reason; surely it makes them feel better or the world wouldn't have a zillion therapists.
Who would I be without my anxiety? That's just who I am. I'm an anxious person; it's just me.	Anxiety doesn't define who I am. It just gets in my way. I have many fine qualities that won't change.

Which side wins the debate? We think the reasons for moving forward deserve a clear victory.

If you have some excuses for staying stuck, try subjecting them to debate like Miguel did in Table 3-2 in this chapter. List your "Excuses for Staying Stuck" on the left side of a blank sheet of paper and your "Reasons for Moving Forward" on the right. The following questions may help you with developing your arguments for moving forward.

- ✔ Does my excuse catastrophize? In other words, am I exaggerating the truth?
- ✔ Can I find any evidence that would contradict my excuse?
- ✔ Can I think of people to whom my excuse doesn't apply? And if it doesn't apply to them, why should it to me?
- ✔ Am I trying to predict the future with negative thinking when no one can ever know the future?

Taking off from the starting blocks

Some excuses for staying stuck sap your motivation and will to change. One of our top ten excuses for staying stuck hits this issue head on, specifically number five: "I'll do something about my anxiety when I feel the motivation. Right now, I don't really feel like it. I'm sure the motivation will come; I just have to wait for it."

This excuse is based on a common but pernicious misconception. Most people think that they need to wait until motivation hits them before acting. Unfortunately, if you operate on that assumption, you could be in for a long wait. That's because facing your fears doesn't particularly feel good. It can even increase your anxiety for a little while. You may never *feel* like tackling it. However, if you start to take action and feel a little progress, your motivation surges.

Ellen can't face driving on freeways. She spends an extra hour each day getting to work and back because she takes the side roads. She really can't afford the time or the extra gas and wear on her car.

Ellen decides to get over her fear once and for all. However, each day when she gets in her car, the very thought of trying to drive even a little on the freeway makes her anxious, and she loses her resolve. So she rationalizes that she'll do something about her problem when the commute gets so bad that she feels sufficient motivation to deal with her fear.

Many months pass, the commute remains the same, and so does Ellen's fear of driving on freeways. She realizes that she may never *want* to confront her phobia. So she decides to force herself to drive on the freeway for just a short distance, whether she feels like it or not. Ellen decides to drive a half-mile stretch of the freeway near her home on a Sunday. After she gets home, she is surprised to find herself feeling proud of her small accomplishment and actually wants to do more. Each step she takes increases her motivation.

Action generally precedes motivation; if you wait to feel like overcoming your anxiety, you may wait a lifetime.

Taking baby steps

If you find that the idea of dealing with your anxiety is just too much to handle, you may be struggling with the number eight excuse for staying stuck: "My anxiety feels too overwhelming to tackle. I just don't know if I could handle the additional stress of even thinking about it." If so, putting one foot in front of the other may help; take baby steps.

Stop dwelling on the entire task. For example, if you think about all the steps that you'll take over the next five years, that's an incredible amount of walking. Hundreds, if not thousands, of miles await you. The mere thought of all those miles could stress you out.

You may, like many folks, wake up early in the morning on some days with a huge list of tasks that you need to do in the coming week. Ugh. A sense of defeat sets in and you feel like staying in bed for the rest of the day. Dread replaces enthusiasm. If instead, you clear your mind of the entire agenda and concentrate on only the first item on the list, your distress is likely to diminish, at least a little.

Paula, for example, is about to put this strategy into play. Paula has a Social Phobia. She can't stand the idea of attending social functions. She feels that the moment that she walks into a group, all eyes focus on her, which sends her anxiety through the roof. She desperately wants to change. But the idea of attending large parties or company functions overwhelms her with terror. Look at Table 3-3 to see how Paula broke the task down into baby steps.

Table 3-3	Paula's Baby Steps to Success
Goals	*Step-by-Step Breakdown of Actions*
Ultimate goal	Going to a large party, staying the entire time, and talking with numerous people without fear.
Intermediate goal	Attending a small party, staying a little while, and talking to a couple of people although feeling a little scared.
Small goal	Going to a work-related social hour, staying 30 minutes, talking to at least one other person in spite of some anxiety.
First baby step	Calling a friend and asking her to go to lunch in spite of anxiety.

This simple strategy works because the overwhelming task is broken down into manageable pieces. Sit down and chart out your ultimate goal, and then chart a goal that isn't quite so lofty that could serve as a stepping stone — an intermediate goal. Then chart out the action that would be required of you to meet a small goal. If your intermediate goal feels doable, you can start with it. If not, break it down further. It doesn't matter how small you make your first step. Anything that moves you just a little in the right direction can get you going and increase your confidence with one step at a time.

Considering the cons and pros

Maybe you suffer from anxiety, but when it comes to doing something about it, you start thinking that yours isn't all that bad after all. If so, you may be *rationalizing* and letting excuse number ten get in the way: "Anxiety isn't really that big of a problem for me. I thought it was when I bought this book, but my anxiety isn't as bad as some of the people that I've been reading about. Maybe it's not that big of a deal."

Persevering through the peaks and valleys

A group of psychologists conducted extensive research on how people make important changes, such as quitting smoking, losing weight, and overcoming emotional difficulties. They found that change isn't a straightforward process. It includes a number of stages.

Precontemplation: In this stage, people haven't even given a thought to doing anything about their problem. They may deny having any difficulty at all. If you're reading this book, you're probably not in this stage.

Contemplation: People start thinking about tackling their problem. But in this stage, it feels a little out of their reach to do anything about it.

Preparation: In preparation, people develop a plan for change. They gather their resources and make resolutions.

Action: The real work begins, and the plan goes into action.

Maintenance: Now is the time to hold one's ground. People must hang tough to prevent sliding back.

Termination: The change has become habit, so much so that relapse is less likely and further work isn't particularly necessary.

These stages look like a straight line from precontemplation to termination, but what these psychologists found is that people bounce around the stages in various ways. They may go from contemplation to action without having made adequate preparation. Others may reach the maintenance stage and give up on their efforts, slipping back to the precontemplation stage.

Many successful changers bounce back and forth in these stages a number of times before finally achieving their goals. So don't get discouraged if that happens to you. Keep your goal in mind and reinitiate your efforts if you slip. Yep. Try, try, and try again.

On the other hand, perhaps your anxiety doesn't warrant doing anything about it. If so, then that's wonderful! Give this book to a friend who needs it more than you! But how can you figure out if you're in denial or not? Pondering the pros and cons of conquering your anxiety can help you.

Ed directs the accounting department of a large manufacturing plant. He has huge responsibilities, multiple deadlines, and difficult people to supervise. He depends on many people to submit figures for his quarterly report, but sometimes, they fail to deliver on time, and Ed needs to confront them. Unfortunately, Ed dreads conflict and avoids speaking. The stress of waiting makes Ed feel nauseous, tense, and irritable. He knows that he has anxiety, but he figures that he's gotten by so far, so he questions whether it's worth trying to change.

Ed ponders the pros and cons of tackling his problem. Putting his concerns in perspective, he organizes his thoughts for taking action versus his fears on paper. (Look at Table 3-4 in this chapter to see how Ed mapped out his pros and cons.) Ed starts by listing the cons of taking action because he's more fully aware of what those are.

Table 3-4	Ed's Cons and Pros for Taking Action
Cons of Taking Action	*Pros of Taking Action*
It will make me more anxious to confront people.	I suffer from anxiety anyway and worry that I'll get in trouble if I can't get these people to produce on time. If I confront the people that I need to, I'll get more help.
People may not like me if I confront them.	I avoid people so much that they don't even know who I am. So what if a few people don't like me? Feeling less worried about people liking me sounds pretty good.
I'm not terribly unhappy at my job most of the time. My quarterly report just happens once a quarter.	Yes, it only happens once a quarter, but I dread the quarterly report for weeks in advance. Getting rid of the dread sounds worth doing.

When Ed considers his cons and pros carefully, he makes the decision to do something about his discomfort. You can use Ed's chart in Table 3-4 as a sample means of charting out your reasons for and against taking action. If your motivation wanes because you're not sure how serious your problem is, take the time to reflect thoroughly. Generate as many reasons as you can.

Chapter 4

Watching Worries Come and Go

Anxiety may feel like it will never go away. Believing that you have no control over it and that stress invades your every waking moment is easy. This chapter helps you to realize that anxiety actually has an ebb and flow. Then we show you how taking a few minutes to write down your feelings each day may discharge a little of your anxiety and possibly improve your health. Finally, we help you understand that progress, like anxiety, ebbs and flows.

Following Your Fears All the Way Down the Line

One of the best early steps that you can take to conquer anxiety is to simply follow it everyday in a couple of different ways. Why would you want to do all that? After all, you already know full well that you're anxious. Watching your worries starts the process of change. You discover important patterns, triggers, and insights into your anxiety.

Observing your anxiety from stem to stern

Observing anxiety fulfills several useful functions. First, monitoring forces you to be aware of your emotions. Avoiding and running away from troubling emotions only causes them to escalate. Second, you'll see that your anxiety goes up and down throughout the day — not quite as upsetting as thinking it rules every moment of your life. And you're likely to discover that recording your ratings can help you to take charge and feel more in control of what's going on inside of you. Finally, keeping track helps you to see how you're progressing in your efforts to quell your distress. Virginia's story shows you how.

Virginia complains to her friends that she's the most nervous person on the planet and that she's close to a nervous breakdown. Recently, her father had heart surgery and her husband lost his job. Virginia feels completely out of control and says that her anxiety never stops. When her counselor suggests that she start tracking her anxiety, she told him, "You've got to be kidding. I don't need to do that. I can tell you right now that I'm anxious all the time. There's no let up." He urges her to go ahead and try anyway.

Table 4-1 shows what Virginia comes up with in her first week of tracking. On a scale of one to ten — ten being total panic and one being complete calm — Virginia rates the level of anxiety that she experiences at around the same time in the morning, then again in the afternoon, and later in the evening.

Table 4-1	Virginia's Day-by-Day Anxiety Levels			
Day	**Morning**	**Afternoon**	**Evening**	**Daily Average**
Sunday	4	6	8	6
Monday	6	7	9	7.3
Tuesday	5	6	6	5.7
Wednesday	4	5	7	5.3
Thursday	3	8	8	6.3
Friday	5	9	9	7.7
Saturday	3	5	5	4.3
Average	**4.3**	**6.6**	**7.4**	**6.1**

Virginia discovers a few things. First, she notices that her anxiety is routinely less intense in the morning. It also tends to escalate in the afternoon and peak in the evenings. With only one week's records, she can't discern if her anxiety level is decreasing, increasing, or remaining stable. However, she notices feeling a little better simply because she feels like she's starting to take charge of her problem. She also realizes that some days are better than others and that her anxiety varies rather than overwhelming her all the time.

Track your anxiety in a notebook for a few weeks. Notice patterns or differences in intensity. Carry your anxiety-tracking notebook with you and try to fill it out at the same times each day.

Writing about your worries — warts and all

Millions of people keep a diary at some point in their lives. Some develop daily writing as a lifelong habit. Logically, people who keep journals must feel that they get something out of their writing or they wouldn't do it.

Keeping a journal of life's emotionally significant events has surprising benefits.

- Journal writing appears to decrease the number of visits people make to the doctor for physical complaints.

- It increases the production of T cells that are beneficial to the immune system.

- Keeping a journal about emotional events improved the grades of a group of college students as compared to those who wrote about trivial matters.

- Recently, unemployed workers who wrote about the trauma of losing their jobs found new employment more quickly than those who did not.

Throwing out the rule book

Journal writing doesn't have rules. You can write about anything, anywhere, and anytime. However, if you want the full benefits of writing in a journal, we encourage you to write about feelings and the emotionally important events of your life. Write about anything that troubles you during the day and/or past difficulties. Spend a little time on it.

Writing about past traumas may bring considerable relief. However, if you find that the task floods you with overwhelming grief or anxiety, you'll probably find it helpful to seek professional assistance.

Counting your blessings: An antidote for anxiety

Writing about your distressing feelings makes a great start. However, if you'd like more bang for your buck, take a few extra minutes and write about what you feel grateful for each day. Why? That's because positive emotions helps counteract negative emotions. Writing about your boons and blessings improves mood, increases optimism, and may benefit your health.

Boosting booster shots

Research on the value of expressing emotions in journals (reported in Volume 63, 1995, of the *Journal of Consulting and Clinical Psychology*) spans a wide range of populations and problems. One of the more interesting studies looked at healthy medical students who had not yet had their required Hepatitis B vaccinations. The researchers speculated that writing about traumatic events might result in improved immunity. Hepatitis B vaccinations come in a series of three shots. Prior to receiving the first shot, researchers assigned one group of students to write about past traumatic events in their lives daily for four days. The other group wrote about nonpersonal issues. At four months and even after six months following the shots, the blood of the students in the traumatic writing group had more antibodies against the Hepatitis B virus than did the blood of those in the other group.

At first blush, you may think that you have little to be grateful for. Anxiety can so easily cloud vision. Did your mother ever urge you to clean your plate because of the "starving kids in China?" As much as we think that pushing kids to eat is a bad idea, her notion to consider those less fortunate has value. Take some time to ponder the positive events and people in your life.

- ✔ **Kindnesses:** Think about those who have extended kindness to you.

- ✔ **Education:** Obviously, you can read; that's a blessing compared to the millions in the world with no chance for an education.

- ✔ **Nourishment:** You probably aren't starving to death, while, as your mother may have noted, millions are.

- ✔ **Home:** Do you live in a cardboard box or do you have a roof over your head?

- ✔ **Pleasure:** Can you smell flowers, hear birds sing, or touch the soft fur of a pet?

Sources of possible gratitude abound — freedom, health, companionship, and so on. Everyone has a different list. You can find yours by following Corrine's example.

Corrine, a single mother, worries about money, keeping up her house, and especially about her children, Trenton, age 15, and Julia, 12. She obsesses about the effect that her divorce has had on her kids and tries to be mother and father, as well as teacher, and police officer to them. Sometimes, she just feels like crying. When the principal called to tell her that a teacher had caught her son smoking pot in the parking lot, she fell apart. The court ordered counseling for the entire family. The therapist suggested keeping a journal of hassles and blessings for both mother and her son Trenton. Look at Corrine's first entries in Table 4-2 in this chapter.

Table 4-2	Corrine's Daily Hassles and Gratitude Journal	
Time of Day	**Hassles**	**Blessings**
Morning	As usual, I had to wake Trenton three or four times even though his alarm went off earlier. He barely talked to me at breakfast and was almost late for school. I worry so much that he'll fail everything. What would I do then? I want so much for him to be happy in life.	I can at least appreciate the fact that my kids are healthy. We have a nice home, and although I feel strapped sometimes, no one is starving here.
Afternoon	At work, I got put in charge of the new Dudley account. I don't know if I can handle this much responsibility. It makes me nervous just thinking about organizing all the people involved.	Hey, I have a great job and a new promotion. The boss must think I do good work even if I worry about it.
Evening	Dinner was the usual frozen stir-fry. Trenton didn't come home from practice until everything was cold. Julia watched TV and said little.	I am grateful for the fact that Trenton is interested in soccer. It will help keep him away from the wrong crowd. Julia is the sweetest kid there ever was, even though she watches too much TV.

Certainly, Corrine needs to work with her son about the incident at school and a few other issues. But when her anxiety rises to extremes, she can't be the parent she wants to be.

Writing in a journal helps Corrine put a different perspective on her problems. She realizes that she has been so uptight about her kids that she hasn't taken the time to notice the good things about them and her own life. Like most people, Corrine has her share of hassles and blessings. Writing about her hassles discharges a little of the emotion that she has bottled up about her concerns. Writing about what she feels grateful for helps to counteract some of her negative obsessions.

Consider keeping a journal as Corrine did. You can use Table 4-2 as a format for your own daily notes. Even if you don't think it could help you, try it for a few days. You might be surprised.

The power of positive psychology

The field of psychology focused on negative emotions for most of the twentieth century. Psychologists studied depression, anxiety, schizophrenia, behavior disorders, and a slew of other maladies. Only recently has the field looked at the pluses of positive emotions, the characteristics of happy people, and the components of well-being. People who feel grateful usually say they feel happier as well.

One study assigned people to three groups. The first group wrote only about the hassles of everyday life. The researchers asked the second group to write about emotionally neutral events.

The third group journaled about experiences that they were grateful for. All the groups performed this task merely once a week for ten weeks. At the end of the experiment (reported in full in Volume 19, 2000, of the *Journal of Social and Clinical Psychology)*, the group that wrote about gratitude exercised more, had fewer physical complaints, and felt more optimistic than those in the other two groups. That such an easy, simple task could be so beneficial is surprising.

Consider giving thanks and appreciating life's gifts from small to large.

Sizing Up Success

You may feel some benefit from simply rating your anxiety on a daily basis and from your journal, but don't expect large improvements overnight. Change takes time. Sometimes, it takes a number of weeks before a positive direction emerges. After all, you spent much of your life feeling anxious; give change time as well.

You should also know that improvement does not happen in a constant, smooth fashion. Rather, it takes a jagged, mountainous course with many ups and downs. You'll have peaks — times when you feel that you're on top of the world and on the verge of conquering your anxiety. But you'll also slip into valleys, and you may feel as though you're on the edge of failure and despair.

Realize that if you're standing in the middle of one of the valleys, it looks like a long climb. You could even feel like you're making no progress at all because all that you see are peaks around you. These are not the times for evaluating your progress. However, the advantage of a valley is that it can tell you much about what trips you up. So if you're in a valley, rather than catastrophize, take the opportunity to reflect and know that things will get better.

If you don't start feeling better after a number of weeks, or if you start feeling utterly hopeless, you should consider seeking professional advice.

Part II
The Thought Remedies

The 5th Wave   By Rich Tennant

"Dora's anxiety has always manifested itself in the 'flight response'."

In this part . . .

We talk about one of the most effective therapies for anxiety and show you methods for tracking your anxiety-arousing thoughts along with ways to change anxious thoughts into calmer thinking. Next, we describe the agitating assumptions that underlie many anxious thoughts. You can discover which agitating assumptions plague you and how you can do something about them.

Furthermore, you'll see that the very words you use to think about yourself and the world can intensify anxiety. The good news is that you can replace your worry words with more reasonable language. In so doing, your anxiety decreases.

Chapter 5

Becoming a Thought Detective

Some time ago, we took a cruise to reward ourselves for completing a major project. One evening, we sat on deck chairs enjoying a fabulous sunset: Brilliant red and orange clouds melted into the deep blue sea. The wind picked up ever so slightly, and the ship rolled gently. We sat relaxed, quietly enjoying the scene and the cradle-like motion. We reflected that in our lifetimes, we had rarely felt so at peace.

The captain's weather announcement interrupted our tranquil state of mind. Apologizing for the inconvenience, he informed us that due to a hurricane, he would have to steer a slightly different course, and we may feel some choppy seas. Still, he assured us that the storm presented no threat.

The breeze suddenly felt chilling. The clouds, once spectacular, appeared ominous. The gentle roll that had relaxed us, generated nervousness. Yet nothing about the sky or the sea had changed from moments earlier.

Our thoughts jerked us from blissful relaxation to mounting anxiety. We pulled our jackets tighter and commented that the weather looked nasty, perhaps we'd be better off inside. Only our thoughts about the sky, the sea, and the breeze had shifted, not the weather.

In this chapter, we show you how powerfully your thoughts influence your emotions and perceptions. You can become a thought detective, able to uncover the thoughts that contribute to anxious feelings. We show you how to gather evidence and put your thoughts on trial. You can see how thoughts all too easily trigger your anxiety, and we give you proven techniques for transforming your anxious thoughts into calm thoughts.

Distinguishing Thoughts from Feelings

Psychologists, often query their clients to find out how they feel about recent events in their lives. Frequently, they answer with how they *think* about the events rather than how they *feel.* For example, Dr. Wolfe had a highly anxious client named Jim who complained about his marriage in the following manner:

Dr. Wolfe: How did you feel when your wife said you were irresponsible?

Jim: I thought she was really out of line.

Dr. Wolfe: I see. But how did you *feel* about what she said?

Jim: She's at least as irresponsible as I am.

Dr. Wolfe: I suppose that's possible. But again, what were your *feelings,* your emotional reaction to what she said? Were you anxious, even angry, or upset?

Jim: Well, I couldn't believe she could accuse me of that.

Dr. Wolfe: I wonder if we should take some time to help you get in touch with your feelings?

Perhaps Jim is extremely anxious and worried that his wife will leave him, or possibly, he's angry with her. Maybe her stinging criticism hurt him. Whatever the feeling, both Jim and Dr. Wolfe could find out plenty from knowing what emotion accompanies his upset.

This example shows that people may not always know how to describe what they're feeling. If you don't always know what you're feeling, that's okay.

Blocking the blues

People often have trouble identifying and labeling their feelings and emotions, especially negative ones. Actually, the difficulty makes sense for two reasons.

First, emotions often hurt. No one wants to feel profound sadness, grief, anxiety, or fear. One simple solution — *avoid* feelings entirely, and many creative ways to avoid emotion are available. Unfortunately, most of these methods can be destructive.

✔ **Workaholism:** Some folks work all the time rather than think about what's disturbing them.

✔ **Alcoholism and drug abuse:** When people feel bad, numbing their emotions with drugs and alcohol provides a temporary, artificial emotional lift; of course, habitually doing so can lead to addiction, ill health, and sometimes, even death.

✔ **Denial and repression:** One strategy for not feeling is to fool yourself and pretend that nothing is wrong.

✔ **Sensation seeking:** High-risk activities, such as sexual promiscuity and compulsive gambling, can all push away distress for a while.

✔ **Distraction:** Athletics, entertainment, hobbies, television, surfing the Internet, and many other activities can cover up bad feelings. Unlike the preceding strategies, distraction can be a good thing. It's only when distractions are used in excess to cover up and avoid feelings that they become problematic.

The second reason that identifying, expressing, and labeling feelings is such a struggle for people is because they're taught from an early age that they "shouldn't" feel certain feelings. Parents, teachers, friends, and relatives bombard kids with "don't feel" messages. See the examples that follow of "don't feel" messages that you've probably heard before:

✔ Big boys don't cry.

✔ Don't be a baby.

✔ Get over it!

✔ It couldn't possibly hurt that bad.

✔ Don't be a scaredy-cat.

✔ Grow up.

✔ Don't be a chicken.

✔ Stop crying, or I'll give you something to cry about!

That many people are described as "out of touch with their feelings" is no wonder. The problem with the habitual tendency to avoid feelings is that you don't find out how to cope with or resolve the underlying issue. Chronic avoidance creates a certain kind of low-level stress that builds over time.

"Denial" isn't just a river in Egypt

In *Gone with the Wind,* Scarlet O'Hara said time and again, "I'll think about that tomorrow. After all, tomorrow is another day." What a nice, easy solution to tough times — shove the issue out of the way. But we're discovering more about the costs of avoiding and repressing emotions. According to researchers at Adelphi University and the University of Michigan, people who declare themselves as mentally healthy over the years when other evidence shows they're not have higher heart rates and blood pressure in response to stress than folks who own up to their emotional difficulties or those who truly don't have problems at the time. Studies also show that when people write about their emotions on a daily basis, their immune system improves. Amazing stuff.

Getting in touch with your feelings

Noticing your emotions can help you gain insight and discover how to cope more effectively. If you don't know what your feelings are, when they occur, and what brings them on, then you can't do much about changing them.

We realize that some people are aware of their feelings and know all too well when they're feeling the slightest amount of anxiety or worry. If you're one of those, feel free to skip or skim the rest of this section.

Take some time right now to assess your mood. First, notice your breathing. Is it rapid and shallow or slow and deep? Notice your posture. Are you relaxed or is some part of your body in an uncomfortable position. Check out all your physical sensations. Look for sensations of tension, queasiness, tightness, dizziness, or heaviness. No matter what you find, just study it and sit with the sensations a while. Then you might ask yourself what *feeling* captures the essence of those sensations. Of course, at this moment, you may not have any strong feelings. If so, your breathing is rhythmic and your posture relaxed. Even if that's the case, notice what it feels like to be calm. At other times, notice your stronger sensations.

Feeling words describe your physical and mental reaction to events.

Perhaps we're presuming too much, but because you're reading this book, we guess that you or someone close to you wants to know about anxiety. So we've given you the following vocabulary list for describing anxious feelings. The next time that you can't find the right words to describe how you feel, one of the words that follow may get you started.

Afraid	Out of it
Anxious	Panicked
Agitated	Self-conscious
Apprehensive	Shaky
Disturbed	Tense
Dread	Terrified
Fearful	Timid
Insecure	Uneasy
Nervous	Uptight
Obsessed	Worried

We're sure that we've missed a few dozen possibilities on the word list, and maybe you have a favorite way to describe your anxiety. That's fine. What we encourage you to do is to start paying attention to your feelings and bodily sensations. You may want to look over this list a number of times and ask yourself if you've felt any of these emotions recently. Try not to make judgments about your feelings. They may be trying to tell you something useful.

Anxiety and fear also have a positive function; they ready your mind and body for danger. Bad feelings only cause problems when you feel bad chronically and repeatedly in the absence of a clear threat.

Negative emotions have an adaptive role to play. They alert you to danger. They prepare you to respond. For example, if King Kong knocks on your door, adrenaline floods your body and mobilizes you to fight him or run like hell! That's good for situations like that. But if you feel like King Kong is knocking on your door on a regular basis and he's not even in the neighborhood, your anxious feelings cause you more harm than good.

Whether King Kong is knocking at your door or not, identifying anxious, fearful, or worried feelings can help you deal with them far more effectively than avoiding them. When you know what's going on, you can focus on what to do about your predicament more easily than you can sitting in the dark.

Getting in touch with your thoughts

Just as some people don't have much idea about what they're feeling, others have trouble knowing what they're thinking when they're anxious, worried, or stressed. Because thoughts have a powerful influence on feelings, psychologists like to ask their clients what they were thinking when they start to feel upset. Sometimes clients describe feelings rather than thoughts. For example, Dr. Baker had the following dialogue with Susan, a client who had severe anxiety:

> **Dr. Baker:** So when your supervisor reprimanded you, you said you felt panicked. What thoughts went through your mind?
>
> **Susan:** Well, I just felt horrible. I couldn't stand it.
>
> **Dr. Baker:** I know; it must have felt really awful. But I'm curious about what thoughts went through your mind. What did you say to yourself about your supervisor's comments?
>
> **Susan:** I felt my heart pounding in my chest. I don't think I really had any thoughts actually.
>
> **Dr. Baker:** That's possible. Sometimes our thoughts escape us for a while. But I wonder if you think about it now, what did those comments mean to you? What did you think would happen?
>
> **Susan:** I'm shaking right now just thinking about it.

As this example illustrates, people don't always know what's going on in their heads when they feel anxious. Sometimes you may not have clear, identifiable thoughts when you feel worried or stressed. That's perfectly normal.

The challenge is to find out what the stressful event *means* to you. That will tell you what your thoughts are. Consider the example prior example. Susan might have felt panicked because she feared losing her job, or she may have thought his criticism meant that she was incompetent. The boss's reprimand may have also triggered memories of her abusive father. Knowing what thoughts stand behind the feelings can help both Dr. Baker and Susan plan the next step.

Tapping your triggers

If you're like Susan, you don't always know what's going on in your mind when you feel anxious. To figure it out, you need to first identify the *situation* that preceded your upset. Zero in on what had just transpired moments before your troublesome feelings. Perhaps you:

- Opened your mail and found that your credit card balance had skyrocketed.
- Heard someone say something that bothered you.
- Read the deficiency notice from your child's school.
- Are wondering why your partner is so late coming home.
- Just got off the scales and saw a number that you didn't like.
- Noticed that your chest feels tight and your heart is racing for no clear reason.

On the other hand, sometimes your anxiety-triggering event hasn't even happened yet. You may be just sitting around and *wham* — an avalanche of anxiety crashes through. Other people wake up at 4 a.m. with worries marching through their minds. What's the trigger then? Well, it can be an image or a fear of some future event. See the following examples of anxiety-triggering thoughts and images:

- I'll never have enough money for retirement.
- Did I turn off the stove before I left the house?
- We'll never finish writing this book on time!
- No one is going to like my speech tomorrow.

✔ What if I get laid off tomorrow?

✔ What if my partner leaves me?

Listen in as Veronica searches for her anxiety-triggering event.

Veronica works in the college admissions office. The college offers her free tuition for two classes per semester. One day, Veronica's supervisor suggests that she consider taking a class in business administration to increase the chances of her getting a promotion in the department. Later, she finds herself feeling unusually anxious. She doesn't know why.

However, after she thinks about it a while, Veronica realizes that the trigger for her anxiety is the thought of taking a class and having to sit through exams. She has always hated tests. Veronica never considered going to college because she's so anxious about taking tests. Veronica's anxiety trigger is the image of a future event — the idea of taking a test.

Snaring your anxious thoughts

If you know your feelings and the triggers for those feelings, you're ready to become a thought detective. Thoughts powerfully influence emotions. The event may serve as the trigger, but it isn't what directly leads to your anxiety. It's the meaning that the event holds for you, and your thoughts reflect that meaning.

For example, suppose your spouse is 45 minutes late coming home from work. You could think *anxious* thoughts:

✔ Maybe she's had an accident.

✔ She's probably having an affair.

Or you might have different thoughts that don't cause so much anxiety:

✔ I love having time alone with the kids.

✔ I like having time alone to work on house projects.

✔ Traffic must be really bad tonight.

Some thoughts create anxiety; others feel good; still others don't stir up much feeling at all. Capturing your thoughts and seeing how they trigger anxiety and connect to your feelings is important. If you're not sure what thoughts are in your head when you're anxious, you can do something to find them.

First, focus on the anxiety trigger. Think about it for a while; don't rush it. Then ask yourself some questions about the trigger. The following list of what we call *minding-your-mind questions* can help you to identify your thoughts or the meaning that the event holds for you:

- ✔ Specifically, what about this event do I find upsetting?
- ✔ What's the worst that could happen?
- ✔ How might this event affect my life?
- ✔ How might this affect the way that others see me?
- ✔ Does this remind me of anything in my past that bothered me?
- ✔ What would my parents say about this event?
- ✔ How might this affect the way that I see myself?

Veronica (you remember her name from earlier in this chapter) suffers from test anxiety. Look at her answers to a few of the following questions from the minding-your-mind list. Her answers indicate what thoughts she has about exams.

- ✔ **What's the worst that could happen?**

  I could fail the test and my boss would find out.
- ✔ **How might this event affect the way others see me?**

  My boss and my coworkers will know how stupid I am.
- ✔ **How might this event affect the way I see myself?**

  I'll finally know for sure that I'm the loser I've always thought I might be.

Even though earlier, Veronica couldn't explain why tests made her so anxious, answering these questions brings her hidden thoughts about test taking to light. No wonder she feels so anxious. Perhaps you'll discover some hidden thoughts of your own if you ask yourself these questions about your anxiety triggers.

Here's Andrew's story.

Andrew loves his work. He designs computer systems for a living and relishes creating complex computer systems to meet the clients' needs. The management appreciates Andrew's expertise and rewards him with a promotion and the opportunity to design a major system for one of the national laboratories. Andrew can't wait to begin at least until he realizes that part of the project involves giving a number of talks to groups of managers and scientists. Andrew's heart races and he perspires profusely at the mere thought of speaking in front of a group. Andrew has been terrified of speaking in front of an audience since elementary school, but he had no idea why.

Andrew has a rather common fear — the fear of speaking in public. He answers a few of the minding-your-mind questions:

> ✔ **Specifically what about this event do I find upsetting?**
>
> I'll look silly and forget what I wanted to say.
>
> ✔ **How might this event affect my life?**
>
> They'll think I'm incapable of putting this system together, and I'll lose the sale.
>
> ✔ **How might this affect the way that others see me?**
>
> They'll know how scared I am and think I'm a fool. Those scientists know more than I do.

When you work with the minding-your-mind questions, use your imagination. Brainstorm and take your time. Even though our examples don't answer all the questions, you may find it useful to do so.

Tracking Your Thoughts, Triggers, and Feelings

Monitoring your thoughts, feelings, and whatever triggers your anxiety paves the way for change. This simple strategy helps you focus on your personal pattern of stress and worry. The very act of paying attention brings your thinking process to light. This clarification helps you gain a new perspective.

If recording your thoughts, feelings, and triggers makes you more anxious, that's okay. It's common. Many other techniques in this book should help, especially the ones for challenging your thoughts in this chapter.

But if the techniques in this book don't help you, consider seeking professional help.

Try using the Thought-Therapy Chart in Table 5-1 to connect your thoughts, feelings, and anxiety triggers. To show you how to use the chart, we've filled it in with Veronica's notes. When you monitor the triggers, include the day, time, place, people involved, and what was going on. When you record your anxious thoughts, use the minding-your-mind questions in the "Snaring your anxious thoughts" section, earlier in this chapter. Finally, write down your anxious feelings and physical sensations, and rate the severity of those feelings. Use 1 to represent almost no anxiety at all and 100 to indicate the most severe anxiety imaginable. (Sort of like how you might feel if 100 rattle snakes suddenly appeared slithering around your bedroom!)

Table 5-1	Thought-Therapy Chart		
Anxiety Triggers	*Anxious Thoughts*	*Feelings & Sensations*	*Rating*
Tuesday morning.	If I take this class, I'll fail, and my boss will find out.	Anxious	70
At work.	I'll never get ahead in this job.	Queasy stomach	60
My boss suggested that I take the class.	I'm really stupid.	Tension	65

You can use this simple technique to monitor your anxious feelings, thoughts, and triggers. Simply design your own Thought-Therapy Chart using the headings of Table 5-1. Keep track and look for patterns.

Raymond discovers that he feels anxious on most Mondays. He realizes that he tends to sleep late on Sunday morning, and therefore, he has trouble falling asleep Sunday nights. A lack of sleep usually makes him more susceptible to anxiety triggers. What doesn't bother him on Tuesdays, stresses him out on Mondays. Raymond changes his sleep habits and feels a little less anxious on Mondays.

Madison, an elementary school teacher, tracks her triggers, thoughts, and feelings for a month. She isn't surprised to discover that she feels anxious about the possibility of receiving criticism. She notices herself shaking the day that the principal observes her class for her yearly evaluation. She finds it difficult to nail down her thoughts at first, so she uses the minding-your-mind questions in the "Snaring your anxious thoughts" section, earlier in this chapter. She asks the question, "What would your parents say about this?" Madison actually hears her mother's caustic voice in her head saying, "You'll never amount to anything if you can't even clean your bedroom right."

Madison realizes how critical her mother had been and how much her mother's harshness hurt her. Just figuring that out helps Madison see that she is expecting the principal to be like her mother. When she thinks about it, she remembers the principal giving her a number of compliments about her teaching. She understands that a negative evaluation is unlikely. This insight alone reduces her anxiety.

Although monitoring may produce useful insights that reduce your anxiety a bit, you, like most people, may need a little more assistance. The next section shows you how to tackle your anxious thoughts and make them manageable.

Tackling Your Thoughts: Thought Therapy

We have three simple strategies for tackling your anxious thoughts.

- **Thought court:** Take your thoughts to court and sift through the evidence.

- **Rethink risk:** Recalculate the odds of your anxious thoughts coming true — most people overestimate the odds.

- **Worst-case scenarios:** Re-examine your ability to cope — if the worst does occur. Most folks underestimate their coping resources.

Veronica tracks her anxious thoughts about test taking. But she never questions them. She remains anxious and convinced that if she takes a class, she will surely fail. And everyone will realize how stupid she is. Veronica needs more than monitoring to deal with her anxious thoughts. She must go to thought court to review the evidence for and against her habitual way of thinking.

Weighing the evidence: Thought court

The thoughts that lead to your anxious feelings have most likely been around a long time. Most people consider their thoughts to be true. They don't question them. You might be surprised to discover that many of your thoughts don't hold up under scrutiny. If you carefully gather and weigh the evidence, you just may find that your thoughts rest on a foundation made of sand.

Keep in mind that gathering evidence when you're feeling really anxious isn't always easy to do. At those times, it's hard to consider that your thoughts might be inaccurate. When that's the case, you'll be better off waiting until you calm down before hunting for the evidence. At other times, you may be able to find evidence if your anxiety isn't too out of control. You may also find it useful to consider the following *evidence-gathering questions* when judging the accuracy of your anxious thoughts.

- Have I had thoughts like these at other times in my life? Have my dire predictions come true?

- Do I have experiences that would contradict my thoughts in any way?

- Is this situation really as awful as I'm making it out to be?

- A year from now, how much concern will I have with this issue?

- Am I thinking this will happen just because I'm feeling anxious and worried? Am I basing my conclusion mostly on my feelings or on the true evidence?

Feelings are always valid in the sense that you feel what you feel. But they are not evidence for supporting anxious thoughts. For example, if you feel extremely anxious about taking a test, the anxiety is not evidence of how you will perform.

These evidence-gathering questions can help you discover evidence for and against your anxious or worrisome thoughts. Take a look at Veronica's notes again in Table 5-1, earlier in this chapter, and her collection of evidence that follows in Table 5-2. Veronica used the evidence-gathering questions in this section to list the evidence against her anxious thoughts in the second column of the table.

Table 5-2	Weighing the Evidence
Evidence Supporting My Anxious Thoughts	*Evidence Against My Anxious Thoughts*
I know my boss will find out if I don't pass because the University pays for my tuition.	Evidence that my boss won't find out if I don't pass doesn't exist. However, even if she does, she'll probably just feel bad for me.
I almost failed chemistry my senior year in high school.	In four years of high school, chemistry was the only class that gave me trouble. I did get pretty good grades.
My father always said that I was slow to learn.	The reason that I feel stupid is probably because of my father; no one else ever said that. Besides, feelings aren't really evidence!
I don't feel smart.	My boss wouldn't have suggested that I take this class unless she thought I could do it. Besides, feelings are not evidence.
My best friend made better grades than I did, and she's in college now. I must be an idiot.	My best friend was just more confident than me; that's why she's in college. My grades were high enough.
I've been at this job for two years and haven't gotten promoted.	Nobody gets promoted here unless they take these classes. That's the only reason I haven't been promoted.

After completing the task, Veronica makes a new judgment about her anxious thoughts. Veronica realizes that the evidence supporting her anxious thoughts doesn't hold up to scrutiny. Upon reflection, she sees that much of her feelings of inferiority stem from a critical father. Furthermore, she's surprised by how much evidence actually supports an alternative view — that she's actually quite capable. Thus, she has a change of heart and more importantly, her anxiety decreases. She decides to take the class and do the best she can.

Consider filling out your own chart so that you can weigh the evidence carefully. Use the same column headings and format of Table 5-2. Be creative and come up with as much evidence for and against as you can.

Don't forget to use the evidence-gathering questions listed earlier in this section if you need help generating ideas.

Make a decision as to whether you truly think your anxious thoughts hold water. If they don't, you just might start taking them less seriously, and your anxiety could drop a notch or two.

Although charting your anxious thoughts and weighing the evidence just once may prove to be helpful, practice magnifies the effect. The longer you stay at it and the more times that you chart your anxious thoughts versus the real evidence, the more you'll gain. Many of our clients find that charting these out regularly for three or four months alleviates a considerable amount of their negative feelings.

Rethinking risk

Another important way to challenge your anxious thoughts is to look at how you assess probabilities. When you feel anxious, like many people, you may *overestimate the odds* of unwanted events actually occurring. It's easy to do. For example, when's the last time you heard a news bulletin reporting that no one got bitten by a snake today, or that half a million airplanes took off and landed today and not a single plane crash? No wonder people overestimate disaster. Because they grab our attention, we focus on dramatic events rather than routine ones. That's why it's useful to think about the real, objective odds of your predicted catastrophe.

Thoughts are just thoughts. Subject them to a reality test.

Mary fears flying. Mary lives in Philadelphia. Her father-in-law, who lived in California, died unexpectedly. Mary drives across the country to the funeral rather than join her husband who chose to fly. Not only is Mary less available to help her family with arrangements, she misses several extra days of work. Her choice is ironic because by driving, she greatly increases her odds of being hurt or even dying. Flying is still the safest form of travel available.

Larry enjoys walking his dog. Unfortunately, Larry also worries that he may have forgotten to lock the door when he leaves the house. More often than not, after he turns the first corner, he goes back to check the lock. Some days, he checks the doorknob four or five times. He feels almost panicked at the idea of someone breaking into his house. Larry doesn't realize that he's over-estimating two risks. First, although his *thoughts* tell him, he probably left the door unlocked; *reality* says that he has never done that. Second, only a few break-ins have occurred in his neighborhood in the past several years. The odds of a burglar plotting to rob Larry's home during the thirty-minute foray with the dogs are astronomically small.

Both Larry and Mary spend too much time and effort on avoiding facing their fears, and what they fear is unlikely to occur. Subject your fears to a reality test. Weigh the odds carefully.

Whenever possible, look up the statistical evidence as it relates to your fears. Unfortunately, you can't always find statistics that help you.

The following story shows how people overestimate the probability of a horrible outcome.

Dennis rudely grabs the pan from his wife, Linda. He snaps at her, "I'll finish browning the meat. Go ahead and set the table." His abrupt demeanor stings Linda's feelings, but she knows how anxious he gets when company comes over for dinner. Dennis tightly grips the pan over the stove, watching the color of the meat carefully. He feels irritable and anxious, "knowing" that the dinner will turn out badly. He frets that the meat is too tough and that the vegetables look soggy from overcooking. The stress is contagious, and when the company arrives, Linda shares his worries.

What are the odds?

On any given day, the odds of being struck by lightning are about 1 in 250 million, and the lifetime odds of being killed

- ✔ By a dog are about 1 in 700,000

- ✔ By a poisonous snake, lizard, or spider are about 1 in 700,000

- ✔ By a firearm are about 1 in 202

- ✔ In air or space transport are about 1 in 5,000

- ✔ In an auto accident are about 1 in 81

Notice how the actual odds don't match very well with what people fear. Many more people fear thunderstorms, snakes, spiders, and flying in airplanes than fear driving a car or being killed by a firearm. It doesn't make a lot of sense does it? Finally, we should note that your individual odds may vary. If you regularly stand out in thunderstorms, holding your golf clubs in the air, your chances of being struck by lightning are a little higher than average.

What outcome does Dennis predict? Almost every time that he and Linda entertain, Dennis believes that the food that they prepare will be terrible, their guests will be horrified, and he'll be humiliated. The odds of this outcome can't be looked up in a table or a book. So how can Dennis assess the odds realistically? You or Dennis can ask the following *questions to recalculate the odds* and then write some answers:

- ✔ How many times have I predicted this outcome and how many times has it actually happened to me?

- ✔ How often does this happen to people I know?

- ✔ If someone I know made this prediction, would I agree?

- ✔ Am I assuming this will happen just because I fear that it will, or is there a reasonable chance that it will really happen?

- ✔ Do I have any experiences from my past that would suggest my dire prediction is unlikely to occur?

In Dennis's case, he realizes that both he and his wife have never actually ruined a dinner although he predicted it numerous times before. Furthermore, he tested his second prediction that his guests would feel horrified if the dinner did turn out badly. He recalled that one time he and Linda attended a barbeque when the meat was burned to the extent that it was inedible. Everyone expressed genuine sympathy and shared stories about their own cooking disasters. They ended up ordering pizza and considered it one of the more enjoyable evenings they'd spent in a long time. The hosts, far from humiliated, basked in the glow of goodwill.

Deconstructing the worst-case scenario

Yes, but you may be thinking, bad things do happen. Lightning strikes. Bosses hand out bad evaluations. Airplanes crash. Some days are just "bad hair days." Ships sink. People stumble and get laughed at. Some lose their jobs. Lovers break up.

The world gives us plenty of reasons to worry. Recalculating the true odds often helps. But you're still stuck with, "What if?" What if your concern truly happens?

Small-potatoes scenarios

What do people worry about? Most of the time they worry about inconsequential, *small-potatoes scenarios.* In other words, outcomes that while unpleasant, hardly qualify as life threatening. Nevertheless, these small scenarios manage to generate remarkable amounts of stress, apprehension, and worry.

Listen to what's worrying Gerald, Sammy, Tricia, and Carol:

Gerald worries about many things. Mostly, he worries about committing a social blunder. Before parties, he obsesses over what to wear. Will he look too dressed up or too casual? Will he know what to say? What if he says something stupid and people laugh? As you might imagine, Gerald feels miserable at social events. When he walks into a crowd, he feels as though a spotlight has turned his way and everyone in the room is staring at him. He imagines that people not only focus on him, but that they also judge him disparagingly.

Sammy worries as much as Gerald; he just has a different set of worries. Sammy obsesses over the idea that he'll lose control and have to run away from wherever he's at. If he's sitting in a classroom, he wonders whether he'll get so anxious that he'll have to leave, and of course, he assumes everyone will know why he left and think something is terribly wrong with him. If he's at a crowded shopping mall, he's afraid he'll "lose it," and start screaming and running out of control.

Seventeen-year-old **Tricia** obsesses over the possibility that her current boyfriend will leave her someday. If he's tired and in a bad mood, she instantly assumes he's upset with her. If he arrives 15 minutes late, she figures he's been spending time with another girl. Not only does she assume he'll eventually leave her, but when he does, she can't imagine that life could go on without him.

Carol is a journalist. She feels anxiety almost every day. She feels pressure in her chest when each deadline approaches and dreads the day when she fails to get her story in on time. Making matters worse, she sometimes has writer's block and can't think of the next word to type for 15 or 20 minutes; all the while, the clock advances and the deadline nears. She's seen colleagues lose their jobs when they consistently failed to reach their deadlines and she fears meeting the same fate one day. It's hard for Carol to stop thinking about her deadlines.

What do Gerald, Sammy, Tricia, and Carol have in common? First, they all have considerable anxiety, stress, and tension. They worry almost every single day of their lives. They can't imagine the horror of dealing with the possibility of their fears coming true. But, more importantly, they worry about events that happen all the time and that people manage to cope with when they do.

Gerald, Sammy, Tricia, and Carol all underestimate their own ability to cope. What if Gerald spills something at a party and people around him notice? Would Gerald fall to the floor unable to move? Would people point and laugh at him? Not likely. He'd probably blush, feel embarrassed, and clean up the mess. The party and Gerald's life would go on. Even if a few rude people laugh at Gerald, most would forget the incident and certainly would not view Gerald any differently.

Carol, on the other hand, has a bigger worry. Her worst-case scenario involves losing her job. That sounds serious. What would she do if she lost her job? The following *coping questions* help Carol to discover her true coping resources. You can use these questions to help deal with your own worst fears.

1. Have I ever dealt with anything like this in the past?

2. How much will this affect my life a year from now?

3. Do I know anyone who has coped with something like this and how did they do it?

4. Do I know anyone who I could turn to for help or support?

5. Can I think of a creative, new possibility that could result from this challenge?

Trying to come to terms with her fears, Carol wrote her answers to these coping questions one through five:

1. **No, actually I've never lost a job before.**

   The first question didn't help Carol discover her hidden coping resources, but it did help her see that possibly she was overestimating the risks of losing her job.

2. **If I did lose my job, I'd probably have some financial problems for a while, but I'm sure I could find another job.**

3. **Well, my friend Janet lost her job a few months ago.**

   She got unemployment checks and asked her parents for a little assistance. Now she has a new job that she really likes.

4. **I'd hate to do it, but my brother would always help me out if I really needed it.**

5. **When I think about it, I really sort of hate these daily deadlines at the newspaper.**

   I do have a teaching certificate. What with the shortage of teachers right now, I could always teach high school English and have summers off. Best of all, I could use those summers to write the novel I've always dreamed about writing. Maybe I'll quit my job now and do that!

It's amazing how often asking yourself these questions can *decatastrophize* your imagined worst-case scenario. Answering these questions can help you see that you can deal with the vast majority of your worries — at least the small potatoes. But how about the worst-case scenarios? Could you cope with real disasters?

Worst-case scenarios

Some peoples' fears involve issues that go way beyond social embarrassment or temporary financial loss. Severe illness, death, terror, natural disasters, disfigurement, major disabilities, and loss of a loved one are worst-case scenarios. How would you possibly cope with one of these? We're not going to tell you it would be easy because it wouldn't be.

Marilyn's mother and grandmother both died of breast cancer. She knows her odds of getting breast cancer are higher than most. Almost every day of her adult life, she worries about her health. She insists on monthly checkups, and every stomach upset, bout of fatigue, or headache becomes an imagined tumor.

Her stress concerns both her family and her physician. First, her doctor helps her to see that she is overestimating her risk. Unlike her mother and grandmother, Marilyn goes for yearly mammograms and she performs regular self-exams. Not only that, she exercises regularly and eats a much healthier diet than her mother or grandmother did.

But still, Marilyn realistically has a chance of getting breast cancer. How would she possibly cope with this worst-case scenario? You might be surprised to know that the same questions used to deal with the small-potatoes scenarios can help you deal with the worst-case scenarios. Take a look at how Marilyn answered our five coping questions:

Question: Have I ever dealt with anything like this in the past?

Marilyn's **answer:** Unfortunately, yes. I helped my mother when she was going for chemotherapy. It was horrible, but I do remember laughing with her when her hair fell out. I understand chemotherapy isn't nearly as bad as it used to be. I never felt closer to my mother than during that time. We talked out many important issues.

Question: How much will this affect my life a year from now?

Marilyn's **answer:** Well, if I do get breast cancer, it will have a dramatic affect on my life a year from now. I may still be in treatment or recovering from surgery.

These first two questions focus Marilyn on the possibility of getting cancer. Even though she obsesses and worries about cancer, the intensity of the anxiety has prevented her from ever contemplating how she would deal with cancer if it actually occurred. Although she certainly hates the thought of chemotherapy or surgery, after she imagines the possibility, she realizes she could probably cope with them.

The more you avoid a fear, the more terrifying it becomes.

Question: Do I know anyone who has coped with something like this and how did they do it?

Marilyn's answer: Of course, my mother died of breast cancer. But during the last three years of her life, she enjoyed each moment. She got closer to all of her kids and made many new friends. It's funny, but now that I think about it, I think she was happier during that time than any other time I can remember.

Question: Are there people I could turn to for help or support?

Marilyn's answer: I know of a cancer support group in town. And, my husband and sister would do anything for me.

Question: Can I think of a creative, new possibility that could result from this challenge?

Marilyn's answer: I never thought of cancer as a challenge, it was a curse. But I guess I realize now that I can choose to be anxious and worried about it or just take care of myself and live life fully. If I do get cancer, I can hopefully help others like my mother did, and I'll use the time I have in a positive way. Besides, there's a good chance that I could beat cancer and with medical advances, those chances improve all of the time. Meanwhile, I'm going to make sure that I don't wait until my final days to get close to my family.

When you have anxiety about something dreadful happening, it's important to stop avoiding the end of the story. Go there. The more you avoid contemplating the worst, the bigger the fear gets. In our work, we repeatedly find that our clients come up with coping strategies for the worst-case scenario, even the big stuff. When people avoid grappling with their fears instead of becoming copers, they turn into victims.

George, for example, fears flying. He recalculates the risks of flying and realizes they're low. He says, "I know it's relatively safe and that helps a little, but it still scares me." Recently, George got a promotion. Unfortunately for George, the new position requires considerable travel. George's worst nightmare is that the plane will crash. George asked himself our coping questions and answered them as follows:

- **Have I ever dealt with anything like this in the past?**

  No, obviously I've never been in a plane crash before.

- **How much will this affect my life a year from now?**

  Not much, I'd be dead!

> ✔ **Do I know anyone who has coped with something like this and how did they do it?**
>
> No. None of my friends, relatives, or acquaintances has ever been in a plane crash.
>
> ✔ **Are there people I could turn to for help or support?**
>
> Obviously not. I mean, what could they do?
>
> ✔ **Can I think of a creative, new possibility that could result from this challenge?**
>
> How? In the few minutes I'd have on the way down, it's doubtful that many creative possibilities would occur to me.

Hmmm. George didn't seem to get much out of our coping questions did he? These questions don't do much good for a small number of worst-case scenarios. For those situations, we have the *ultimate coping questions:*

1. What is it about this eventuality that makes you think you absolutely could not cope and could not possibly stand it?

2. Or is it possible that you really could deal with it?

George answers,

1. Okay, I can imagine two different plane crashes. In one, the plane would explode and I probably wouldn't even know what happened. In the other, something would happen to the engine, and I'd experience several minutes of absolute terror. That's what I really fear.

2. Could I deal with that? I guess I never thought of that before; it seemed too scary to contemplate. If I really put myself in the plane, I'd probably be gripping the seat, maybe even screaming, but I guess it wouldn't last for long. I suppose I could stand almost anything for a short while. At least if I went down in a plane, I know my family would be well taken care of. When I really think about it, as unpleasant as it seems, I guess I could deal with it. I'd have to.

Most people fear dying to some extent — even those with strong religious convictions (which can help) rarely welcome the thought. Nevertheless, death is a universal experience. Although most people would prefer a pain-less, quick exit during sleep, many deaths aren't as easy.

If you have a particular way of dying that frightens you, actively contem-plating it works better than trying to block it out of your mind. If you do this, you're likely to discover that, like George, you can deal with and accept almost any eventuality.

If you find yourself getting exceptionally anxious or upset by such contemplation, professional help may be useful.

Cultivating Calm Thinking

Anxious thoughts capture your attention. They hold your reasonable mind hostage. They demand all your calmness and serenity as ransom. Thus, when you have anxious thoughts, it helps to pursue and destroy them by weighing the evidence, recalculating the odds, and reviewing your true ability to cope.

Another option is to crowd out your anxious thoughts with calm thoughts. You can accomplish this task by using one of two techniques. First, you can try what we call the friend perspective, or you can construct new, calm thoughts to replace your old anxious thoughts.

Being your own best buddy

Sometimes, simple strategies work wonders. This can be one of them. When your anxious thoughts hold most of your reasonable mind hostage, you still have a friend in reserve. Where? Within yourself.

Pick a worry. Any worry. Listen to that worry and everything outrageous it has to say to you. For example, **Juan** worries about his bills. He has a charge card balance of a few thousand dollars. His car insurance comes due in a couple of weeks and he doesn't have the money to pay for it. When Juan contemplates his worry, he thinks that maybe he'll go broke, his car will be repossessed, and that eventually, he'll lose his house. He feels he has no options and that his situation is hopeless. Juan loses sleep because of his worry. Anxiety shuts down his ability to reason and analyze his dilemma.

Now, we ask Juan to help an old friend. We tell him to imagine Richard, a friend of his, is sitting in a chair across from him. His friend is in a financial bind and needs advice on what to do. Richard fears he will lose everything if he can't come up with some money to pay his car insurance. We ask Juan to come up with some ideas for Richard.

Surprising to Juan, but not to us, he comes up with a cornucopia of good ideas. He tells Richard, "Talk to your insurance agent about monthly payments instead of every six months. Also, you can get an advance on your credit card. Furthermore, isn't there an opportunity to do some overtime work? Talk to a credit counselor, and couldn't one of your relatives loan you a few hundred dollars? In the long run, you need to chip away at that credit-card debt and pull back a little on your spending."

Try this technique when you're all alone — alone that is except for your friend within. Truly imagine that good friend is sitting across from you and talk out loud. Take your time and really try to help. Brainstorm with your friend. You don't have to come up with instant or perfect solutions. Seek out any and every idea you can, even if it sounds foolish at first — it just might lead you to a creative solution. This approach works because it helps you pull back from the overwhelming emotions that block good, reasonable thinking.

Don't dismiss this strategy just because of its simplicity!

Creating calm

Another way to create calm thoughts is to simply look at your anxious thoughts and develop an alternative, more reasonable perspective. The key with this approach is to put it on paper. It will not do nearly as much good to leave it in your head.

This strategy doesn't equate with mere positive thinking because it won't help you to simply create a Pollyanna alternative. Be sure that your reasonable perspective is something that you can at least partially believe in. In other words, your emotional side may not fully buy into your alternative view at first, but the new view should be something that a reasonable person would find believable. Your task will be easier if you have already subjected your anxious thinking to weighing the evidence, recalculating the odds, and reevaluating your coping resources for dealing with your imagined worst-case scenarios.

In Table 5-3 are some examples of anxious thoughts and their reasonable alternatives. We also provide you with a Pollyanna perspective that we *don't* think is useful.

Table 5-3	Developing a Reasonable Perspective	
Anxious Thought	*Reasonable Alternative*	*Pollyanna Perspective*
If I wear a tie and no one else does, I'll look like an idiot.	If no one else wears a tie, some people will no doubt notice. However, they probably won't make a big deal out of it. Even if a couple people do, it really won't matter to me at all a few weeks from now.	Everyone will think I look great no matter what!

Anxious Thought	*Reasonable Alternative*	*Pollyanna Perspective*
If I get a C on this exam, I'll be humiliated. I have to be at the top of my class. I couldn't stand it if I weren't.	If I get a C, I certainly won't be happy. But I'll still have a good grade average and a good chance at a scholarship. I'll just work harder the next time. I'd love to be at the top of my class, but life will go on just fine if I fall short of that.	There's no way that I won't get an A. I must, and I shall.
If I lose my job, in a matter of weeks, I'll be bankrupt.	If I lose my job, it will cause some hardship. However, odds are good I'll find another one. And my wife has offered to increase her her hours to help out if I need her to.	I could never lose my job.
I'd rather walk down twenty flights of stairs than take this elevator. The thought of the doors closing terrifies me.	It's time I tackled this fear because the odds of an elevator crash are infinitesimally small. Taking the elevator is pretty scary, but perhaps I can start by just riding up or down a couple of floors and working my way on from there.	I need to quit being such a wimp. I'm just going to jump on this thing and take it to the top!

We showed you the Pollyanna perspective because it's important not to go there. You could think the last example of the Pollyanna perspective looks great. Just get over your fear in an instant. That would be nice we suppose, if only it worked that way. The problem with that approach is that you set yourself up for failure if you try it. Imagine someone truly terrified of elevators trying to jump on and take it to the top floor all at once. More likely than not, the person would do it that once, feel horror, and make the fear even worse.

Be gentle with yourself; go slowly when confronting your anxious thoughts and fears.

Chapter 6

Busting Up Your Agitating Assumptions

In This Chapter

▶ Understanding how some beliefs make you anxious

▶ Discovering your agitating assumptions

▶ Challenging your anxious beliefs

▶ Replacing your worry convictions

Driving in heavy traffic, disagreeing with the boss, flying in airplanes, paying bills, fighting with your partner, receiving a poor grade, going to a job interview, making a speech, getting bad news from the doctor, or noticing that your pants are unzipped while leaving church may make many people anxious. While one person may become anxious about traffic, airplanes, or health, another becomes anxious about speeches and embarrassments, and a few people rarely become anxious at all.

This chapter explains why certain activities or events make you anxious while others don't. You'll see how certain beliefs or assumptions generate excessive worry and anxiety. These beliefs come from your life experiences — not because you're defective. Questionnaires help you discover which assumptions may agitate you and create anxiety. We call these your *agitating assumptions* — what can really stir you up. We provide ways for you to challenge those assumptions. Replacing your agitating assumptions with calming assumptions can reduce your anxiety.

Understanding Agitating Assumptions

An assumption is something that you presume to be correct without question. You don't think about your assumptions; rather, you take them for granted as basic truths. For example, you probably believe that fall follows summer and that someone who smiles at you is friendly and someone who scowls at you isn't. Therefore, your assumptions provide a map for getting you through life.

And that's not necessarily a bad thing. Your assumptions guide you through your days with less effort. For example, most people assume their paychecks will arrive more or less on time. That assumption allows them to plan ahead, pay bills, and avoid unnecessary worry. If people didn't make this assumption, they'd constantly check with their payroll department or bosses to ensure timely delivery of their checks and to the annoyance of all concerned.

Similarly, most people assume that food that's sold in the grocery store is safe to eat. Otherwise, they'd boil away germs and flavor to protect them from harm. Food that couldn't be boiled would be subjected to intense scrutiny and tests.

And when you go to the doctor, you probably assume that the doc will provide good care and has your best interests at heart. Otherwise, you'd think twice before allowing inspection of delicate regions.

Unfortunately, sometimes assumptions fail to provide useful information. They may even distort reality so much that they arouse considerable distress. For example, before giving a speech, you may tremble, quiver, and sweat. You worry that you may stumble over your words, drop your notes, or even worse, faint from fear. Even though little of that has ever happened on your previous speeches, you always assume that it will this time. That dread of embarrassment comes from an agitating assumption.

Unquestioned beliefs that you hold to, *agitating assumptions* assume the worst about yourself or the world.

When activated, these beliefs cause anxiety and worry. Unfortunately, most people don't even know they have these beliefs. Therefore, agitating assumptions can go unchallenged for many years, thus leaving them free to fuel anxiety.

Finding Your Agitating Assumptions

Perhaps you're curious as to whether you hold any agitating assumptions. People usually don't even know if they have these troubling beliefs so they don't question them. Challenging agitating assumptions has to start with knowing which ones you have. In our work with clients, we found that five major agitating assumptions plague them:

✔ **Perfectionism:** Perfectionists assume that they must do everything right or they will have failed totally and the consequences will be devastating. They ruminate over minor details.

✔ **Approval:** Approval addicts assume they must win the approval of others at any cost to themselves. They can't stand criticism.

✔ **Vulnerability:** Those afflicted with the vulnerability assumption feel at the mercy of life's forces. They worry all the time about possible disasters.

✔ **Control:** Those with the control assumption feel that they can't trust or rely on anyone but themselves. They always want to be the driver — not the passenger.

✔ **Dependency:** Those with the dependency assumption feel they can't survive on their own and turn to others for help.

Assumptions have a powerful influence on the way that you respond to circumstances. Suppose, for example, that the majority of comments that you get on a performance review at work are quite positive, but one sentence describes a minor problem.

✔ If you have the perfectionism assumption, you severely scold yourself for your failure. You won't even see the positive comments.

✔ If you have the approval assumption, you obsess about whether your boss still likes you.

✔ On the other hand, the vulnerability assumption leads you to believe that you're about to lose your job, and then your house and car.

✔ By contrast, if you have a control assumption, you focus on the utter incompetence of your boss and wonder why you weren't in charge.

✔ Finally, if you have the dependency assumption, you look to others for support and help.

Same event, but various individuals react completely differently depending on which assumption those individuals hold. Just imagine the reaction of someone who simultaneously holds several of these assumptions. One sentence in a performance review could set off a huge emotional storm of anxiety and distress.

You may have one or more of these assumptions to one degree or another. In order to help you find out, we have a set of five quizzes for you to take to see which, if any, agitating assumptions you hold.

Testing Your Beliefs and Assumptions

In Table 6-1, place a checkmark in the column marked "T" if a statement is true or mostly true as a description of you; conversely, place a checkmark in the column marked "F" if a statement is false or mostly false as a description of you. Please don't mark your statement as "T" or "F" simply based on how you think you should be, but rather on the basis of how you think you really do act and respond to events in your life.

Table 6-1		The Agitating Assumptions Quiz
T	*F*	***Perfectionism***
		If I'm not good at something, I'd rather not do it.
		When I make a mistake, I feel terrible.
		I think if something's worth doing, it's worth doing perfectly.
		I can't stand to be criticized.
		I don't want to turn my work into anyone until it's perfect.
T	*F*	***Approval***
		I often worry about what other people think.
		I sacrifice my needs to please others.
		I hate speaking in front of a group of people.
		I need to be nice all the time or people won't like me.
		I can rarely say no to people.
T	*F*	***Vulnerability***
		I worry about things going wrong.
		I worry a great deal about my safety, health, and finances.
		Many times, I feel like a victim of circumstances.
		I worry a great deal about the future.
		I feel pretty helpless much of the time.

T	F	Control
		I hate taking orders from anyone.
		I like to keep my fingers in everything.
		I hate to leave my fate in the hands of others.
		Nothing would be worse than losing control.
		I do much better as a leader than a follower.

T	F	Dependency
		I'm nothing unless someone loves me.
		I could never be happy on my own.
		I ask advice about most things that I do.
		I need a great deal of reassurance.
		I rarely do things without other people.

Most people endorse one or more of these items as true. So don't worry too much if you found quite a few statements that apply to you. For example, who doesn't hate embarrassing themselves? And most people worry at least a little about the future.

So how do you know if you have a problem with one of these assumptions? You start by looking at each assumption one at a time. If you checked one or more items as true, that raises the possibility that this assumption causes you some trouble. Just how much trouble depends on how much distress you feel.

I, Laura Smith, coauthor of *Overcoming Anxiety For Dummies*, battled with the vulnerability assumption. One evening I sat in the beauty shop. Suddenly, a thug stormed in, demanding that everyone lie on the floor and hand over their money and jewelry. He brandished a .44 Magnum pistol to emphasize his point. Not long after the incident, I realized that I had acquired the agitating assumption of vulnerability. I found myself worrying about my safety much more than I had in the past. I started to nervously scan parking lots for miscreants and jumped at loud noises. When I found myself waking up from nightmares, I knew the vulnerability assumption was creating trouble and that I needed to do something about it. I used some of the techniques described in Chapter 8. These strategies included gradually returning to the scene of the crime, talking about the crime, and relaxation. Soon, I found my vulnerability assumption abating.

Ask yourself what makes you feel especially anxious, and does it have to do with one or more items that you checked as true? If so, you probably struggle with that agitating assumption.

If you have a number of these agitating assumptions, don't get down on yourself! You likely developed your agitating assumptions for good reasons. And you should congratulate yourself for starting to figure out the problem. That's the first step toward feeling better.

Coming Down with a Case of Agitating Assumptions

If you have too much anxiety, one or more agitating assumptions undoubtedly cause you problems. But it's especially important to know that you're not crazy for having agitating assumptions! That's because people acquire these assumptions in two completely understandable ways:

- When shocking, traumatic events *shatter* previously held assumptions.
- When experiences in childhood prevent the development of a reasonable sense of safety, security, acceptance, or approval.

Shattering your reasonable assumptions

The following example illustrates how life can create an agitating assumption.

Bill had always assumed, like most people do, that a green light signals that it's safe to proceed through an intersection. Bill drove for twenty years without mishap. One day on the way to work, Bill drove through an intersection that he'd safely traversed hundreds of times before. Suddenly, an SUV barreled through the red light and broadsided Bill's sedan. Bill sustained serious injuries but recovered.

When Bill returns to driving, he finds himself creeping through intersections with intense feelings of anxiety. He can barely make himself drive to work and back each day and avoids driving whenever possible. Bill's doctor tells him he now has high blood pressure and that he needs to reduce his stress. Bill worries about his worry but doesn't know what he can do about it.

Bill has formed a new assumption — an agitating assumption. The vulnerability assumption plagues him. He now worries that driving is dangerous and requires the utmost vigilance. Bill had good reason to form that assumption, and like most agitating assumptions, Bill's belief contains a grain of truth — driving can be dangerous. However, as with all agitating assumptions, the problem lies in the fact that Bill overestimates the dangers of driving. Therefore, he feels excessive anxiety whenever he gets into the car.

Bill's anxiety didn't emerge until he was an adult, but anxiety can begin at any age. Many adopt their agitating assumptions in childhood.

Acquiring assumptions in childhood

You may have been one of the lucky ones who glided through childhood feeling loved, accepted, safe, and secure. Perhaps you lived in a home with two loving parents, a dog, a station wagon, and a white picket fence. Or maybe not. You probably didn't have a perfect childhood. Not many do. For the most part, your parents probably did the best they could, but they were human. Perhaps they had bad tempers or ran into financial difficulties. Or possibly, they had addictions or failed to look out for your safety as well as they should have. For these and numerous other reasons, you may have acquired one or more agitating assumptions.

Unlike Bill, **Harold** didn't have to wait until adulthood to suffer from his agitating assumption. Harold's mother rarely gave him much approval. She harshly criticized almost everything he did. For example, his room was never quite clean enough and his grades were never quite stellar enough. Even when he brought his mother a gift, she told him it was the wrong color or size. He felt he could do almost nothing right.

Slowly but surely, Harold acquired an agitating assumption — "I must be absolutely perfect, or I will be a total failure." Being perfect is pretty hard. So you can imagine why he now feels anxious most of the time.

Cars: A dangerous mode of transportation?

Although Bill now overestimates the risks of driving, you should know that driving does involve significant dangers. The National Safety Council compared travel on buses, planes, trains, and cars. Deaths from automobile accidents far exceed deaths from all of these other modes of transportation combined. Sounds scary, doesn't it? However, the odds of dying in your car don't look all that bad. For every 100 million miles driven, there is less than one fatality.

If you have agitating assumptions, you don't question them. You believe in them wholeheartedly. Just as he assumes the sky is blue, Harold believes that he's perfect or a complete failure. When Harold undertakes a project, he feels intense anxiety due to his morbid fear of making a mistake. Harold's agitating assumption is that of painful perfectionism, and it makes him miserable, but he doesn't know why.

Challenging Those Nasty Assumptions: Running a Cost/Benefit Analysis

Now you have a better idea about which agitating assumptions may be giving you trouble. In the old days, many therapists would have told you that insight is enough. We disagree. Pretend you just took an eye test and found out that you suffer from severe nearsightedness. Wow, you have insight! But what does that change? Not much. You still walk around bumping into the furniture.

You're about to get a prescription for seeing through your problematic assumptions. It starts with a cost/benefit analysis. This analysis paves the way for making changes.

Perhaps you think your painful perfectionism assumption is a good and appropriate. Maybe you believe that you have profited from your perfectionism and that it has helped you accomplish more in your life. If so, why in the world would you want to challenge or change it? The answer is simple. You wouldn't.

Therefore, you need to take a cold, hard look at the costs as well as any possible benefits of perfectionism. Only if the costs outweigh the benefits does it make sense to do something about your perfectionism. Take a look at Prudence, a painful perfectionist.

Prudence the perfectionist

Prudence, a successful trial attorney, works about seventy hours per week. Her closet is full of power suits; she wears her perfectionism like a badge of honor. Prudence works out to maintain her trim figure and manages to attend all the right social events. At 43 years of age, Prudence stands on top of her profession. Too busy for a family of her own, she dotes on her 9-year-old niece and gives her lavish presents on holidays. Prudence is shocked when her doctor tells her that her blood pressure has gone out of control. Her doctor wonders about the stress in her life. She says it's nothing that she can't handle. He inquires about her sleep habits, and she replies, "What sleep?"

Prudence is in trouble, and she doesn't even know it. She believes that her high income is due to her relentless standards and that she can't let up in the slightest way. Take a hypothetical look at Prudence's cost/benefit analysis of perfectionism.

A cost/benefit analysis starts with listing every imaginable benefit of an agitating assumption. Including every benefit your imagination can possibly conjure up is important. Then and only then, should you start thinking about the costs of the assumption. Once again, include any and every benefit that you can imagine. Take a look at Table 6-2 to see what Prudence wrote in defense of her perfectionism.

Table 6-2	Cost/Benefit Analysis of Prudence's Painful Perfectionism
Benefits	**Costs**
My income is higher because of my perfectionism.	
I rarely make mistakes.	
I'm widely respected for my work.	
I always dress professionally and look good.	
Other people admire me.	
I'm a role model for my niece.	

Prudence's fondness for her perfectionism is no small wonder. Filling out the benefits in her cost/benefit analysis (see Table 6-2) is easy for her, but what about the costs? Prudence will probably have to expend much more effort and work to complete the costs, and she may even have to ask other people for ideas. Now, review what she writes after she worked at the task and consulted others in Table 6-3.

Table 6-3	Cost/Benefit Analysis of Prudence's Painful Perfectionism
Benefits	**Costs**
My income is higher because of my perfectionism.	I don't have much time for fun.
I rarely make mistakes.	I'm anxious and maybe that's why my blood pressure is running so high.

(continued)

Table 6-3 *(continued)*

Benefits	Costs
I'm widely respected for my work.	I don't have many friends.
I always dress professionally and look good.	I spend plenty of time and money on clothes and makeup.
Other people admire me.	I get very irritable when people don't measure up.
I'm a role model for my niece.	Some people hate me for my harsh standards and expectations of them. I've lost several secretaries in the last six months.
	I hardly ever see my niece because I'm so busy.
	Sometimes I drink too much to unwind.
	Actually, I think my focus on work has kept me from finding a meaningful relationship.

Don't get anxious about how you'll manage to prepare your own cost/benefit analysis. Read the following examples; they'll give you some good ideas. Then we give you some simple guidelines.

The cost/benefit analysis helps you to know if you really want to challenge your agitating assumptions. You would probably agree that Prudence's example shows more costs than benefits. But wait, it isn't finished. The final step is to examine carefully whether you would lose all the benefits by changing the assumption.

For example, Prudence attributes her high income to her dedication and long work hours. Perhaps she's partly right, but would her income evaporate if she worked just a little less? Most likely, if she worked less, her income might drop a bit, but with less anxiety, she might increase her efficiency enough to make up the difference. If she were less irritable, she would be able to retain her secretarial staff and gain efficiency once again. And would Prudence actually start making more mistakes if she relaxed her standards? Research suggests that excessive anxiety decreases performance. With respect to her niece, Prudence isn't really getting the benefit that she thinks she is because she's not around enough to serve as an effective role model. Finally, more people fear Prudence than admire her. So you see, many times the perceived benefits of an assumption evaporate upon close inspection.

Anxiety: How much is too much?

A little bit of anxiety seems to improve performance and reduce mistakes. Some anxiety channels attention to the task at hand. However, when perfectionism reaches extreme levels, so does anxiety, and performance drops off. Excessive anxiety interferes with the ability to recall previously learned information and mistakes multiply.

Anne's approval addiction

Anne craves approval and abhors the idea of rejection. Anne, a graduate student in social work, has to meet each week with her advisor for supervision of her casework. She dreads those supervision sessions, always fearing her advisor's criticism. Anne does plenty for her clients; she would do anything that she thinks they may need help with — spending hours of her own time, even running errands for them if they ask. Her supervisor tries to tell her to pull back from giving excessive help to her clients; he says that her bending over backwards to assist clients doesn't help her or her clients. She cries after hearing her supervisor's comments. However, Anne's worst fears surround the required presentations in front of graduate school classmates. Before giving talks to her classmates, she spends an abundance of time in the bathroom feeling ill. During lively discussions in her class, Anne remains quiet, and almost never takes sides. Anne is addicted to approval.

Anne walks quietly through life. People rarely criticize her. She avoids embarrassment by not taking risks. She is kind hearted and people like her. What's wrong with that?

Well, a cost/benefit analysis of Anne's agitating assumption, in particular her addiction to approval (see the bulleted list in the "Finding Your Agitating Assumptions" section, earlier in this chapter), reveals that people walk all over her. It also shows that fellow students fail to appreciate how bright she is because she rarely speaks up in class. Anne neglects her own needs and at times feels resentful when she does so much for others and they do so little to return the favor. Anne's approval addiction doesn't give her what she expects. Sure, she rarely receives criticism, but because she takes so few risks, she never gets the approval and praise that she really wants.

Peter's feeling of vulnerability

Peter, a college graduate with a business degree, receives a promotion that requires him to move to California, but he turns it down because he fears big cities and earthquakes. Peter watches the weather channel and listens to the news before he ventures any distance from home and avoids driving if the radio reports any chance of inclement weather. Peter's worry restricts his life. He also worries about his health and often visits his doctor, complaining of vague symptoms, such as nausea, headaches, and fatigue. Peter's doctor suggests that his worry may be causing many of his physical problems. He tells Peter to fill out a cost/benefit analysis of his agitating vulnerability assumption.

Table 6-4	Cost/Benefit Analysis of Peter's Vulnerability Assumption	
Benefits	**Costs**
I keep myself safe.	I worry all the time.
I work hard to stay healthy.	Sometimes I can't stop thinking about my health.
I stay away from harm.	I'm so concerned about getting hurt that I've never enjoyed what other people do, such as skiing or trips abroad.
I am more careful than most about saving for retirement.	I worry so much about tomorrow that I forget to enjoy today.
I don't take unnecessary risks.	My doctor tells me that my worry probably harms my health more than anything else.

Someone as entrenched as Peter in his agitating vulnerability assumption certainly isn't going to give it up just because of his cost/benefit analysis. However, this analysis starts the ball rolling by showing him that his assumption is costing him big time. The exercise motivates him to start thinking about doing something different.

Jeff's need for control

Jeff, the head of a division at his engineering company, likes order in his life. His employees know him as a taskmaster who micromanages. Jeff takes pride in the fact that, although he asks for plenty, he demands more of himself than he does of his employees. He issues orders and expects immediate results. His division leads the company in productivity.

You may think that Jeff has it made. It certainly sounds like his issue with control pays off handsomely. But scratch beneath the surface, and you see a different picture. Although known for productivity, his division is viewed as lacking in creativity and leads all others in requests for transfers. The real cost of Jeff's control assumption comes crashing down upon him when at 46 years of age, he suffers his first heart attack.

Jeff has spent many years feeling stressed and anxious, but he never looks closely at the issue. Jeff's quest for control nets him the opposite of what he wanted. Ultimately, he loses control of his life and health.

If control is one of your agitating assumptions, do a cost/benefit analysis. Jeff's fate doesn't have to be yours, too.

Daniel's dependency

Daniel lived with his parents until, at 31 years of age, he married Dorothy. He met Dorothy through his church singles group and decided immediately to marry her. Dorothy seemed independent and secure, something that Daniel craved but lacked. At the beginning of their relationship, Dorothy became fond of Daniel's constant attention. Today, he still calls her at work three or four times everyday, asking for advice about trivia and sometimes seeking reassurance that she still loves him. If she's five minutes late, he's beside himself. He often worries that she'll leave him. Dorothy's friends tell her that they aren't sure that Daniel could go to the bathroom by himself. Daniel believes that he can't survive without her.

Table 6-5	Cost/benefit Analysis of Daniel's Dependency Assumption
Benefits	*Costs*
I get people to help me when I need it.	I never find out how to handle difficult problems, tasks, situations, and people.
Other people take care of me.	Sometimes people resent having to take care of me.
Life is not as scary when I have someone to lean on.	My wife hates me calling her all the time.
It's not my fault when problems arise or plans don't work out.	My wife gets angry when I don't take initiative.
I'm never lonely because I always make sure that I have someone around.	I might drive my wife away if I continue to cling to her so much.
It makes life easier when someone else takes care of business.	Sometimes I'd like to take care of something, but I think I'll screw it up.
	I haven't discovered how to master very much. Sometimes I feel like a Mama's boy.

Someone like Daniel is unlikely to give up his defective dependency assumption without more work than this. However, a cost/benefit analysis can provide an initial impetus. Meaningful change takes time and work.

Challenging your own agitating assumptions

You can run your own cost/benefit analysis. See the list of agitating assumptions in the "Finding Your Agitating Assumptions" section, earlier in this chapter. Which ones trouble you? If you haven't already taken the Agitating Assumptions Quiz in Table 6-1, earlier in this chapter, do so now and look at your answers. Do you tend towards perfection, seeking approval, vulnerability, control, or dependency?

First, if one of these applies to you, select one. Then, using the format of Table 6-5, for example, fill out all the benefits that you can think of for your agitating assumption in the left-hand column. Then fill in the costs in the right-hand column. If you get stuck, ask a trusted friend or partner for help. It won't necessarily mean that you operate on the dependency assumption or that you're overly dependent. Refer to the cost/benefit analyses that Prudence, Peter, and Daniel (refer to Tables 6-3, 6-4, and 6-5, respectively) filled out earlier in the chapter.

When you've finished your cost/benefit analysis, take another look at each of the benefits. Ask yourself whether those benefits will truly disappear if you change your agitating assumption. Prudence the perfectionist believes that her income is higher because of her perfectionism, but is that really true? Many people report that they make far more mistakes when they feel under pressure. Perfectionism, if nothing else, certainly causes pressure. So, it's probably not the case that perfectionists earn more money and make fewer mistakes. As often as not, they end up not doing as well as they could because their perfectionism leads them into making more mistakes.

When you look carefully at your perceived benefits you're likely to find, like Prudence, that the presumed benefits will not evaporate if you change your assumption.

Similarly, Anne thinks she avoids embarrassment by never speaking in class. But she finds herself even more frightened and embarrassed when she's required to present in class than if she took more risks earlier. Avoiding what she fears seems to increase her worries. So Anne receives a double dose of what she so desperately wanted to avoid.

Agitating assumptions often get you the *opposite* of what you want.

Agitating assumptions cause worry and stress and rarely give you any true benefits. If you're going to give up your assumptions, you'll need to replace them with a more balanced perspective.

Designing Balanced Assumptions

So, do you think you have to be perfect or that everyone has to like you all the time? Do you always need to be in charge? Do you feel that you can't manage life on your own? Or do you sometimes feel that the world is a dangerous place? These are the agitating assumptions that stir up worry, stress, and anxiety.

Another problem with these assumptions is that they do contain a kernel of truth. For example, it *is* nice when people like you, and it *is* nice to be in charge sometimes. We all need to depend on others sometimes as well. That sliver of truth makes people reluctant to abandon their assumptions.

The solution is to find new, balanced assumptions that hold even greater truth, but old assumptions are like habits — they're hard to break. To do so requires finding a new habit to replace the old. It also takes plenty of practice and self-control, but it isn't that difficult. We'll show you how to do it. You just need a little persistence.

We'll go over each of the assumptions and help you to see how to formulate an alternative, more reasonable assumption to replace your old one. Try using these reasonable, balanced perspectives to talk back to your agitating assumptions when they occur. Finally, once you develop a new assumption, try acting in ways that are consistent with that new belief.

For the perfectionist

Perfectionists believe they have to be the best in everything they do. They feel horrible when they make mistakes, and if they're not outstanding at something, they'll generally refrain from trying. Fortunately, a good cost/ benefit analysis can often help them see that perfectionism exacts a terrible toll.

But if not perfect, then what? Some people think it would mean going to the other extreme. Thus, if not perfect, these folks assume that they would become sloths with no standards at all.

If you're worried about giving up on your perfectionism assumption, we have good news for you. The alternative is not the other extreme! You may find it helpful to copy the following statements, or what we call "balanced views" on an index card. Or, you may want to think of your own alternatives. Just be sure they aim for the middle ground. Carry your card around with you as a reminder for when you start to get hung up on perfectionism.

> ✔ I like to do well at things, but it's silly to think that I have to be the best at everything.
>
> ✔ I'll never be good at everything, and sometimes it's really fun just to try something new.
>
> ✔ Everyone makes mistakes; I need to deal with it when I do.

In other words, if you currently hold the assumption that you must be perfect and do everything right or you've failed totally; try to think in less extreme terms. A more balanced assumption would be that you like doing things well, but that *all humans make mistakes and so do you.* You don't want to be above the rest of us humans. *Collect evidence* that refutes your perfectionist assumption. For example, think about all the people you admire, yet who make numerous mistakes over time. When they make mistakes, do you suddenly see them as defective? Doubtful. Use the same standard for yourself.

Balancing an approval addict

Approval addicts desperately want to be liked all the time. They sacrifice their own needs in order to please others. Standing up for themselves is hard because to do so would risk offending someone. When criticized, even unfairly, they tend to fall apart.

But isn't it good to want people's approval? As with all agitating assumptions, it's a matter of degree. Taken too far, the approval assumption can ruin your life.

The deadly secrets of perfectionism

Perfectionism pays off . . . sometimes. A little bit of perfectionism probably can improve the quality of your work, sports, and other endeavors as long as you don't let it get out of hand. How bad is it when perfectionism gets too extreme? Worse than you may think. Perfectionists often become extreme procrastinators just to avoid making mistakes. Not only that, perfectionists more often develop Obsessive-Compulsive Disorder (see Chapter 2), various types of anxiety disorders, depression, physical ailments, and eating disorders. Worst of all, it appears that adolescents who suffer from perfectionism have a higher rate of suicide.

But if you quit worrying about getting people's approval, what will happen then? Will you end up isolated, rejected, and alone? Is rudeness and boorish behavior the alternative to being nice all the time?

If you worry about giving up on your approval addiction, we have a palatable alternative, and you just may want to carry these ideas in your pocket. Feel free to make some up on your own as well.

- ✔ What other people think matters, but it's not usually crucial.

- ✔ Some people won't like me no matter what I do. That's true for everyone.

- ✔ I need to start paying attention to my needs at least as much as other people's.

In addition, consider *collecting evidence* that refutes your approval addiction assumption. For example, think about people whom you like and admire who manage to speak their minds and look out after their own needs. Why do you like them? It's probably not because they bow and scrape to your every whim. Besides, someone who did that would probably turn you off.

If you feel addicted to approval and assume you must have the approval of others at all times and at virtually any cost, consider a more balanced perspective. Sure, everyone likes to be liked, but you need to realize that no matter what you do, some people won't like you some of the time. Try thinking that your needs matter and that what other people think of you does not define your worth.

Balancing vulnerability

People who hold the vulnerability assumption feel unsafe and worry constantly about every conceivable mishap. They might worry about safety, health, natural disasters, or the future; they often feel like victims of life's circumstances. They feel helpless to do much about their lot.

People with this assumption fail to understand that worry never stopped a single catastrophe. Nor does excessive worry help you prepare for the inevitable bad luck and misfortune that occur in everyone's life.

However, a better alternative assumption can keep you reasonably safe, and without all that worry. If you want to give up your vulnerable assumption, try carrying these ideas with you and use them like mantras.

- ✔ I need to take reasonable precautions but stop obsessing over safety. The amount of preparedness that I or anyone else can take action on is limited.

✔ I will go to the doctor for an annual physical, pay attention to nutrition and exercise, and after that, worrying about my health is pointless.

✔ Some unfortunate mishaps are unforeseen and out of my control. I need to accept that bad things happen; worry is no shield.

Again, if you hold the vulnerability assumption and feel that you're at the mercy of life's dangerous forces, then you may want to consider a more balanced point of view. Try thinking that no one can prevent the trials and tribulations of life, but that you can usually cope when they do occur. Collect evidence about the many unpleasant incidents that you were able to cope with in the past. For example, when you had high blood pressure, perhaps you exercised or took medication to control it, or when you lost someone that you cared for, you grieved, but you survived.

Relaxing control

Some people always want to take charge. They can't stand taking orders. When in a group, they dominate the conversation. They always want to know everything that's going on around them in their families and at work. They don't delegate well. Some fear flying because they aren't in the cockpit.

Being a control freak is tiring and causes plenty of anxiety, too. Perhaps you have trouble with this agitating assumption. Many highly successful, intelligent folks do, and this assumption isn't easy to give up, but the costs to health, well-being, and relationships are staggering.

As for all agitating assumptions, we have an alternative, balanced view that will serve you better than control ever did. Review our suggestions. And if you must take control and rewrite them, that's okay, too!

✔ I can usually trust other people to do what they need to do. I don't have to manage everyone, and they're likely to resent me if I do.

✔ Asking for help or delegating a task isn't the end of the world, and sometimes, delegating is much more efficient.

✔ I don't have to know every single detail of what's going on in order to feel in charge. Letting go reduces stress.

✔ Letting others lead can make them feel better and take a load off me.

Diminishing dependency

People with the agitating dependency assumption believe they can't make it on their own. They ask for advice when they don't really need it and seek reassurance that they're loved or that what they've done is right. The thought of not having a close relationship terrifies them. They can barely imagine trying to live life alone. You're not likely to find someone with an agitating dependency assumption eating alone at a restaurant.

Many agitating assumptions ironically backfire. Excessively dependent people eventually annoy and irritate those that they depend on. Partners of dependent people often distance themselves from the relationship after they become weary of constant clinging and helplessness.

If you battle with dependency, consider some of our alternative thoughts. Write these on an index card and keep them handy for frequent review. Feel free to embellish these or come up with some of your own.

- ✔ It's nice to have someone who loves me, but I can survive on my own and have done so in the past.

- ✔ Seeking advice can be useful; working through an issue on my own is satisfying.

- ✔ I prefer to be with other people, but I can find out how to appreciate time alone.

If you buy into the defective dependency assumption — that you can't be all right on your own and that you need help with all that you do — try thinking in a more reasonable fashion. Realize that it's nice to have someone to depend on, but that you're capable of many independent actions. Collect evidence on your capabilities. Do you put gas in your own car? Do you manage your own checkbook? Do you get to work and back on your own? Can you remember the times that you did well without someone? Realizing that you have taken independent action successfully and remembering that you have pulled yourself through a difficult spot all alone can boost your confidence enough to take more independent action in the future.

If you find that your agitating assumptions rule your life and cause you intense anxiety and misery, you may wish to consult a professional psychologist or mental health counselor. But first, start with your primary care doctor to rule out physical causes. Sometimes anxiety does have a physical base, and your primary care doctor can give you a referral after physical causes have been looked into. Should you consult a professional, you'll still find this book useful because most anxiety experts are familiar with the tools that we provide, and they'll help you implement them.

Above All: Be Kind to Yourself!

In our work with clients, we found that these agitating assumptions are surprisingly common, and many successful people, who don't even have a full-blown anxiety disorder, tend to fall under the influence of one or more of these assumptions. Therefore, it's important that you don't beat up on yourself for "being under the influence."

The origins of your belief could be in your childhood or the result of a traumatic event. Possibly your parents peppered you with criticism and that caused you to crave approval. Perhaps you had an unfortunate accident or trauma that caused you to feel vulnerable. Maybe your parents failed to provide you with consistent care and love, leading you to feel insecure and as a result, you yearn for help and affection. These represent merely a few out of an infinite number of explanations for why you develop agitating assumptions. The point is that you didn't ask for your assumptions and you came by them honestly.

You have started on the road to overcoming anxiety. However, go slowly; take pleasure in the journey, and realize that change takes time and practice. Be patient with yourself.

Chapter 7

Watching Out for Worry Words

. . . .

In This Chapter

▶ Recognizing anxiety-arousing words

▶ Understanding how language disturbs

▶ Tracking worrisome words

▶ Substituting calm phrases

. . . .

I'll never get this right . . . I always stumble over my words . . . I should really lose some weight . . . How can I be so stupid? . . . It will be terrible if I don't get that raise . . . I must get this finished, or I'll be in big trouble . . . What if I flunk? . . . I'm a klutz at sports.

Imagine inner conversations like these. How would you feel talking to yourself like this? Probably not very good. This chapter explains how words alone can stir up a whirlwind of anxiety. We help you discover worry words to look out for. They come in several forms and categories, and you'll see how to track these words down. Then we give you alternative words and phrases to quell your anxiety.

Stacking Little Sticks into Bonfires of Anxiety

"Sticks and stones can break my bones, but words can never hurt me." Perhaps you heard this saying as a child. Parents often try to assuage their kids' hurt feelings through this catch phrase, but it usually doesn't work because words do have power. Words can frighten, judge, and hurt.

If only those words just came from other people, that would hurt enough. But the words that you use to describe yourself — your world, your actions, and your future — may have an even greater impact on you than what you hear from others.

At breakfast, a little worried about her husband's blood pressure, **Jason's wife Beverly** mentions that it looks like he's gained a little weight. "Oh, really?" Jason queries. "Maybe just a little bit; it's no big deal. I just worry about your health," she replies.

A simple conversation between husband and wife. Or is it? Now, see what Jason thinks to himself about her comment over the course of the next few hours. "I'm a *pig* . . . She's *totally disgusted* with me . . . She'll *never* want to have sex with me again . . . Losing weight is *impossible* for me . . . I'm *certain* that she'll leave me; that would be *unbearable*."

By the afternoon, Jason feels intense anxiety and tension. He's so upset that he withdraws from Beverly and sulks through the rest of the day. Beverly knows that something's wrong and worries that Jason is losing interest in her.

What happened? First, Beverly delivered a fairly mild statement to Jason. Then Jason pounded himself with a slurry of anxiety-arousing words — *pig, totally, disgusted, impossible, certain,* and *unbearable.* Rather than ask Beverly for clarification, Jason's mind overflowed with powerful words that grossly distorted Beverly's original intention. His inner thoughts no longer had any connection to reality.

The worry words that you use when you think to yourself inflame anxiety easily and are rarely supported by evidence or reality. They become bad habits that people use unwittingly. However, we have good news: Like any habit, the anxiety-arousing word habit can be broken.

Worry words come in four major categories. We'll go through each of them with you carefully:

- ✔ **Extremist:** Words that exaggerate or catastrophize
- ✔ **All-or-none:** Polar opposites with nothing in between
- ✔ **Judging, commanding, and labeling:** Stern evaluations and name calling
- ✔ **Victim:** Underestimating your ability to cope

Extremist words

It's amazing how selecting certain words to describe events can literally make mountains out of molehills. Extremist words grossly magnify troubling situations. In doing so, they aggravate negative emotions.

Emily, pulling out of a tight parking spot at the grocery store, recognizes a neighbor coming out of the store and honks to get her attention. As the sound of the horn dies away, Emily hears metal scraping metal. Her bumper dents a side panel of the late model SUV parked next to her. Emily stomps on the brake, jams her car into park, and leaps out to inspect the damage — a four-inch slash.

Using her cellphone, she calls her husband, Ron, immediately. Hysterical, she cries, "There's been a *horrible* accident. I *destroyed* the other car. I feel *awful;* I just *can't stand it.* You have to come here right away." Ron attempts to calm his wife and rushes to the scene from work. When he arrives, he's not that surprised to find the damage is far more minor than his wife described. He's well aware of her habit of using extreme words, but that doesn't mean Emily isn't upset. She is. But neither she nor Ron realize how Emily's language lights the fuse for her emotional response.

Most of Emily's problematic language falls under the category of extremist words. See the following list for a sampler of extremist words.

Abhorrent	Dreadful
Agonizing	Ghastly
Appalling	Hopeless
Awful	Horrible
Calamitous	Intolerable
Devastating	Ruinous
Disastrous	Unbearable

Of course, reality can be horrible, appalling, and downright awful. It would be hard to describe the Holocaust, September 11th, famine, or the worldwide AIDS epidemic in milder terms. However, all too often, extremist words like these reshape reality. Think about how many times that you or the people that you know use these words to describe events that while certainly unpleasant, can hardly be described as calamitous.

Life presents challenges for you to deal with: Loss, frustration, aggravation, and pain routinely drop in like unwelcome guests who annoy you considerably. You may try to banish them from your life, but your best efforts won't keep them from stopping by uninvited as usual. When they arrive, you have two choices. First, you can magnify and catastrophize and tell yourself how *horrible, awful, unbearable,* and *intolerable* they are. When you do that, you'll only manage to intensify your anxiety and distress. Your other option is to think in more realistic terms. (See the "Exorcising your extremist words" section, later in this chapter, for more on realistic options.)

All-or-none, black-or-white words

Pick up a black-and-white photograph. Any photo will do. Look carefully, and you'll see many shades of gray that likely dominate the picture. Most photos contain very little pure black or white at all. Calling a photo black and white oversimplifies and fails to capture the complexity and richness of the images. Just as calling a photograph black and white leaves out much of the aesthetics, describing an event in black-and-white terms ignores the full range of human experience. Like a photograph, little of life is black or white.

Nevertheless, people so easily slip into language that oversimplifies, just as black and white do. Like extremist language, this dichotomizing intensifies negative feelings.

Thomas puts his newspaper down, unable to concentrate, and tells his wife that he'd better get going. "I didn't sleep a wink last night. I've been *totally* freaked about my sales quota this month. I'll *never* make it. There's *absolutely* no way. Sales *entirely* dried up with the slower economy, but the boss has *zero* tolerance for extenuating circumstances. I'm *certain* he's going to jump my case. It would be *absolutely* impossible to find another job if he fires me." If Thomas is at a loss for additional all-or-none words, he can borrow from the following list:

Absolute/absolutely	Forever
All	Invariably
Always	Never
Ceaseless/ceaselessly	None
Complete/completely	Perpetual/perpetually
Constant/constantly	Total/totally
Continuous/continuously	Without exception
Entire/entirely	Zero
Everyone/no one	

Few things (other than death and taxes) occur with absolute certainty. You may recall pleading with your parents for a later curfew. We bet that you told them that *everyone* stays out later than you. If so, you did it for good reason, hoping that the exaggeration would make a more powerful statement. Nevertheless, your parents probably saw through your ploy.

Everyone exaggerates sometimes; our language has many words for inflating reality. Thomas exaggerates by declaring that he'll *never* make the sales quota. Then his anxiety escalates. When Thomas states that he'll never make the quota and that a job would be absolutely impossible to find, he concentrates on the negative rather than searching for positive solutions. (For an all-or-none antidote, see the "Disputing all or none" section, later in this chapter.)

Judging words

You *should* read this book more carefully than you've been doing. Not only that, but you *should* have read more of it by now. And you *should* have taken the exercises more seriously. You're a *pathetic jerk*. *Shame* on you! . . . WE'RE JUST KIDDING.

What authors in the world would take their readers to task like that? None that we can think of. That sort of criticism is abusive. People react with dismay when they witness parents humiliating their children by calling them *stupid* or *rotten*. Many would view a teacher who calls his students *fools* and describes their best effort as *awful, pathetic, and disgusting,* as equally abusive. That kind of harsh judgment hardly inspires; berating crushes the will.

However, many people talk to themselves this way or even worse. Some hear a steady stream of critical commentary running through their minds. You may be your own worst critic. Many folks take the critical voice that they heard in childhood and turn it on themselves, often magnifying the critique in the process.

Steve, balancing his checkbook, discovers that he neglected to enter a check a few days ago. Fretting and worrying about the possibility that the check that he wrote will bounce, Steve thinks, "I *should* be more careful. It's *pathetic* that someone with a Master's degree could do something this *stupid*. I *ought* to know better. I'm such a *jerk*. I *disgust* myself. I *must* never, ever make this kind of mistake again." By the time he finishes his self-abusive tirade, Steve feels more anxious and even a little depressed.

Judging words come in the following three varieties, and we show you examples in Table 7-1 in this chapter.

- ✔ **Judgments:** These are harsh judgments about yourself or what you do. For example, when you make a human mistake and call it an utter failure, you're judging your actions rather than merely describing them.

- ✔ **Commandments:** This category contains words that dictate absolute, unyielding rules about your behavior or feelings. If you tell yourself that you *should* have or *must* have taken a particular action, you're listening to an internal drill sergeant. This zealous drill sergeant tolerates no deviation from a dogmatic code of conduct.

✔ **Labels:** Finally, self-degrading labels put the icing on the cake. Steve's checkbook mistake, for example, leads to all three types of condemnations: He judges his error as *stupid,* he shouldn't have allowed it to happen, and he declares himself a *jerk* when it does. It's no wonder that Steve feels anxious when he works on his checkbook. Ironically, the increased anxiety makes further mistakes more likely.

Table 7-1	The Three Categories of Judging Words	
Judgments	*Commandments*	*Labels*
Bad	Have to	Fool
Despicable	Must	Freak
Failure	Ought	Idiot
Inadequate	Should	Jerk
Pathetic	Or else!	Monster
Stupid		A nobody
Undeserving		Pig
Wrong		

Victim words

You may remember the story *The Little Engine That Could* by Watty Piper about the train that needed to climb a steep hill. The author of the book wisely chose not to have the engine say, "I think I *can't;* I'll never be able to do it; this hill is impossible."

The world feels like a much scarier place when you habitually think of yourself as a victim of circumstance. Certain words can serve as a flag for that kind of thinking, such as the list of victimizing words that follows:

Can't	Incapacitated
Defenseless	Overwhelmed
Frail	Powerless
Helpless	Shattered
Impossible	Vulnerable
Impotent	Worn out

Marlene, suffering from severe, generalized anxiety, jumps whenever she hears loud noises. Married for 20 years to a husband who's cheated on her repeatedly, Marlene doesn't consider leaving him because she worries that she *can't* survive on her own. She feels *helpless* to deal with the demands of life on her own and believes that it would be *impossible* for her to handle working and caring for her two teenage kids. Even now, she feels *overwhelmed* by housework.

Victim words demoralize. They offer no hope. With no hope, there's little reason for positive action. When victims believe themselves defenseless, they feel vulnerable and afraid.

However, people who describe themselves as victims do enjoy a few advantages: They don't feel compelled to do much about whatever predicaments they face; people express sympathy for them; and some people offer to take care of them.

Tracking Your Worry Words

You probably don't realize how often you use worry words inside your head. Because worry words contribute to stress and anxiety, performing a checkup on your use of these words is a good idea. You can start by tuning in to your self-talk. Get a small notepad and carry it with you for a few days. Listen to what you say to yourself when you feel stressed or worried. Take a few minutes to write the internal chatter down.

Now, check your monologue for worry words. You may discover that you use a few worry words that we haven't listed, and some words could fit into more than one category. That's okay. Just look for the relevant themes. Underline them and then put them into these general categories (which we repeat from earlier in the chapter to save you time):

- ✔ **Extremist:** Words that exaggerate or catastrophize

- ✔ **All-or-none:** Polar opposites with nothing in between

- ✔ **Judging, commanding, and labeling:** Stern evaluations and name-calling

- ✔ **Victim:** Underestimating your ability to cope

Frank, a talented mechanic, works for an automobile repair shop. After his promotion to shop supervisor, he feels an enormous responsibility resting on his shoulders. Frank's punctuality, attention to detail, and perfectionism reflect his stellar work ethic. Unfortunately, Frank's perfectionism goes too far. He obsesses over the quality of his employees' work. He checks and rechecks everything. In order to feel like he's doing his job properly, he starts working sixty hours or more each week. His blood pressure starts to rise, and his doctor tells him that he needs to reduce his stress and anxiety.

So Frank picks up his copy of *Overcoming Anxiety For Dummies* and refers to Chapter 7 for help on tracking and trapping his worry words. This is what he writes:

The workload is <u>dreadful</u>. It's <u>impossible</u> to keep up; I'm <u>overwhelmed</u>. But I <u>should</u> be able to do everything. I'm an <u>absolute failure</u> if I can't get the work out. Because I'm the boss, I <u>must</u> be responsible for all of the workers. If everyone doesn't do their job, I'm <u>totally</u> responsible. If someone else makes a mistake I <u>should</u> be on top of it. I <u>can't stand</u> the idea of a dissatisfied customer. When someone complains, it feels like a <u>calamity</u>. I feel like a <u>loser</u> and a <u>jerk</u> if I can't make things right.

- ✔ **Extremist words:** *dreadful, calamity, can't stand it*
- ✔ **All-or-none words:** *totally, absolute*
- ✔ **Judging, commanding, and labeling words:** *loser, jerk, should, must*
- ✔ **Victim words:** *overwhelmed, impossible*

Frank is surprised to see how many worry words pepper his thoughts. Yet he remains convinced that these words fit his reality. Frank needs to go a little further to overcome his anxiety.

Refuting and Replacing Your Worry Words

Ask yourself how you truly wish to feel. Few people like feeling anxious, worried, and stressed. Who would choose those feelings? So perhaps you agree that you prefer to feel calm and serene rather than wound up. Set that as your goal.

A good way to start on your way toward feeling better is to change your worry words. However, you aren't likely to stop using worry words just because we told you that they create anxiety. That's because you still may think that these words accurately describe yourself and/or your world. Many people go through life without questioning their self-talk, simply assuming words equate with reality.

In order to refute the accuracy of your internal chatter, consider a small change in philosophy. This shift in philosophy entails questioning the idea that thoughts, language, and words automatically capture truth. Then substitute that idea with a new one — using logic and evidence-gathering to structure your reality. At the same time, keep in mind that your goal is to experience more calm.

Exorcising your extremist words

The vast majority of the time when people use extremist words, such as *intolerable, agonizing, horrible, awful, hopeless,* and *ghastly,* they use them to describe everyday events. When you hear yourself using those words, subject them to a logical analysis.

For example, few events in life are unbearable. After all, you managed to get through every single difficult time in your life up to now or you wouldn't be alive and reading this book. Many circumstances feel really bad, but somehow, you deal with them. Life goes on.

When you think in extreme terms, such as *unbearable, intolerable, can't stand it, awful,* and *disastrous,* you lose hope. Your belief in your ability to manage and carry on diminishes. Consider whether your unpleasant experiences are actually described more accurately in a different way:

- ✔ Difficult but not unbearable
- ✔ Uncomfortable but not intolerable
- ✔ Disagreeable but not devastating
- ✔ Distressing but not agonizing

Recall Emily from the section on extremist words earlier in the chapter. She dented her car in a parking lot accident and reacted with extreme distress, due in part to her thoughts based on extremist words. After she works on her exaggerated style, she learns to view minor problems for what they are — minor. For example, when her purse is stolen from a dressing room, she tells herself, "Well, this is sure a hassle. I don't like having to call credit card companies and wait two hours to get a new driver's license. But, at least I wasn't hurt and I can imagine far worse things." Emily discovers she's far less upset when she thinks in these terms; she now can distinguish between a catastrophe and an inconvenience.

Remember your goal of feeling calmer. When you drop extreme language, your emotions also drop. Moderate descriptors soften your reactions.

Less-extreme portrayals lead you to believe in your ability to cope. Humans have a surprising reservoir of resilience. You cultivate your capacity for problem solving and survival when you have hope.

Disputing all or none

People use all-or-none words, such as *never, always, absolute, forever, unceasing,* and *constant,* because they're quick, easy, and they add emotional punch. But these terms have insidious downsides: They push your thinking to extremes, and your emotions join the ride. Furthermore, all-or-none words detract from coping and problem solving.

Rarely does careful gathering of evidence support the use of all-or-none words. Many people use all-or-none words to predict the future or to describe the past. For example, "I'll *never* get promoted," or "You *always* criticize me." Whether you're talking to yourself or someone else, these words hardly facilitate calmness, nor do they describe what has happened or what's likely to happen in the future. So try to stay in the present. Table 7-2 illustrates the switch between all-or-none words and calm, evidence-gathering words that keep you *in the present without exaggeration.*

Table 7-2	Switching to the Present
All or None	*In the Present without Exaggeration*
I'll *never* get promoted.	At this moment, I don't know whether I'll be promoted. However, I'll do everything that I can to see to it that it happens.
You *always* criticize me.	Right now, your criticism makes me feel bad.
I always panic when I'm in a crowd.	Right now, I can't know for certain if I'll panic the next time I'm in a crowd. I may panic, and I may not. If I do, it's not the worst thing in the world, and I won't die from it.

Remember Thomas from the earlier section of this chapter on all-or-none, black-or-white words? Thomas thought he'd never make his sales quota and that he'd likely get fired. Once fired, he assumed he would never find another job. After reading *Overcoming Anxiety For Dummies,* Thomas realizes his words hurt him. He changes his words to reflect shades of gray. A few months later, he actually fails to reach his sales quota. Rather than catastrophize, he thinks, "Okay, this wasn't a great month. I wasn't the only one to miss quota, and it's very unlikely I'll be fired. If I do get fired, my sales record can land me another job. I'm going to quit worrying and focus on making quota next month."

Thomas moves from despair to reasonable optimism. His stress goes down and his sales increase. You can do the same for yourself, no matter what your problem.

Judging the judge

Words that judge, command, or label, such as *should, must, failure, fool, undeserving,* and *freak,* inflict unnecessary pain and shame on their recipients. You may hear these words from others or from your own critic within.

Labels and judgments describe a person as a whole, but people usually use them to describe a specific action. For example, if you make a mistake, you may say to yourself, "I can't believe that I could be such an *idiot!*" If you do, you just made a global evaluation of your entire being based on a single action. Is that useful? Clearly, it's not accurate, and most importantly, the judgment doesn't lead you to feel calm or serene.

Like the other types of worry words, commandments don't inspire motivation and improved performance. Yet people use these words for that very purpose. They think that saying "I *must* or *should,*" will help them, but more likely, those words cause them to feel guilty or anxious. Self-scolding merely increases guilt and anxiety, and guilt and anxiety inevitably decrease both motivation and performance.

Try replacing your judging, commanding, and labeling words with more reasonable, accurate, and supportable alternatives.

- ✔ **Judging:** I got a pathetic score on my ACT test. I must be stupid.

  Reasonable alternative: It wasn't the score that I wanted, but I can study more and retake it. Given that I studied little, the score was actually reasonable.

- ✔ **Commanding:** I must have a happy marriage. I should have what it takes to keep it happy.

  Reasonable alternative: Much as I'd like to have a happy marriage, I was okay before I met my wife, and I can learn to be okay again if I have to. Being happily married is just my strong preference, and I don't have complete control over the outcome; it does take two, after all.

In the section on judging words, Steve made an error in his checkbook. He promptly condemned himself by calling himself a jerk and telling himself he should never make an error like that again. Once Steve tackles this bad habit, he changes his views. Like most people, Steve makes another mistake in his checkbook three months later. This time he realizes the world will not end and that he is not stupid. He stops and reflects. Reflection allows him to see that most of his mistakes happen when he tries to do two or three tasks at once. He decides to slow down a little. Using less harsh judgment allows Steve to learn from his mistakes rather than berate himself.

Vanquishing victim words

Victim words, such as *powerless, helpless, vulnerable, overwhelmed,* and *defenseless,* put you in a deep hole and fill you with a sense of vulnerability and fear. They make you feel as though finding a way out is impossible and that hope remains out of reach. Yet, as with other worry words, only rarely do they convey unmitigated truth.

Nevertheless, victim words can become what are known as self-fulfilling prophecies. If you *think* a goal is impossible, you're not likely to achieve it. If you *think* that you're powerless, you won't draw upon your coping resources. Instead, you're likely to wallow in your adversity. As an alternative, consider the logic of your victim words. Is there anything at all that you can do to remedy or at least improve your problem?

Gather evidence for refuting victim words that appear in your self-talk. Ask yourself whether you've ever managed to cope with a similar situation before. Think about a friend, an acquaintance, or anyone at all that has successfully dealt with a burden like yours.

After you consider the logic and the evidence, ask if victim words make you feel better, calmer, or less anxious. If not, replace those words with new ones.

> ✔ **Victim:** I have a fatal disease, and I'm totally powerless to do anything about it.
>
> **Reasonable alternative:** I have a disease that's indeed often fatal. However, I can explore every avenue from clinical trials to alternative treatments. If that doesn't work, I can still find meaning with the rest of my life.
>
> ✔ **Victim:** I feel overwhelmed by debt. I feel helpless and have no options other than declaring bankruptcy.
>
> **Reasonable alternative:** I do have a considerable debt. However, I could go to a credit-counseling agency that specializes in renegotiating interest rates and payments. I might also be able to get a second, part-time job and chip away at the bills. If ultimately I do have to declare bankruptcy, I can slowly rebuild my credit.

A survivor's story

A large storm window shattered and sliced Karen Smyers' hamstring, requiring surgery. That was in 1997. In 1998, an 18 wheeler hit Karen, riding her bike, from behind, leaving her with six broken ribs and a separated shoulder. In 1999, she broke her collarbone and found out that she had thyroid cancer. The year after the surgery to remove her thyroid gland, doctors discovered cancerous lymph nodes in her neck. Karen considers herself lucky. In October 2001, at age 40, she won a triathlon in Austin, Texas. Karen focused on her goals and her family in spite of adversities that many would consider overwhelming.

Recall Marlene from the earlier section on victim words. She remains married to a husband who cheats on her repeatedly. Marlene feels there's no way out because she could never be okay on her own. After considerable therapy, Marlene no longer views herself as a victim. She stands up to her husband, insists they seek marital therapy, and tells him if he continues to cheat on her she will leave him. She knows she can survive on her own. Stunned by her new found assertiveness, her husband finds her more attractive. He agrees to marital therapy and recommits to the marriage.

Part III
Anti-Anxiety Actions

ATTEMPTING TO REDUCE THE ANXIETY IN HIS LIFE, WALDO "WHIP" GUNSCHOTT GOES FROM BEING A WILD ANIMAL TRAINER, TO A WILD BALLOON ANIMAL TRAINER.

In this part . . .

We show you that changing what you're doing is another powerful way to attack anxiety. We provide you with a set of tools for challenging your fears by facing them head-on. Don't worry; we help you do this gradually, one step at a time. This part helps you to figure out what's important to you; then you can find out how to streamline your life in ways that fit your goals.

You'll also see how exercise can reduce your anxiety. If you struggled in the past with getting yourself to exercise, we help you see why and what you can do to find the motivation.

Finally, after all that activity, you're going to need some sleep. That's one reason why we show you various ways of improving your sleep.

Chapter 8

Facing Fear One Step at a Time

• •

• •

Tori sets out to master riding a bicycle without training wheels. Grandpa holds the bike steady and jogs alongside her. Tori beams with pride. She does fine, but the second that he tells her that she's doing great without his help, Tori gets scared, realizing that she's on her own. Before Grandpa can grab on, Tori and the bike crash into a heap. Both knees bloody, she cries in real pain.

Grandpa comforts Tori and tells her, "There's an old saying, 'When you fall off a horse, get right back on.' So let's get you cleaned up and bandaged; then we'll give it another try."

Good advice, but Tori finds herself paralyzed with fear, unable to go along. Nevertheless, a few days pass, and she manages to get back at it again. Not everyone who gets scraped up in life can do that.

When life hands you lemons, make lemonade. But is this advice really as easy to put into action as it seems? Is turning a situation around for the better after a series of hurts or even bouncing back after one difficulty a realistic self-expectation?

This chapter explains how you can get back in the saddle and overcome your fears in manageable steps. We discuss how to face fears in your imagination. That often prepares you for the next step — tackling your fears by going straight at them but in small steps. This chapter also provides a recipe called *exposure* for overcoming your personal anxiety problem.

Exposure: Coming to Grips with Your Fears

No single strategy discussed in this book works more effectively in the fight against anxiety than exposure. Simply put, exposure involves putting yourself in direct contact with whatever it is that makes you anxious. Well now, that may just sound a little ridiculous to you.

After all, it probably makes you feel pretty anxious to even think about staring your fears in the face. We understand that reaction, but please realize that if you're terrified of heights, exposure doesn't ask you to lean over the edge of the Grand Canyon tomorrow. Or if you worry about having a panic attack in crowds, you don't have to sit in the stands of the World Cup Football (soccer) Tournament as your first step.

If you find yourself procrastinating with the recommendations in this chapter, read Chapter 3 to build motivation and overcome obstacles to change. If you still find these ideas difficult to consider, you may want to consult a professional for help.

Stepping into exposure

Exposure involves a systematic, gradual set of steps that you can tackle one at a time. You don't move from the first step until you master it. Then, when you're comfortable with the first one, you move to the second. Each new step brings on anxiety but not an overwhelming amount.

Don't try exposure if your anxiety is severe. You'll need professional guidance. If any step raises your anxiety to an extreme level, stop any further attempt without help. Also, don't attempt exposure if you're in the midst of a crisis or have a current problem with alcohol or substance abuse.

Getting ready

Before you do anything else, we suggest that you practice relaxing. Consider reading Chapters 12 and 13 for a thorough review of how to do this. But for now, you can use a couple of simple, quick methods.

Why practice relaxing? Exposure makes you anxious. No way around that. Figuring out how to relax can help you feel more confident about dealing with that anxiety. Relaxation can help keep the inevitable anxiety within tolerable limits.

First, we suggest a breathing strategy:

1. Inhale slowly, deeply, and fully through your nose.

2. Hold your breath for a slow count of six.

3. Slowly breathe out through your lips to a count of eight, while making a slight hissing or sighing sound as you do. That sound can be ever so soft.

4. Repeat this type of breath ten times.

Try practicing this type of breathing several times a day. See how it makes you feel. If it doesn't help you feel calmer, stop doing it. Instead, try our next suggestion, which tightens and loosens muscle groups, an abbreviation of the method discussed in Chapter 12.

If you have any physical problems, such as low back pain, recent injury, surgery, muscle spasms, or severe arthritic conditions, don't use the technique that follows. Or you can consider it, but do so gently and be sure to avoid tensing to the point of pain. Finally, even if you're in good condition, you shouldn't allow yourself to feel pain when you tighten the muscles in the ways that we suggest.

1. Find a comfortable place to sit or lie down.

2. Loosen any tight clothing.

3. Pull your toes up toward your knees.

4. Clamp your legs together.

5. Tighten all the muscles in your legs and buttocks.

6. Hold the tension for a count of eight.

7. Now release the tension all at once.

8. Allow relaxation to slowly come in and replace the tension.

9. Notice the relaxed feeling for a few moments.

10. Next, squeeze your fists, bring your hands up to your shoulders, pull in your stomach, and pull your shoulder blades back as though you're trying to make them touch. Tighten all the muscles between your waist and your neck. Hold for eight seconds.

11. Release the tension, allow relaxation to replace the tension, and notice the relaxed feeling.

12. Finally, tense your neck and facial muscles. Scrunch your face into a ball.

13. Hold the tension for eight seconds.

14. Release the tension and relax. Be aware of the relaxation as it slowly replaces the tension.

15. Sit with the new, relaxed feelings for a few minutes.

16. If you still feel tense, repeat the procedure one more time.

Most folks find that one or both of the breathing or the muscle tensing exercise techniques relax them, even if only a little. If by any chance, these techniques fail to relax you or even make you more anxious, Chapters 12 and 13 may give you more ideas. Work through those chapters carefully.

However, even if no relaxation technique works for you, it doesn't mean that exposure won't be effective. Exposure can work on its own. Without relaxation, you simply need to proceed slowly and carefully.

Building blocks

Breaking up the exposure process into manageable steps is important. To start the breakdown process:

1. **Pick one and only one of your worries, such as from out of the following list of examples:**

   Enclosed spaces

   Financial ruin

   Flying

   Having a panic attack (a fear of a fear)

   People

2. **Think about every conceivable aspect of your fear or worry.**

   What starts up your fear? Include all the activities surrounding your fear. For example, if you're afraid of flying, perhaps you fear driving to the airport or packing your luggage. Or if you're afraid of dogs, you avoid walking near them, and you probably don't visit people who have dogs loose in their homes. Wherever the fear starts, take some notes on it. Think about all the anticipated and feared outcomes. Include all the details — other people's reactions and the setting.

Leeann's story is a good illustration of how to break down the exposure process into manageable steps.

Leeann, a 32-year-old pharmaceutical representative, receives a promotion, which means a large increase in salary and plenty of air travel. During her interview, Leeann doesn't mention her intense fear of flying, somehow hoping that it will just go away. Now, she faces her first flight in three weeks, and her distress prompts her to seek help.

Lucky for her, Leeann picks up a copy of *Overcoming Anxiety For Dummies*. She reads about exposure and concludes that it's the best approach for her problem. To see how Leeann completes the first task — describing her fear and all its components — see Table 8-1.

Table 8-1	What I'm Afraid Of
Question	*Answer*
How does my anxiety begin?	The very thought of flying makes me anxious. Even driving on the same road that leads to the airport gets me worked up.
What activities does your fear include?	First, I'd have to make a reservation; that would be difficult. Then I'd have to pack my luggage, drive to the airport, go through security, spend some time in the waiting area, hear my flight called, and board the plane. Then I'd take a seat and go through takeoff. Finally, I'd endure the flight.
What outcomes do I anticipate?	I fear that I'll go crazy, throw up on the passengers next to me, or start screaming, and they'll have to restrain me. Of course, the plane could crash, and I'd die or sustain horrible burns and pain, unable to get out of the plane.

You can see that Leeann's fear of flying consists of a number of activities from making a reservation to getting off the plane. Her anticipated outcomes include a range of unpleasant possibilities.

Using the Table 8-1 question-answer format, you can describe what you're afraid of. Use your imagination. Don't let embarrassment keep you from including the deepest, darkest aspects of your fears, even though they may sound silly to someone else.

Now, you're ready to take your fear apart and stack your building blocks. Use your blocks to construct a tower of fear (see Figure 8-1). Make a list of each aspect of your fear. Then rate each one on a scale of 0 to 100. Zero represents the total absence of fear, and 100 indicates a fear that's unimaginably intense, totally debilitating. Then stack your blocks with the lowest ranked block on the bottom and the highest ranked one at the top. This constitutes your exposure hierarchy.

Figure 8-1 shows how Leeann stacked the blocks for her fear of flying:

Landing:
92

Takeoff:
92

Boarding
the
airplane:
88

Waiting to
board:
75

Checking
in:
65

Packing:
48

Making a
reservation:
28

Visiting the
airport,
without flying:
20

Figure 8-1:
How Leeann
ranks her
fears about
flying.

Leeann's tower contained only eight building blocks. You may want to break the task down into 15 or 20 steps. For example, Leeann's steps jump from packing to checking in. She could add an in-between step or two, such as driving to the airport and parking in the airport garage.

For a phobia like Leeann's, the building blocks represent tasks that all directly lead to her ultimate fear. But some people have different types of anxiety. For example, someone with Generalized Anxiety Disorder (GAD; see Chapter 2), may have a variety of fears — fear of rejection, fear of getting hurt, and worry about financial calamity. The best tower of fear chooses one of those fears and includes everything relevant to that fear.

So, now you have your tower of fear. What do you do next? Choose between the two kinds of exposure — the kind that occurs in your imagination and the exposure that occurs in real life. In a sense, you get to pick your poison.

Imagining the worst

Many times, the best way to begin exposure is through your imagination. That's because imagining your fears usually elicits less anxiety than actually confronting them directly. In addition, you can use your imagination when it would be impossible to replicate your real fear. For example, if you fear getting a disease, such as Hepatitis C, actually exposing yourself to the virus wouldn't be a good idea.

You may think that viewing your fears through your mind's eye wouldn't make you anxious. However, most people find that when they picture their fears in rich detail, their bodies react. As they gradually master their fears in their minds, generally the fears reduce when confronting the real McCoy.

Imaginary exposure follows just a few basic steps:

1. If you think that it would make you more comfortable, use one of the brief relaxation strategies described in the "Stepping into exposure" section, earlier in this chapter, before you start.

2. Choose the lowest building block from your tower of fear.

3. Picture yourself as if you actually confront your fear. Leeann's was visiting the airport without any intention of flying.

4. Imagine as many details about your fear building block as you can — the sights, sounds, smells, and anything that brings your imaginary experience to life. If you have difficulty picturing the experience, see Chapter 13 for ideas on how to sharpen your mind's eye.

5. Rate your anxiety on a scale of 0 to 100 after you have a good picture in your mind that gives you an idea of what being exposed to your fear would be like.

6. Keeping the picture in your mind until you feel your anxiety drop significantly is important. Waiting until your rating decreases by around half or more is best. It will come down that much as long as you stay with the imaginary exposure long enough. For example, if you experience anxiety at a level 60, keep thinking about the exposure until it drops to around 30.

7. Finish the session with a brief relaxation technique described in the "Stepping into exposure" section, earlier in this chapter.

8. If the imaginary experience went easily, you may want to choose the building block that's a step up in your tower of fear, and perhaps another one after that. Continue daily practice. Always start with the last building block that you completed successfully (in other words, one where your anxiety level dropped by half or more).

Facing your fears (gulp)

Although we usually recommend starting exposure in the imagination, the most effective type of exposure happens in real life. The strategy works in much the same way as imaginary exposure; you break your fears down into small steps and stack them into a tower of fear from the least problematic to the most intensely feared. Now, it's time to face your fears head on. Gulp.

1. Start with a brief relaxation procedure such as the ones described earlier in this chapter.

2. Select a fear or a group of worries with a similar theme such as fear of rejection or risk of personal injury.

3. Next, you break the fear into a number of sequential steps — each step being slightly more difficult than the prior step.

4. Finally, you take one step at a time. If your anxiety starts to rise to an unmanageable level, try using one of the brief relaxation techniques. You keep working on each step until your anxiety drops, generally by at least 50 percent.

See the following hints to help you get through the exposure process:

- Get an exposure buddy, but only if you have someone you really trust. This person can give you encouragement and support.

- If you must, back off your step just a little. Don't make a complete retreat unless you absolutely feel out of control.

- Your mind will tell you, "Stop! You can't do this. It won't work anyway." Don't listen to this chatter. Simply study your body's reactions and realize that they will not harm you.

- Find a way to reward yourself for each successful step that you take. Perhaps indulge in some desired purchase or treat yourself in some other way.

- Use a little positive self-talk to help quell rising anxiety, if you need to. See Chapter 5 for ideas.

- Understand that at times, you will feel uncomfortable. View that discomfort as progress; it is part of how you overcome your fears.

- Practice, practice, and practice.

- Don't forget to practice brief relaxation before and during the exposure.

- Remember to stay with each step until your anxiety drops. Realize that your body can't maintain anxiety forever. It will come down if you give it long enough.

- Expect exposure to take time. Go at a reasonable pace. Keep moving forward, but you don't have to conquer your fear in a few days. Even with daily practice, exposure can take a number of months.

Remember to make realistic goals. For example, let's say that you're afraid of spiders, so much so that you can't enter a room without an exhaustive search for hidden horrors. You don't have to get to the point where you let tarantulas crawl up and down your arms. Let yourself feel satisfied with the ability to enter rooms without unnecessary checking.

Finally, try to avoid using "crutches" during exposure. People use crutches, such as alcohol and drugs, to avoid fully exposing themselves to the steps in their tower of fear. Some of the popular crutches that people use include the following:

- Drinking

- Taking tranquilizers, especially the benzodiazepines discussed in Chapter 15

- Distracting yourself, with rituals, song lyrics, or chants

- Holding onto something to keep from fainting

If you absolutely feel the need to use one of these crutches, use as little as you can. Sometimes, a reasonable in-between step is to use lyrics or chants at first and then to make the next step in your tower of fear — without the chants.

In your later steps, it would be good to even drop relaxation and self-talk as a way to completely master your fear.

Conquering Your Fears

Confronting your fears directly is one of the most powerful ways of overcoming them. The exposure plan can look just a little different, depending on the particular type of anxiety that you have. This section lays out example plans for six types of anxiety. You'll no doubt need to individualize these for dealing with your problem. However, they should help you to get started.

You may want to review the descriptions of the seven major types of anxiety in detail in Chapter 2. We are omitting one of them: Post-Traumatic Stress Disorder. That's because, for the most part, people with this disorder should seek professional advice. The list that follows offers a brief synopsis of each anxiety category for which we suggest the use of real-life exposure:

- **Generalized Anxiety Disorder (GAD):** A chronic, long-lasting state of tension and worry.

- **Social Phobia:** A fear of rejection, humiliation, or negative judgment from others.

- **Specific Phobia:** An exaggerated, intense fear of some specific object, animal, spiders, needles, or a situation, such as being high off the ground — acrophobia.

- **Panic Disorder:** A fear of experiencing repeated panic attacks in which you feel a variety of physical symptoms, such as lightheadedness, racing heartbeat, or nausea. You may also fear losing control, dying, or going crazy.

- **Agoraphobia:** This problem often, but not always, accompanies Panic Disorder. You worry about leaving home, feeling trapped, or unable to get help if you should need it.

- **Obsessive-Compulsive Disorder:** Repetitive, unwanted thoughts jump into your mind and disturb you. It can also involve various actions or rituals that you do repeatedly as a way to prevent something bad from happening. However, these actions don't make much sense.

Waging war on worry: GAD

People with Generalized Anxiety Disorder worry about most everything. As a result of that worry, they usually end up avoiding a variety of opportunities and other tasks of everyday life. These worries can rob their victims of pleasure and enjoyment.

Maureen's friends call her a "worry wart," and her children call her "the prison guard." Maureen frets constantly, but Maureen's biggest worry is the safety of her 16-year-old twin boys. Unfortunately, Maureen's worry causes her to restrict her kids' activities far more than most parents do. She doesn't allow them out of the house after dark, so they can't participate in extracurricular activities. Maureen interrogates them about every new friend. As the kids get older, they rebel. Squabbles and fights dominate dinner, but the biggest bone of contention revolves around learning to drive. Although both are eligible to take driver's education, Maureen declares that they can't drive until they're at least 18 years old.

Maureen is surprised when the school counselor calls her to discuss her sons' concerns. He meets with her for a few sessions and helps Maureen to realize that her worries are overblown. She knows she has a problem and she decides to tackle it head on.

After helping her understand that her worries are overblown, the counselor suggests that Maureen talk to other parents at her church to get a reality check. She finds out that most parents allow their 16-year-old kids to attend supervised evening activities, to take driver's education, and even drive if they maintain good grades.

Maureen constructs her tower of fear, stacking the blocks from the least fearful to the most terrifying (see Figure 8-2). She rates the anxiety that each block causes her on a 1 to 100 point scale. Then she rates her anxiety again with repeated exposures. She doesn't go to the next step until her anxiety comes down about 50 percent.

Realize that Maureen's entire tower of fear consists of 20 blocks. She tries to make sure that each step is within five to ten anxiety points of the previous one.

If you have Generalized Anxiety Disorder, pick one of your various worries. Then construct your personal tower of fear.

Construct your tower with enough blocks so that the steps are small. If you find one step insurmountable, try coming up with an in-between step. If you can't do that, try doing the next step through repeated imaginary exposure before tackling it in real life.

Figure 8-2:
Maureen's tower of fear, with the most fearful situations at the top.

Allowing her teenage twins to drive unsupervised.
Anxiety: 95

Allowing her sons to get a driver's license.
Anxiety: 90

Letting her sons take driver's education classes.
Anxiety: 84

Letting her twins go to a school dance.
Anxiety: 75

Letting her sons have a new friend without interrogating the parents.
Anxiety: 65

Allowing her sons to attend a sports game in the early evening at school.
Anxiety: 58

Fighting phobias, Specific and Social

You fight both Specific and Social Phobias in pretty much the same way. Take the feared situation, object, animal, or whatever, and approach it in graduated steps. Again, you construct a tower of fear out of steps or building blocks.

Ruben's story is a good example of how the tower of fear can help someone with a Specific Phobia — a fear of heights.

Ruben met Diane through a singles chat room online. They e-mail back and forth for several weeks. Finally, they decide to meet for coffee. Several hours pass in what seems like minutes to both of them, and Ruben offers to walk Diane home.

As he holds the door open for her, her body brushes against him. Their eyes meet and Ruben almost kisses her right there in the doorway. As they walk toward her apartment, she asks, "Do you believe in love at first sight?" Ruben doesn't hesitate, "Yes," he answers, wrapping her in his arms. The kiss is so intense that Ruben thinks he might collapse on the spot.

"I've never done this before on a first date, but I think I'd like you to come up to my place," Diane strokes his arm, "I have a wonderful view of the entire city from my penthouse apartment."

Ruben looks up at the 25-story apartment building. His desire shrinks. "Ah, well, I've got to pick up mom, I mean the cat at the vet," he stammers. Diane, obviously hurt and surprised, snaps, "Fine. I've really got to wash my socks."

Ruben decides to fight his phobia. He constructs a tower of fear out of building blocks that start at the top and go all the way to the least fearful step:

- ✔ Visiting Diane in her penthouse apartment and looking out from the balcony. Anxiety: 95

- ✔ Visiting Diane in her penthouse apartment but not going out onto the balcony. Instead, looking out at the city from inside her living room, or better yet, her bedroom! Anxiety: 82 from her living room, 92 from her bedroom.

- ✔ Riding the elevator by myself at the downtown hotel up to the tenth floor and looking out. Anxiety: 80

- ✔ Taking the glass elevator with Diane at the downtown hotel up to the tenth floor and looking out. Anxiety: 75

- ✔ Imagining visiting Diane in her penthouse apartment and going out onto the balcony, as well as peering down. Anxiety: 68

- ✔ Walking up three flights of stairs and peering down. Anxiety: 62

- ✔ Walking across a pedestrian bridge that has a chain-link fence around it. Anxiety: 55

- ✔ Imagining visiting Diane in her penthouse apartment without going onto the balcony. Anxiety: 53

- ✔ Calling Diane and telling her about my phobia, and hopefully, soliciting her understanding and support. Anxiety: 48

Confessing his problem to Diane is a building block that may appear unrelated to Ruben's fear. However, not admitting to his fear is avoidance, which only fuels fear. Including any building block that's connected to your fear is good. Ruben also included building blocks in his tower that require him to use his imagination to face his fear. It's fine to do that. Sometimes, an imaginary building block can help you take the next behavioral step.

Imagining the real-life steps before actually doing them doesn't hurt.

Pushing through panic and agoraphobia

Even if you only have Panic Disorder without Agoraphobia, you can approach it in much the same way as you do Agoraphobia. That's because your panic attacks are likely to have predictable triggers. Those triggers can form the basis for your tower of fear.

Tanya, for example, experiences her first panic attack shortly after the birth of her baby. Always somewhat shy, she begins to worry about something happening to herself when she takes the baby out. She fears that she might faint or lose control, and the baby would be vulnerable to harm.

Her panic attacks start with a feeling of nervousness and sweaty palms, and then progress to shallow, rapid breathing, a racing heartbeat, lightheadedness, and a sense of dread and doom. Ventures away from the house trigger her attacks, and the more crowded the destination, the more likely that she'll experience panic. By six months after her first attack, she rarely leaves the house without her husband.

One day, Tanya's baby girl spikes a serious fever, and she needs to take her to the emergency room. Panic overtakes her; she frantically calls her husband, but he's out on a business call. Desperate, she calls 911 to send an ambulance, which she and her husband can't afford on their limited budget.

Tanya knows that she must do something about her Panic Disorder and its companion — Agoraphobia. She constructs a tower of fear out of a set of building blocks, starting with the least problematic to the top, most difficult goal.

- Taking baby by myself to the mall on Saturday afternoon, when it's most crowded. Anxiety: 98

- Taking the baby to the grocery store during the day when it's only moderately crowded. Anxiety: 92

- Going to the mall without the baby or my husband, when it's crowded. Anxiety: 88

- ✔ Going to the grocery store with the baby when it first opens, when hardly anyone is there. Anxiety: 86

- ✔ Going to the grocery store by myself when it's only moderately crowded. Anxiety: 84

- ✔ Taking the baby to the pediatrician by myself. Anxiety: 80

- ✔ Taking the baby on three errands in one day. Anxiety: 74

- ✔ Taking the baby to the bank when it's crowded. Anxiety: 65

- ✔ Taking the baby in the car to my mother's house, five miles away, for the afternoon. Anxiety: 30.

- ✔ Walking the baby around the block. Anxiety: 25

Notice that Tanya's tower of fear contains quite a few steps between 80 and her top item of 98. That's because she needed to make each step very gradual in order to have the courage to proceed. She could have made the steps even smaller if necessary.

You can break your tower of fear down into as many small steps as you need in order for you to not feel overwhelmed by taking any single step.

One final type of exposure with panic attacks involves experiencing the sensations of the attacks themselves. How do you do that? You intentionally bring them on through a number of strategies that follow:

- ✔ **Running in place:** This accelerates your heartbeat, just as it does during many panic attacks.

- ✔ **Spinning yourself around until you feel dizzy:** Panic attacks often include sensations of dizziness and lightheadedness.

- ✔ **Breathing through a small cocktail straw:** This strategy induces sensations of not getting enough air, which also mimics panic.

- ✔ **Putting your head between your knees and rise up suddenly:** You may also feel lightheaded or dizzy.

After you experience these physical sensations repeatedly, you discover that they don't harm you. You won't go crazy, have a heart attack, or lose control. Frequent, prolonged exposures tell your mind that sensations are just sensations.

Don't bring on these physical sensations if you have a serious heart condition or any other physical problem that could be exacerbated by the exercise. For example, if you have asthma or a back injury, some of these strategies would be ill advised. Check with your doctor if you have any questions or concerns.

Overriding an obsessive-compulsive disorder

Obsessive-Compulsive Disorder (OCD) sometimes overwhelms and dominates a person's life, and commonly requires help from a professional with experience treating this disorder. Only attempt the strategies that we describe in this section on your own if your problems with OCD are relatively mild. Even then, you may want to enlist a friend or partner to help you.

Chapter 2 discusses this disorder, which often starts with obsessive, unwanted thoughts that create anxiety. People with this problem then try to relieve the anxiety caused by their thoughts by performing one of a number of compulsive acts. Unfortunately, it seems that the relief obtained from the compulsive acts only fuels the vicious cycle and keeps it going.

Therefore, for Obsessive-Compulsive Disorder, exposure is only the first step. Then you must do something even harder — prevent the compulsive, anxiety-relieving actions. This strategy has a rather obvious name, *exposure and response prevention.*

But let's start with the first step — exposure. Because OCD has an obsessional component, in other words, feared thoughts, images, and impulses — exposure often starts with imaginary exposure as described in the "Imagining the worst" section, earlier in this chapter. Imaginary exposure may be the only strategy that you can use if your obsessions couldn't or shouldn't be acted out in real life, such as in the following examples:

- Thoughts that tell you to violate your personal religious beliefs.
- Repetitive thoughts of harm coming to a family member or loved one.
- Frequent worries about burning alive in a home fire.
- Unwanted thoughts about getting cancer or some other dreaded disease.

Now, do the following:

1. **List your distressing thoughts and images, and then rate each one for the amount of distress it causes.**

2. **Next, select the thought that causes the least upset and dwell on the thought over and over, ad nauseam until your distress abates at least 50 percent.**

   Sometimes, listening over and over to a tape recorded description of your obsession is useful.

3. **Then proceed to the next item on your list that causes a little more discomfort and keep working your way up the list.**

This approach is quite the opposite of what people with OCD usually do with their unwanted obsessions. Normally, they try to sweep the haunting thoughts out of their minds the moment that they appear, but that only succeeds ever so briefly, and it maintains the cycle.

Give imaginary exposure enough time — keep the thoughts and images in your head long enough for your anxiety to reduce at least 50 percent before moving to the next item.

If you also suffer from compulsive acts, or avoidance due to obsessive thoughts, it's now time for the more difficult, second step — exposure and response prevention. Again, make a hierarchy of feared events and situations that you typically avoid — a tower of fear — then proceed to put yourself into each of those situations but without performing the compulsive act.

For example, if you fear contamination from dirt and grime, go to a beach, play in the sand, and build sand castles, or go out in the garden, plant flowers, and keep yourself from washing your hands. Remain in the situation until your distress drops by 50 percent. If it doesn't drop that much, stay at least an hour and a half and try not to quit until a minimum of a third of your distress goes away. Don't proceed to the next item until you conquer the one that you're working on.

Although using relaxation procedures with initial exposure attempts is a good idea, you shouldn't use relaxation with exposure and response prevention for OCD. That's because one of the crucial lessons is that your anxiety will come down — if and only if — you give exposure enough time. Furthermore, some of those with OCD actually start to use relaxation as a compulsive ritual itself. Thus, it's fine if you want to practice a little relaxation for anxieties not related to your OCD, but don't use it with exposure and response prevention.

Preparing for exposure and response prevention

Prior to actual exposure and response prevention, you may find it useful to alter your compulsive rituals in ways that start to disrupt and alter their influence over you. Methods for initiating this assault on compulsions include:

- ✔ Delay performing your ritual when you first feel the urge. For example, if you have a strong compulsion to wipe the doorknobs and the phones with Lysol, try putting it off for at least 30 minutes. The next day, try to delay acting on your urge for 45 minutes.

- ✔ Carry out your compulsion at a much slower pace than usual. For example, if you feel compelled to arrange items in a perfect row, go ahead and do it, but lay them out with excruciating slowness.

 ✔ Change your compulsion in some way. If it's a ritual, change the number of times that you do it. If it involves a sequence of checking all the door locks in the house, try doing them in a completely different order than usual.

Going right at exposure and response prevention for OCD

Cindy obsesses incessantly about getting ill from dirt, germs, and pesticides. Whenever she imagines that she's come into contact with any of these to the slightest degree, she feels compelled to wash her hands thoroughly, first with soap containing pumice to abrade the dirty layer of skin, and then with antibacterial soap to kill the germs. Unfortunately, this ritual leaves her hands cracked, sore, and bleeding. When she goes out into public she wears gloves to hide the self-inflicted damage. Not only that, she's discovering that her hand washing consumes increasing amounts of time. Her 15-minute breaks at work are too short to complete her hand-washing ritual. Cindy finally decides to do something about her problem when her supervisor at work tells her that she must take shorter breaks. Cindy prepares for her exposure and response prevention exercise by doing the following first for a week:

 ✔ She delays washing her hands for 30 minutes when she feels the urge. Later, she delays washing for 45 minutes.

 ✔ She changes her washing by using a different type of soap and starting with the rubbing alcohol instead of ending with it.

Cindy is surprised to find that these changes make her hand-washing urges a little less frequent, but they haven't exactly disappeared, and they continue to cause considerable distress. She needs to muster up the courage to do exposure and response prevention.

First, she approaches Dolores, a trusted friend for help. She tells Dolores about her problem and asks her to coach her through the exercises by lending support and encouragement. Then she makes a tower of fear for her exposure and response prevention that includes touching the following "dirty dozen":

 ✔ Toilet seats with her bare hands. Anxiety: 99

 ✔ Cans of pesticide. Anxiety: 92

 ✔ Her cat's liter box. Anxiety: 90

 ✔ Motor oil. Anxiety: 87

 ✔ Dirty carpets. Anxiety: 86

 ✔ Doorknobs. Anxiety: 80

 ✔ Handrails on an escalator. Anxiety: 78

> ✔ The wheel of a car driven by someone else. Anxiety: 72
>
> ✔ Unwashed fruits and vegetables. Anxiety: 70
>
> ✔ The seat of a chair that a sick person sat on. Anxiety: 67
>
> ✔ The seat of a chair that a healthy person sat on. Anxiety: 60
>
> ✔ A telephone receiver that someone else has used. Anxiety: 53

Dolores helps Cindy with her tower of fear by having her start with the easiest building block — touching a telephone receiver that someone else used. She has Cindy do this a number of times and encourages her to resist the urge to wash her hands. After an hour and a half, the urge to wash drops significantly. The next day, Dolores has Cindy take on the next building block.

Each day they tackle one new building block if Cindy succeeds on the previous day. When she gets to touching the cat's liter box, Cindy balks at first. Dolores says she won't "make" Cindy do it, but she thinks it just might help her. In other words, she urges her on. The cat litter box takes many attempts. Finally, Cindy manages to touch it and stay with it. However, it takes a total of three hours of repeatedly attempting and finally touching the liter box numerous times for as long as ten minutes each time for her anxiety to come down by half.

Now and then, exposure and response prevention takes a while, so you have to have plenty of time set aside. In Cindy's case, the final two items didn't require as much effort because her earlier work had seemingly cracked the compulsion enough so that it lost some of its power over her.

Upping the ante

After she gets through her tower of fear, Cindy takes one more initiative. She tackles the toughest building blocks again. But this time, she asks Dolores to describe scenes of Cindy getting sick and dying a slow death from some dreaded disease because of her contamination, while Cindy is actually doing the exposure task.

We call this "upping the ante." It gives you the opportunity to practice your exposure while bombarding yourself with your worst fears. Why in the world would you want to do that? Mainly because doing so reduces the grip those fears have on you. Of course, that's true, *if and only if* you stay with the exposure along with the dreaded outcome pictured in your mind long enough.

If you can't do this on your own or with a friend, please consult a professional for help.

If you get stuck on exposure and response prevention, you may want to consult Chapter 5 and work through it carefully. Pay particular attention to the section on rethinking risk. Usually, those with OCD overestimate the odds of catastrophic outcomes if they halt their compulsions, and this chapter can help you recalculate the odds.

Chasing Rainbows

Sometimes, people come to us asking for a quick fix for their anxiety problems. It's as though they think that we have some magic wand that we can pass over them and everything will get better. That would be so nice, but it isn't realistic.

Other folks hope that with help, they'll rid themselves of all anxiety — another misconception. Some anxiety helps prepare you for action, warn you of danger, and mobilize your resources. The only people who are completely rid of anxiety are unconscious or dead.

Overcoming anxiety requires effort and some discomfort. We have no way around that. No magic wand. But we know that those who undertake the challenge, make the effort, and suffer the discomfort, are rewarded with a new confidence.

Chapter 9

Simply Simplifying Your Life

· ·

In This Chapter

▶ Discovering what's really important to you

▶ Prioritizing goals

▶ Getting help from others

▶ Saying "No"

· ·

Phil answers the phone again for the third time since sitting down for dinner with his family. "Oh, sure," he agrees, "I can help referee the boy's soccer game this Saturday." His wife groans, "I thought you were going to help my brother move this weekend, and the house is a mess; we were going to clean it up together."

"Don't forget Dad, you promised me you'd go with me to sell raffle tickets door to door," whines his daughter, "and I need a ride to the mall in 15 minutes." Phil's stomach starts to burn. He grabs an antacid from his front pocket and sucks on it. "We can drop you off on the way to the grocery store and pick you up when we're done," Phil responds.

Phil and his wife both work full time at demanding jobs. Their two kids are involved in many activities. Phil tries to be a good dad, but sometimes he just gets tired. Does this sound like your family? Do you have too much to do? If so, your stress and anxiety probably increase when demands take over your life. In this chapter, we describe four sound strategies for simplifying your life:

✔ **Exploring your values.** Take our values clarification quiz and decide what areas in life are meaningful to you and how to devote time and energy to those and less to other things.

✔ **Prioritizing and setting goals.** After you figure out what's most important, give these goals top priority to help you get what you want.

✔ **Discovering the importance of delegating.** Doing all the work yourself can be cumbersome and even impossible, so letting somebody else do it can improve the quality of your life.

✔ **Discovering the power of NO.** It's only a two-letter word, but saying "No" when you need to can make your life much more manageable.

Evaluating What's Important Versus What's Not

Everyone would like to have it all, and some book titles promise you that you can. It's a seductive idea. Who wouldn't want everything possible from life?

✔ An abundance of friends

✔ Adventure

✔ A close family

✔ Good health

✔ Happiness

✔ Leisure time

✔ Power

✔ Recognition

✔ Rewarding hobbies

✔ Spirituality

✔ Success

✔ Successful, happy children

✔ True, lasting love

✔ Wealth

Nice list. No doubt, a few exceptionally lucky people do almost have it all. But this book deals with the real world, and the real world throws curve balls at you. Life also doles out a limited amount of time within which to manage all that we need to do. Thus, most people must make tough choices on how to use their time.

Quizzing to find what you hold dear

We can help you prioritize these choices. Take our values clarification quiz, and then compare the results with how you actually spend your time. You may be surprised to see a mismatch between what you value and what you spend your time doing.

Look over the list of values that follow. Circle the eight values that matter the most to you. Then go back and underline the top three.

Achievement	Leisure time
Art	Looking good
Cleaning up the environment	Loving partner
Close friends	Mental or physical stimulation
Competition	Money
Creativity	Pleasure
Donating time or money to others	Political activism
Economic security	Predictability
Entertainment	Recognition
Expensive possessions	Recreation
Family life	Risk taking
Good food	Safety
Having happy kids	Satisfying work
Health	Showing kindness
Honesty	Spirituality
Independence	Showing kindness
Influencing others	Variety
Intellectual pursuits	

Tallying up what you put your teeth into

Which values stand out as most important for you? Now, review a month in your life. You can do this by keeping an activity time log as follows:

1. **Write down every activity and how long you spend on it.**

   Don't worry about trivial details like washing your hands (unless you're obsessive-compulsive about hand washing).

2. **If you forget to write down your activities for a few hours, try to fill your log in from memory.**

   You could even record your activities once a day before bedtime. Perfect accuracy is not important.

3. **When the month is over, add up the total hours spent on each type of activity.**

   What really matters is how much time you devote to what you value. How do your values match up with the amount of time that you spend on them?

Holly, for example, feels stressed and anxious and that she never has enough time for anything. Holly completes the values clarification quiz and chooses close friends, satisfying work, and family life as her most highly prized goals. Then Holly tracks her activities on a time log for a month. The following list shows how Holly spends her time:

- Work: 205 hours
- Watching television: 60 hours
- Eating meals: 45 hours
- Commuting to work and daycare: 44 hours
- Showering and getting ready in the morning: 30 hours
- Meal preparation: 30 hours
- Taking kids to sports and lessons: 24 hours
- Housework: 22 hours
- Shopping/errands: 10 hours
- Exercise: 4 hours
- Paying bills: 3 hours
- Time with friends: 2 hours
- Time alone with husband: 1 hour

As she reviews her time log, Holly realizes that she works 50 hours a week at her job as a financial planner. Although the job provides challenge, satisfaction, and a nice income, Holly doesn't find it particularly meaningful. She's appalled to realize that she spends a mere 30 minutes per week with her friends. Even worse, she spends almost no time alone with her husband. Her time with her children consists of shuttling them to and from daycare and various activities. Hardly what she considers quality family time.

Shame and dismay flood Holly as she notices that television consumes more of her time than any single activity outside of work. She knows she's not living the life that she imagined she would. So Holly decides to do something different.

Ranking Priorities

Try not to let yourself feel ashamed and dismayed like Holly when you review your values and find your life strays from the course. The fact is, most people discover that the way they spend their time differs considerably from what they profess to value. Nevertheless, you can turn things around if you want to.

If you completed a time log, compare what you actually do with what you value. If a discrepancy exists, prioritize and set goals. Simplify your life. Make sure that your goals are specific and obtainable. Don't make goals like "I'll be happier," or "I'll save more money." These are too vague. Instead, state specific ideas for increasing your happiness, such as playing tennis twice a month or reading at least one book per month for pleasure. Or have $100 per month automatically withdrawn from your paycheck to go into savings.

Holly starts by poring over her time log for the past month. Television viewing jumps out as the first candidate for the chopping block. She decides to limit her television viewing and to improve the quality of her family time. She sets the following, concrete goals:

- ✔ I will only watch my favorite news shows that come on after the kids are put to bed.

- ✔ Friday night will be family night. We will order pizzas, play games, and talk.

- ✔ Two nights per month, we'll get a sitter and my husband, and I will go out on a date.

- ✔ Two Saturdays per month, we'll choose a family activity such as roller-skating, hiking, or a movie.

Holly feels good about her new goals and priorities. However, she realizes that she still works too many hours and has not found a way to include friends in her life. Since the kids were born, she's lost contact with most of her good friends. Looking at her schedule, she wonders what to do.

Delegating for Extra Time

Many people with anxiety feel they must always take responsibility for their job, the care of their family, and their home. Unless they have a hand in everything, they worry things might not get done. And if someone else takes over a task, they fear the result will fall short of their standards.

Holly works many long hours and still feels the need to cook, clean, transport her kids, and run most of the household errands. Sometimes her husband offers to do laundry or cook, but she turns him down, thinking that he'll only mess it up. But when Holly makes the decision to reorganize her life, she knows she'll have to start delegating.

She ponders what, how, who, and when. She discovered some brainstorming techniques in some business seminars, so she invites a couple of her friends over and includes her husband. She asks them all to help her devise a list of ways that she can farm out more of her onerous workload. See the following list to find out what they came up with:

- **Take the risk of letting husband do some laundry and cooking.** If he screws up, Holly can show him how to do better next time.

- **Hire a cleaning service to come in once every two weeks.** The service may cost a bit, but her long work hours earn her more than enough money to cover it.

  One friend describes a service she uses called Poop-Busters. They all laugh about it, but Holly delights in the idea of never having to bug her kids to clean up after their two dogs again, and it's surprisingly affordable.

- **Hire a chef to come to the house once every two weeks to prepare seven or eight family meals and store them in the freezer.** Another friend relates that she uses a new personal chef service. She says that they used to eat out that often and the cost compares favorably.

- **Family can spend one hour a week in a frantic, joint cleaning effort.** Her husband suggests that if everyone does it at the same time, it could be kind of fun.

- **Holly's secretary will take on some more responsibilities, including client phone calls and scheduling her appointments.** She figures that she can ask her because she really isn't that busy.

- **Hire a monthly lawn service.** Holly's husband says that he doesn't mind mowing, but that a lawn service could trim, fertilize, aerate, and de-thatch the lawn better than he could, and it would give them more time together.

- **Read *Organizing For Dummies* by Eileen Roth (Wiley Publishing, Inc.).** For some great tips on how to save time and effort and get organized, see the pages of this book. If you don't want to go the route of hiring outside help, this book can help you do it yourself in less time. When you're organized, tasks go smoother and faster.

We realize a number of these ideas cost money. Not always as much as you might think, but still they do cost something. Partly, it's a matter of how high money stacks up on your priority list. Balance money against time for the things that you value.

Nevertheless, not all families can consider such options. You might notice that not all these options entail financial burden. Get creative. Ask your friends, coworkers, and family for ideas on how to delegate. It could change your life.

Come up with two tasks that you could delegate to someone else. It doesn't need to cost money, just relieve one or more of your burdens in a way that can save you time.

Just Saying "No"

We have one more idea. Say "No." If you're anxious, you may have trouble standing up for your rights. Anxiety often prevents people from expressing their feelings and needs. When that happens, resentment joins anxiety and leads to frustration and anger. Furthermore, if you can't say no, other people can purposefully or inadvertently take advantage of you. You no longer own your time and your life.

Holly agrees to do most anything anyone asks of her. When her boss requests her to work late at the last minute, she always agrees. Even if working late impinges on important plans, she rarely expresses unwillingness. She also finds it difficult to hang up on annoying phone solicitors. She gives a few dollars to every solicitation for a charitable donation, even if she's never heard of the organization. She does more driving of other people's children than any of the other parents in the carpool. When her children need last minute help on homework projects because of their own procrastination, she pitches in despite her own fatigue and better judgment.

If you're a little like Holly, we have some suggestions for finding out how to say, "No." Realize it will take you some time to incorporate this new habit. You've probably been agreeing to fulfill everyone's every request for many years, so it will take a while to do something different.

First, notice the situations in which you find yourself agreeing when you don't really want to. Does it happen mostly at work, with family, with friends, or with strangers? When people ask you to do something, try the following:

- **Validate the person's request or desire.** For example, if someone asks you if you would mind dropping off something at the post office on your way home from work, say, "I understand that it would be more convenient for you if I dropped that off." This will give you more time to consider whether you really want to do it.

- **After you make up your mind, look the person who's making the request in the eye.** You don't need to rush your response.

- ✔ **Give a brief explanation, especially if it's a friend or family member.** However, remember that you really don't owe anyone an explanation; it's merely polite. You can say that you'd like to help out, but it just isn't possible, or you can simply state that you really would rather not.

- ✔ **Be clear that you cannot or will not do what you've been asked.** It's a fundamental human right to say "No."

Holly answers the phone and a solicitor for a long distance plan cheerfully begins his spiel. He talks so quickly that Holly can't speak without interrupting him. Then she realizes that she has the right to interrupt. After all, he's interrupting her dinner. So she musters up her courage and declares, "Thank you for calling. I'm just not interested." The salesperson goes right on and says, "Could I ask you why not?" She responds "No" and hangs up the phone. Her husband and children look on in amazement.

When you say "No" to bosses or family members, they may be temporarily unhappy with you. If you find yourself overreacting to their displeasure, it may be due to an agitating assumption. See Chapter 6 for more information.

Chapter 10

Let's Get Physical

*A*t 50 years of age, **Bernice** continues to struggle with tension and feels on edge much of the time. Of course, she's doing much better than she was a few years ago before she went to a therapist for her panic attacks. At that time, she'd been missing quite a few days of work due to her anxiety disorder, and she averaged four panic attacks per week. Her therapist taught her many of the strategies that we discuss in Chapters 5, 6, 7, 8, and 16. These techniques virtually eliminated her panic attacks, but Bernice seems to have a revved up nervous system.

Bernice tries several different medications but doesn't like the side effects. She also notices that she's gaining weight, which is common among women of this age group. A friend cajoles her into joining a gym. Along with the membership come four sessions with a personal trainer. Within a matter of six weeks, Bernice discovers a passion for exercise. Her mood improves; her anxiety and stress abate. She even starts to drop a few pounds, and she feels great.

In this chapter, we review the many benefits of exercise. A solid exercise regimen can help you with anxiety, but it also improves your health, appearance, and sense of well-being. The big rub for most people lies in finding the motivation and time to make exercise a part of their routine. We help you find the motivation and show you how to develop a reasonable plan that can work. We also guide you through the various exercise program options. In large part, it depends upon your personal goals and state of health.

Ready . . . Exorcise!

Please excuse our pun: We're not advising that you attempt to exorcise demons or perform hocus pocus, but like a good housecleaning, exercise can clear out the cobwebs and cast out the cloudy thinking and inertia that may accompany anxiety.

Exercise reduces anxiety. The harder and longer that you go at it — whether you're swimming, jogging, walking, working in the yard or on your home, playing racquetball or tennis, or even walking up the stairs — the less anxious you'll be. Exercise instills a newfound sense of confidence while blowing away anxiety's cloud. With enough exercise, you'll notice your attitude change from negative to positive.

Exercise reduces anxiety in several ways:

✔ Exercise helps to rid your body of the excess adrenaline that increases anxiety and arousal.

✔ Working out increases your body's production of *endorphins* — substances that reduce pain and create a mild, natural sense of well-being.

✔ Exercise also helps to release muscle tension and frustrations.

Of course, everyone has felt that they should exercise more. Most people realize that exercise has some sort of benefits for their health, but not everyone knows how extensive these benefits can be.

✔ Researchers have found that exercise decreases

- Anxiety

- Bad cholesterol

- Blood pressure

- Chronic pain

- Depression

- Low back pain

✔ Researchers have also found that exercise decreases the risk of

- Breast cancer

- Colon cancer

- Diabetes

- Falling, especially among the elderly

- Heart attack
- Stroke
- ✔ Research also supports the claim that exercise increases
  - A sense of balance
  - Endurance
  - Energy
  - Flexibility
  - The functioning of the immune system
  - Good cholesterol
  - Lung capacity
  - Mental sharpness
  - A sense of well-being

Wow! With such extensive, positive effects on anxiety, health, and well-being, why isn't everyone exercising? Millions of people do. Unfortunately, millions do not. The reason is both simple and complex. For the most part, people hit a brick wall when it comes to finding the motivation to exercise and especially for sustaining it. They complain about not having the time and being too embarrassed, too old, too fat, and too tired to exercise. But if our list of benefits appeals to you, the next section, "Don't Wait for Willpower — Just Do It," may help you muster the motivation.

Before beginning an exercise program, you should check with your doctor. This is especially true if you're over 40, overweight, or have any known health problems. Your doctor can tell you about any cautions, limitations, or restrictions that you should consider. Also, if after brief exercise, you experience chest pain, extreme shortness of breath, nausea, or dizziness, consult your physician immediately.

Don't Wait for Willpower — Just Do It

Have you ever thought that you just don't have the willpower to undertake an exercise program? You may be surprised to discover that we don't believe in willpower. That's right. *Willpower* is merely a word, an idea; it's not real.

Your brain doesn't have a special structure that contains so-called willpower. It's not something that you have a set quantity of and that you can't do anything about. The reason that people believe that they don't have willpower is that they merely don't do what they think they should. But reasons other than willpower exist to account for the lack of effort.

People fail to undertake projects for several kinds of reasons:

- ✔ **Distorted thinking:** Your mind may tell you things like "I just don't have the time," "I'm too tired," "It isn't worth the effort," or, "I'll look stupid as compared to the other people who are in better shape than me."

- ✔ **Lack of reward:** This problem comes about when you fail to set up a plan for rewarding new efforts. You may believe that exercise will cost you something in terms of leisure time, rest, or more profitable work. In some ways, this is true. That's why you need to set up a plan for reinforcing your efforts.

- ✔ **Environmental obstacles:** Perhaps you don't know of a good place for exercising, or the weather in your area isn't suitable. Maybe you have young kids that you need to take care of. You'll need to find ways around these obstacles.

- ✔ **Insufficient supports:** We all need support sometimes. Exercising alone can be tough for anyone, especially if your partner doesn't want to participate.

Defeating defeatism

If you're waiting for motivation to come knocking at your door, you could be in for a long wait. Not many people wake up with a burst of new enthusiasm for starting an exercise program. Like the commercial says, "Just do it." That's because motivation frequently follows action; if you think otherwise, you're putting the cart before the horse. Thinking that you should wait for the motivation before taking action is one of the top ten defeatist ideas.

We list the top ten most defeatist ideas and arguments against them in Table 10-1. Look these over carefully to see which if any may be hindering your decision to exercise. Ponder both sides carefully.

Table 10-1	The Top Ten Defeatist Ideas
Defeatist Ideas	*Debunking Defeatist Ideas*
I don't have the motivation. When inspiration comes to me, I'll start exercising.	Motivation follows action, not the other way around. Regular exercise feels great eventually, but that often takes time.
I don't have time.	Time is only a matter of priorities. Exercising for 30 minutes, 3 times a week will give me a good start.

Defeatist Ideas	Debunking Defeatist Ideas
I'm too tired.	I'm tired much of the time because I don't exercise! Exercise increases energy and stamina.
I'm too old for exercise.	No one is ever too old to exercise. Doctors say it's good at every age; even people over the age of 80 can benefit from exercise. They just have to start slowly.
I'll look silly compared to the people who are in better condition.	Everyone starts from somewhere. If I'm too embarrassed, I can start at home. I can join others when I start to get somewhere.
It's too expensive to go to the gym.	As compared to the costs of poor health, it's cheap. Anyway, I can exercise without going to a gym.
It's not worth the effort.	It may feel that way sometimes, but the benefits are indisputable.
I have too much to do at work. I can't take time away for something silly like exercise.	Studies show that people who exercise regularly miss fewer days at work. Besides, they're probably more productive as well.
I don't like exercise.	So far, I haven't enjoyed it, but I don't have to enjoy everything that's good for me. I don't like my annual physical, but I do go through with it, and I can always try different kinds of exercise; maybe I will find one that I do like.
I'm just not an exerciser. It's not who I am.	With all the benefits that exercise holds for me, I need to work out. I don't have to think of myself as some jock, I just need to exercise 3 or 4 times a week.

Table 10-1 contains the ten defeatist ideas that we run into most frequently. If you have one or more of these defeatist ideas running around in your head, perhaps you agree with our debunking arguments. If not, see if you can develop your own way of countering defeatist thoughts and ideas. Chapter 3 has many ideas for overcoming the thoughts that cause resistance to change. If you find motivation elusive, you're not exactly the first person in the world to have that problem.

Willpower is a misnomer; you simply need to tackle the thoughts that stand in your way and then try our other ways of developing motivation that are explained in the rest of this chapter.

Rewarding yourself for exercise

Psychologists have known for decades that people usually do more of what they find rewarding and less of what they find unpleasant whenever they can. That fact may sound like a no-brainer to you. Nevertheless, ignoring the importance of rewards is easy when trying to get started on an exercise program.

If you're out of shape right now, exercise may feel more unpleasant than pleasant, at least in the beginning. During or after your workout, you may be out of breath, your muscles may ache, and you may have soreness for a few days or even longer. Reminding yourself of the benefits of exercise can help, but let's face it: The benefits don't accrue until you've been working out a while.

A large number of the problems that people struggle with involve difficulty in balancing short-term payoffs versus long-term benefits and costs. Don't you think so? Consider the common bad habits presented in Table 10-2. The greater tendency toward immediate gratification overshadows any consideration for the detrimental effects that arise over the long haul.

Table 10-2	The Effects of Bad Habits	
Example	*Short-term payoff*	*Long-term result*
Alcohol abuse	Drinking usually feels better than not to drink.	Alcohol can kill you.
Smoking	Smokers claim that smoking relaxes them.	A wide range of health problems.
Obesity	People wrestling with weight find eating satisfying.	Many health problems.
Drug abuse	Many so-called recreational drugs feel good.	Permanent body and brain damage.
Spending problems	Spending money is usually fun.	Savings and retirement suffer badly.

The banzai self-starter plan

If you really want to exercise but still haven't started, try what we call *the banzai self-starter plan* to test whether you really want to start exercising. The banzai self-starter plan has just a few simple steps:

✔ Write out five checks for some amount that would feel a little bad to lose, but not so much that it would break your budget, perhaps ten or twenty dollars each.

✔ Look up the address of some organization that you personally do not like, perhaps the opposite political party or a local organization that makes you fume.

✔ Write a letter in support of this organization and sign it.

✔ Hand the stamped letters with the checks to a highly trusted friend. Tell your friend that you will report each week for five weeks whether you exercised three or more times. If you did not, ask that your letter be dropped into the mail.

Ouch! Are we serious? Yes. We have tried this strategy with a variety of clients in the past. Trust us; it's a rare person who allows those letters to actually end up in the mail.

The banzai self-starter plan usually works best for relatively short-term motivational requirements that last six weeks or less. Don't rely on it for long-term solutions. The good news is that exercise programs often become self-sustaining within four or five consistent weeks of effort.

Exercise involves the same problem with balancing short-versus long-term payoff, but the payoffs are only apparent after consistent, long-term participation. At first, exercise more often than not feels lousy; whereas, eventually, for those who keep up the routine, a daily workout improves your health and sense of well-being. Unfortunately, people have a hard time doing what may feel unpleasant in the short run even if benefits await them over time.

However, you can work your way around this dilemma: Set up your own personal reward system for exercising. For example, give yourself ten points for each time that you exercise for 30 minutes or more. After you accumulate 100 points, indulge yourself with a treat — a new outfit, going out for dinner at a nice restaurant, planning a special weekend, or setting aside a whole day to spend on your favorite hobby. Over time, as exercise becomes a little more pleasant (which it will!), up the ante — require 200 points before you treat yourself.

Eventually, you'll find that exercise becomes rewarding in its own right, and you won't need to reward yourself as a means of instilling the necessary motivation. As the pain of an out-of-shape body lessens and endurance increases, you'll discover other rewards from exercise as well, such as:

- ✔ It can be a great time to think about solutions to problems.

- ✔ Plan out the day or week while you exercise.

- ✔ Some people report increased creative thoughts during exercise.

- ✔ You may get a great feeling from the sense of accomplishment.

Because exercise often doesn't feel good in the beginning, setting up a self-reward system sometimes helps a great deal; later, other rewards will likely kick in.

However, if you find that even a self-reward program doesn't quite do the trick. What can you do if that's where you end up? We have one more idea that's a bit more severe — the banzai self-starter plan. (See "The banzai self-starter plan" sidebar in this chapter.)

Busting barriers to exercise

Sometimes people struggle with starting exercise because of a few personal or environmental obstacles. You want to exercise, but inconveniences just get in the way, such as

- ✔ Weather that's too cold and precipitous to consider jogging in

- ✔ Overly crowded gyms in your area where equipment is always in use

- ✔ Dangerous neighborhoods that feel unsafe to walk or jog in

- ✔ A lack of exercise equipment and no cash to buy it

However, the real problem with these obstacles lies in your mind-set — not in the hindrances themselves. These are merely inconveniences, hassles, little problems waiting to be solved — not concrete blockades.

Nevertheless, making your environment as exercise-friendly as you can is a good idea. Consider turning an unused room or space in your home into a workout space. Make the room as exercise-friendly as possible. You may want to have a music system or headphones, a television to watch, or simply a book to read.

In addition, you can stock your room with simple, relatively inexpensive equipment; you don't have to spend a fortune on exercise equipment. Consider using:

- ✔ Jump ropes

- ✔ Cans of soup instead of hand weights

- ✔ A concrete cinder block for stepping exercises

- ✔ An inexpensive yoga mat
- ✔ Reasonably priced exercise equipment

Use creativity. Summer yard sales are a good bet for finding reasonably priced exercise equipment. Sometimes it takes a little thought to find the right place, time, and type of equipment that you want to use. But realize that you can solve the problem, and your solution doesn't have to be a perfect one.

Surrounding yourself with a few cheerleaders

Although social supports aren't absolutely essential, many people find that company can increase motivation to exercise. Other people can give you encouragement and provide someone interesting to talk with. You can obtain social support in various ways:

- ✔ **Recruiting an exercise buddy:** If you know someone who has talked about wanting to exercise, you have an instant support system. If you don't, try discussing your problem with your friends. If they don't want to exercise, perhaps they know someone else who does. Leave no stone unturned.

- ✔ **Taking a class:** All kinds of exercise classes are available at the YMCA and YWCA. Look at the continuing education class schedule for an exercise class that's offered at your local high school, community college, or university.

- ✔ **Joining a gym:** You'll find like-minded people at health clubs or gyms, and many of the members are new to exercise or have a hard time sticking to it after they start up a program — just like you. That's especially true in January!

- ✔ **Getting a personal trainer:** It sounds expensive, doesn't it? Personal trainers do cost, but they can help you design a program and push you to stick with it. You may be able to reduce the cost by getting a personal trainer for yourself and a friend for less cost than the two of you would pay separately. You'll find that after four or five weeks, you won't need to use your trainer often or perhaps not at all.

The bottom line — humans are social animals. Undertaking a new but difficult enterprise is easier if you have a support system, which is probably available to you if you give it some thought.

Working in Your Workout

Today, people work longer hours than ever before, so it's tempting to think that the day doesn't hold enough time for exercise. Of course, we covered the distorted belief that "I don't have time to exercise," in Table 10-1, earlier in this chapter. However, even though you may have come to the realization that you have the time and that it's all a matter of priorities, you won't find the time unless you plan for it.

That's right; you have to scrutinize your schedule seriously and work exercise into your life. Perhaps your job offers flex time, whereby you can choose to come in an hour later and stay later two or three times a week to have time to exercise in the morning, or perhaps you can exercise twice on the weekends and find just one time after work during the week.

 Conventional advice suggests that you should do some kind of vigorous exercise for a half hour or more at least three times a week. Perhaps you can work it in on the weekends and find a third time during the week by getting creative. It isn't all that difficult. For example:

- ✔ **Parking at a distance:** Park your car about a 20-minute brisk walk away from your place of work once or twice a week.

- ✔ **Taking the stairs:** If you often take the elevator up five or six floors to work, try a brisk walk up the stairs several times a day instead.

- ✔ **Exercising during your breaks:** If you get a couple of 10- or 15-minute breaks at work, try going for a brisk walk rather than standing around the water cooler. Two or three 10-minute periods of exercise do you the same amount of good that one 20- or 30-minute period does.

Selecting an Exercise — Whatever Turns You On

Choosing the type of exercise that works best for you depends in part on what goals you have. Almost any exercise can reduce anxiety somewhat. However, you're bound to find that you like certain types of exercise more than others. Because any exercise has benefits, we recommend that you start with exercise that seems most appealing to you. Although the array of exercise possibilities is almost infinite, some of the most popular forms of exercise are aerobics, weight training, and yoga.

Pumping up your heart and lungs

One of the best ways to alleviate anxiety is to engage in *aerobic* exercise (also known as *cardiovascular* exercise). *Aerobic* means "with oxygen," and it refers to the kind of hardy exercise that increases your intake of oxygen and thus shapes up your heart and lungs. Aerobic exercise also lowers blood pressure, reduces bad cholesterol while raising your good cholesterol, and develops your energy and endurance.

Aerobic exercise involves your large muscles in rhythmic, repetitive actions and lasts for more than a few minutes. To get the most benefit, you should keep at it for 20 or 30 minutes, although two or three 10-minute periods works pretty well, too. Types of aerobic exercise include

- Basketball
- Bicycling
- Jogging
- Racquetball
- Rowing
- Skating
- Tennis
- Walking briskly

With aerobic exercise, you want to feel winded but still be able to say a five- or six-word sentence without gasping for another breath — an indication that your heart and lungs are working hard enough to improve their condition but not so hard that you pass out. To be precise, you can get an inexpensive heart monitor and track your pulse, or to get a general idea, you can take your pulse yourself by putting your index finger on the artery in your neck that's just below your chin and next to your Adam's apple. The artery isn't hard to find because you'll feel the rhythmic pumping of blood through it with your fingers. Your *pulse* tells you how fast or slow your heart is beating. Look at a clock with a second hand, and with your finger on your artery, count the pulsations that occur within 15 seconds and multiply that number by four to find out the number of beats per minute — known as your pulse.

A basic formula is available to figure out your ideal heart rate zone. Essentially, you subtract your age from 220 and multiply the result by a percentage that depends upon your fitness level.

Everyone should have regular physical checkups. If you're over 40 or have any kind of health concerns, be sure to consult your physician for help in determining your fitness level and target heart rate.

If you're a healthy beginner, but in poor shape, multiply by 0.5. For example, if you're 35 years old and haven't exercised since ninth grade gym class, you would calculate your initial target heart rate zone as follows:

$$220 - 35 = 185 \times 0.5 = 92.5$$

If, on the other hand, you're in moderately good shape, multiply by 0.6. For example, if you're 65 years old, have been fairly active, and have your doctor's blessing, you would calculate your target zone this way:

$$220 - 65 = 155 \times 0.6 = 93.0$$

Finally, if you're already in very good condition, you can multiply by 0.8. For example, if you're 53 years old and have been exercising vigorously for quite some time, you would calculate your target zone this way:

$$220 - 53 = 167 \times 0.8 = 133.6$$

When you're exercising vigorously, your heart rate will likely go over your ideal zone. When that happens, it's time to slow down and bring your pulse back into the zone.

Lifting your way out of anxiety

Weight training builds strength mostly, and it may not reduce anxiety as well as aerobic exercise, but some people believe it helps. They say that their confidence improves and tension reduces.

Probably the easiest way to engage in weight training is by using dumbbells, barbells, or weight machines. However, you can obtain reasonable strength gains from some inexpensive, resistance machines as well as rubber exercise bands, and even no-equipment exercises, such as

- Crunches
- Lunges
- Push-ups
- Squats

You should know that strength and weight training require some knowledge. Before you train with weights, we recommend that you consult a trainer or purchase a book, such as *Weight Training For Dummies,* 2nd Edition, by Liz Neporent, MA, and Suzanne Schlosberg (Wiley Publishing, Inc.). Then you can start pumping and lifting your anxiety up and away.

Yearning to try yoga?

You'd almost have to live in a monastery not to have heard of yoga nowadays. No one knows for sure when yoga actually began, but it's been around at least 3,000 to 5,000 years. The many types and versions of yoga involve a series of poses that you hold for perhaps 30 seconds to a couple of minutes. Various stories abound about the origins of yoga, but most believe it developed in India and was practiced by Buddhist monks.

For many, yoga has a spiritual component. Others practice it merely as an exercise. You can do either or both; there's no fixed rule about how to practice yoga.

 Yoga has some interesting benefits. First, it can be quite relaxing and anxiety alleviating. It also blends nicely with a practice known as "mindfulness," described in Chapter 16. As a combination, yoga and mindfulness can be a powerful tool against anxiety. Second, yoga has positive physiological effects, such as increased strength, flexibility, and balance. Certain versions of yoga can even be somewhat aerobic.

However, perhaps you think of yoga as tying your body up like a human pretzel, or maybe you've seen pictures of people sitting on the floor with their eyes closed and thought that yoga looks more like sleep than exercise. Both of these ideas are myths as we can personally attest.

A couple of years ago, Dr. Smith (the co-author of this book) started dabbling in yoga. She came home and extolled the virtues of yoga to Dr. Elliott (the other co-author of this book). I supported her new interest, but I knew it wasn't for me. After all, I'm 6 feet, 3 inches tall, and at that time, I had as much flexibility in my body as a bronze statue. I imagined looking like a total buffoon or worse.

After a few months, Dr. Smith urged me to join her. I said that may happen . . . when pigs fly. She persisted. (She persists when she's really right about something.) Eventually, when at a professional conference together, she suggested that we arrange a private lesson with the spa connected to the hotel that we stayed in. I decided that perhaps a private lesson wouldn't be quite so humiliating, and I could show her once and for all that I wasn't going to like yoga, much less be capable of do it.

Well, I was wrong. Although my body didn't bend like a pretzel, the instructor showed me how to honor any restrictive signals that my body gave me, and he pointed out that yoga is noncompetitive — you don't have to look great. Today, both of us enjoy yoga and find it quite relaxing. We've experienced increased flexibility, balance, strength, and calm.

Again, yoga requires a little knowledge. You can sign up for a beginner class, read a book, such as *Yoga For Dummies* by Georg Feuerstein, PhD and Larry Payne, PhD (Wiley Publishing, Inc.), or check out one of a variety of videotapes, such as *Basic Yoga Workout For Dummies* with Susan Ivanhoe (Wiley Publishing, Inc.). We think that your investigation will be worth the effort. Yoga just may surprise you like it did me.

How about exercise and panic?

Some people fear that exercise could set off panic attacks. In part, that's because exercise produces a few bodily symptoms, such as increased heart rate, and those with panic attacks sometimes respond to such symptoms with panic. However, if you go at exercise gradually, it can serve as a graded exposure task as discussed in Chapter 8. In other words, it can be an effective treatment approach for panic.

In addition, although the actual risk is somewhat controversial, exercise can cause a build up of lactic acid, which does seem to trigger panic attacks in a few people. However, over the long run, exercise also improves your body's ability to rid itself of lactic acid. Therefore, again, we recommend that if you fear that you'll have panic attacks as a result of exercise, simply go slowly. If you find it absolutely intolerable, stop exercising for a while or use other strategies in this book for reducing your panic attack frequency before going back to exercise.

Chapter 11

Sleep, Sweet Sleep

● ●

In This Chapter

▶ What's keeping you awake?

▶ Making your bedroom cozy and nice

▶ Establishing nighttime routines

▶ Getting rid of nightmares

● ●

Does this little wee-hours script sound familiar? It's 4:07 a.m., and you're thinking . . .

> I'm awake. The alarm goes off in only two more hours. I hope that I can go back to sleep. . . . Let's see . . . I wonder how hot it will be today and what should I wear? Do I have enough gas in the car? I've got four new clients scheduled for this morning and then a consultation at the hospital later on. The next section of the book is due in a week — there goes the weekend. I need to figure out my mother's insurance billing — that means calling the agency and remaining on hold forever. I better make sure that Trevor mailed his college applications; the deadline is almost here. I have to fill out all that financial stuff, too. I wonder whether I can fit in the gym tonight. Did I remember to take out the chicken for dinner? I really need to stop thinking about all of this . . . I need to go back to sleep. Okay, I'll try to concentrate on my breathing. Breathe in to the count of eight and then let it out slowly and then in. . . .

Have you ever experienced "early morning worry"? As if falling asleep isn't hard enough, many people wake up before they want to, driven into high alert as anxious thoughts race through their consciousness. In this chapter, you can find out how to get the best rest possible. Also, we show that what you do in the hours before bed can help or interrupt your sleep. Finally, you will see how to get rid of those repetitive nightmares once and for all.

The tendency toward an early morning awakening with an inability to get back to sleep can be a sign of depression as well as anxiety. If your appetite changes, your energy decreases, your mood swings into low gear, your ability to concentrate diminishes, and you've lost interest in activities that you once found pleasurable, you may be clinically depressed. You should check with a mental health practitioner or a physician to find out.

Giving Sleeplessness a Name

People generally need about eight hours of sleep per night. Seniors may need a little less sleep, but this idea remains controversial among scientists. Besides, the real gauge as to whether you're getting enough sleep is how you feel during the daytime, not the exact number of hours you get. In any case, anxiety frequently disrupts sleep, and a lack of sleep can increase your anxiety. The following list describes the most common sleep disturbances:

- **Circadian rhythm** occurs when your biological sleep clock doesn't jibe with your actual sleep schedule. This condition happens when people work rotating shifts or when traveling across time zones.

- **Hormonal factors** may also play a part. Pregnant or menopausal women may suffer sleep disturbances. Hormonal fluctuations that occur during pregnancy and menopause can cause physical discomfort and changes in bodily temperature that interrupt sleep.

- **Insomnia,** by far the most common sleep problem, may be the result of anxiety, depression, stress, poor sleep habits, discomfort, or an inadequate sleeping environment such as living in a noisy apartment building or sleeping on a lumpy mattress. Insomniacs have difficulty falling asleep and/or staying asleep.

- **Narcolepsy** occurs in the daytime rather than at night. It is a serious condition in which the person experiences sudden lapses of consciousness into sleep or overwhelming feelings of sleepiness. Medications can help.

- **Nightmares** may increase with stress and anxiety. Of course, sometimes they just happen. In either event, if you suffer these frequently, they can disrupt the quality of your sleep.

- **Dreamless sleep** is less restful sleep. Scientists call the state of dreaming *Rapid Eye Movement* (REM) sleep. During this time, the eyes shift rapidly and dreams occur. Interrupted sleep, certain drugs, and alcohol can interfere with getting enough REM sleep.

- **Prostate problems** may be disturbing enough to keep a man awake. Men who have an enlarged prostate may wake up numerous times during the night to urinate. If you wake up more than once a night to urinate, you may wish to consult your doctor.

- **Restless leg syndrome,** more common among middle aged and older adults, produces the urge to keep moving because of uncomfortable feelings in the legs and feet. Certain prescription medications can help, so consult your doctor if you believe that you may suffer from this problem.

- **Snoring** sometimes indicates a more serious problem known as *sleep apnea.* People with sleep apnea actually stop breathing for short periods of time and wake up briefly to take a breath.

Sleep terror in children

Childhood sleep disorders, one of the most common complaints brought to pediatricians, can disrupt the whole family. Children usually outgrow many sleep disorders, such as bed-wetting, frequent awakenings, and problems going to sleep, within a reasonable time period.

Sleep terror, especially strange and frightening to many parents, is relatively common, occurring among 1 to 6 percent of all kids, but the incidence among adults is less than 1 percent. Sleep terror tends to present itself about an hour and a half after going to bed. The child typically sits up suddenly and screams for up to a half an hour. During the episode, the child is actually asleep and is difficult to awaken and to provide comfort to. Children don't remember their sleep terror in the morning. Sleep terror most often occurs when children are between ages 4 and 10. By the time a child is a teenager, it usually disappears.

Direct treatments for sleep terror are unavailable as yet. But then again, because children don't remember it, sleep terror usually doesn't cause the children who have it any daytime distress. Too little sleep may increase the likelihood of sleep terror, so parents should make sure their children get enough sleep. And stress may also contribute to sleep terror, so parents should attempt to alleviate stress and other anxieties in their children. (See Chapter 17 for more information about how to help your kids cope with stress and anxiety.)

Sleep apnea can be a serious problem. If you or your partner snores heavily, you may want to consult a physician or a sleep clinic. Many major hospitals have special clinics where your sleep can be monitored and assessed. Usually, you go there and spend the night in their sleep lab. Your family doctor can refer you to one of these specialized centers.

As you can see, much sleeplessness has a physical basis. At the same time, if your sleep is disrupted for any reason and you have problems with anxiety, returning to sleep is more difficult. Obviously, you should explore the possible physical basis of any sleep problems. However, after you have done what you can with physical causes, you may still need to work on improving your sleep patterns.

The ABCs of Getting Your Zs

Your sleep environment matters. Of course, some rare birds can sleep almost anywhere — on the couch, in a chair, on the floor, in the car, or even at their desk at work. On the other hand, most folks require the comfort of a bed and the right conditions. Sleep experts report that for a restful sleep, you should sleep in a room that's

✔ **Dark:** You have a clock in your brain that tells you when it's time to sleep. Darkness helps set the clock by causing the brain to release melatonin, a hormone that helps to induce sleep. Consider putting up curtains that block out most of the sun if you find yourself awakened by the early morning light or because you need to sleep during the day. Some people even wear masks to keep light out.

✔ **Cool:** People sleep better in a cool room. If you feel cold, adding blankets is usually preferable to a warm room.

✔ **Quiet:** If you live near a busy street or have loud neighbors, consider getting a fan or white noise generator to block out nuisance noises. The worst kind of noise is intermittent and unpredictable. If the noise is consistent, the various kinds of sporadic noise that can be blocked out by a simple floor fan may amaze you.

✔ **Complete with a comfortable bed:** Mattresses matter. If you sleep with someone else or a dog, make sure that everyone has enough room.

In other words, make your bedroom a retreat that looks inviting and cozy. Spoil yourself with high-thread-count sheets and pillowcases. You may want to try aromatherapy (see Chapter 12). No one knows for sure if it works, but many people claim that the fragrance of lavender helps them sleep.

Following a Few Relaxing Routines

Sleep revitalizes your physical and mental resources. Studies show that sleep deprivation causes people to drive as if they were under the influence. Physicians without sufficient sleep make more errors. Sleep deprivation makes you irritable, crabby, anxious, and despondent.

Thus, you need to schedule a reasonable amount of time for sleep — at least seven or eight hours. Don't burn the candle at both ends. We don't care how much work you have on your plate; depriving yourself of sleep can only make you less productive and less pleasant to be around.

So first and foremost, allow sufficient time for sleep. But that's not enough if you have trouble with sleep, so we suggest that you look at the ideas in the subsections that follow to improve the quality of your sleep.

Associating sleep with your bed

One of the most important principles of sleep is to teach your brain to associate sleep with your bed. That means that when you get into bed, don't bring work along with you. Some people find that reading in bed relaxes them, and others like to watch a little TV before bed. That's fine if it works for you, but if those activities don't relax you, avoid doing them in bed.

If you go to bed and lie around for more than 20 or 30 minutes, unable to fall asleep — get up. Again, the point is to train your brain to link your bed to sleep. You can train your brain to dislike getting up by taking on some unpleasant (though fairly passive, even boring) chore while you're awake. If you do this a number of times, your brain will find it easier to start feeling drowsy when you're in bed.

Just before hitting the hay

Some find that taking a warm bath with fragrant oils or bath salts about an hour before hitting the hay is soothing. You may discover that soaking in a scented bath in a dimly lit bathroom while listening to relaxing music before going to bed is just the right ticket to solid slumber. Other people use one of the relaxation techniques discussed in Chapters 12 and 13 quite helpful. Studies show that relaxation can improve sleep.

Whenever possible, go to bed at close to the same time every night. Many people like to stay up late on weekends, and that's fine if you're not having sleep problems, but if you are, we recommend sticking to the same schedule as during the week. You need a regular routine and passive activities before bed.

Therefore, don't do heavy exercise within a few hours of going to sleep. Almost any stimulating activity can interfere with sleep, even mental. For example, we discovered somewhat to our dismay that if we work on writing an article or a book after 9:00 p.m., then our brains continue to spin out thoughts and ideas well after bedtime. So we've changed our routine, and we don't write late in the evening.

Watching what you eat and drink

Obviously, you don't want to load up on caffeinated drinks within a couple of hours before going to bed. Don't forget that many sources other than coffee — colas, certain teas, chocolate, and certain pain relievers — contain caffeine. Of course, some people seem rather impervious to the effects of caffeine while others are better off not consuming any after lunch. Even if you weren't bothered by caffeine in the past, you could develop sensitivity to it as you age. Consider caffeine's effects on you if you're having trouble sleeping.

Nicotine also revs up the body. Try to avoid smoking just prior to bed. Obviously, it's preferable to quit smoking entirely, but because some people haven't been able to stop as yet, at least watch how much you smoke before bedtime.

Alcohol relaxes the body and should be a great way of aiding sleep, but it isn't. That's because alcohol disrupts your sleep cycles. You don't get as much of the important REM sleep (discussed earlier in this chapter in the "Giving Sleeplessness a Name" section), and you may find yourself waking up early in the morning. However, some people find that drinking a glass or two of wine in the evening is relaxing. That's fine, but watch the amount.

Heavy meals prior to bed aren't such a great idea either; many people find that eating too much before bed causes mild discomfort. In addition, you may want to avoid highly spiced and/or fatty foods prior to bed. However, going to bed hungry is also not a good idea; the key is balance.

So what should you eat or drink before bed? Herbal teas, such as chamomile or valerian, have many advocates. We don't have much data on how well it works, but herbal teas are quite unlikely to interfere with sleep, and they're pleasant to drink. Some evidence supports eating a small carbohydrate snack before bedtime to help induce sleep.

Mellowing medication

Many people try treating their sleep problems with over-the-counter medications, many of which contain antihistamines that do help, but they can lead to drowsiness the next day. Occasional use of these medications is relatively safe for most. Herbal formulas, such as melatonin or valerian, may also help. (See Chapter 14 for more information on herbs.)

If sleep problems are chronic, you should consult your doctor. A medication that you're already taking could possibly be interfering with your sleep. Your doctor may prescribe medication to help induce sleep. Many sleep medications become less effective over time, and some carry the risk of addiction. These potentially addictive medications are only used for a short period of time. On the other hand, a few sleep medications work for a longer time as an aid for sleep without fear of addiction. Talk about your sleep problem with your doctor for more information and help.

What to Do When Sleep Just Won't Come

"Ding, ding," goes the clock chime. **Becky** sighs, realizing that it's 2:00 a.m., and she has yet to fall asleep. She turns over and tries to be still, so that she doesn't wake her husband. She thinks, "With everything I have to do tomorrow, if I don't sleep, I'll be a wreck. I hate not sleeping." She gets out of bed, goes into the bathroom, finds the bottle of melatonin, and pops three into her mouth. She's been taking them routinely for months, and they just don't seem to have the same effect that they did before.

She goes back to bed, tries to settle down, and worries about the bags under her eyes and what people will think. Her itchy dry skin starts to crawl. She can't stand the feeling of lying in bed for an eternity without sleeping.

In Becky's mind, her lack of sleep turns into a catastrophe, and her pondering actually makes it far more difficult for her to fall asleep. When you can't sleep, try to de-catastrophize your problem by

- ✔ **Reminding yourself that every single time that you failed to sleep in the past, somehow you got through the next day in spite of your lack of sleep the night before.** It may not have been wonderful, but you did it.

- ✔ **Realizing that occasional sleep loss happens to everyone.** Excessive worry can only aggravate the problem.

- ✔ **Getting up and distracting yourself with something else to do.** This stops your mind from magnifying the problem and can also prevent you from associating your bed with not sleeping.

- ✔ **Concentrating solely on your breathing.** See Chapter 16 for ideas on mindfulness and staying in the present moment as opposed to focusing on thoughts about the negative effects of your sleeplessness.

Many people try taking daytime naps when they consistently fail to sleep at night. It sounds like a great solution, but unfortunately, it only compounds the problem. Frequent or prolonged naps disrupt your body's natural clock. If you must nap, make it a short, power nap — no longer than 20 minutes.

Of course, a few unusual folks find that they can nap for just three or four minutes whenever they want during the day; they wake up refreshed and sleep well at night. If that's you, go ahead and nap. Most people simply can't do that.

Nagging Nightmares

Bad dreams plague almost everyone from time to time. However, some people find that nightmares invade their sleep on a nightly basis. Folks who suffer from Post-Traumatic Stress Disorder (PTSD) are particularly likely to experience nightmares frequently. Many people find nightmares emotionally upsetting, and these visions of horror can cause you to awaken and then wrestle with getting back to sleep.

Psychiatrists Krakow and Neidhardt developed an effective strategy for getting rid of nightmares. You no longer have to feel like a helpless victim to these melodramas in your mind. Instead, you can take action to rid yourself of nightmares once and for all.

Those suffering from Post-Traumatic Stress Disorder (PTSD) may experience the same nightmare night after night. Others suffer nightmares involving new dramas of horror far more often than they wish. Your nightmares may be repetitive or ever changing. Either way, you can use this technique:

1. **Develop your imagination.**

   Practice imagining and describing vivid scenes, just so long as they're pleasant and involve multiple senses. You can also check Chapter 13 for more ideas on developing your imagination.

2. **Record your nightmares.**

   Keep a pad of paper and a pen at your bedside. When you awaken from a nightmare or first thing in the morning, write down as much as you can possibly conjure up about your nightmare. Be sure to write in present tense and first person. Describe the imagery with all your senses if you can. Leave some space on the page to write down any thoughts or memories that you associate with the nightmare.

   For example, **Vic** drives trucks for a living. A few years ago, he drove through a fog-filled stretch of highway. Suddenly, without warning, he saw brake lights in front of him. He slammed on his brakes but couldn't stop in time. No sooner had he hit the rig in front of him, than he felt the impact of another vehicle slamming into his rear end. He heard horns blaring, metal crunching, and people screaming out from the foggy, surreal scene. Although terribly shaken, Vic only sustained minor cuts and bruises. Others in the 40-vehicle accident weren't so lucky.

   Since that time, nightmares have plagued Vic almost nightly. He wakes up in a sweat and often spends the rest of the night sleepless. He records the following:

   > I'm in my rig driving somewhere, but I don't know where. My brakes give out, and I start gaining speed going downhill. I can smell the burning break lining. I see cars start flying off the road in front of me for no reason. Then I see the old car my parents used to drive just ahead. Somehow I know they're in there. My mother's face appears in the rear windshield. At first she's laughing, but then her face turns to horror. I know that I'm going to run into them. I can't stop.

   Now, he writes his thoughts and memories conjured up by the dream.

   > I know the brakes failing must be about the accident and the total lack of control that I felt. I also feel horribly guilty when I awaken. Maybe that's about all the people who got hurt in the multi-car pileup that day. I especially think about the two kids who were killed. I wonder about the car with my parents. I remember learning how to drive in that car. So why would that be in my dream?

Maybe it's because I started to feel that I wasn't that good of a driver after the accident. But why are my parents in the dream, and why do I feel so guilty? I never really hurt them, or maybe I did. I still feel a little guilty about leaving Tulsa to go to Seattle when they were kind of old and didn't want me to go.

3. Take the dream that bothers you and change the ending.

This is the final step toward ridding yourself of nightmares: Create an ending that makes you feel better and puts you more in control; then imagine the new dream in vivid detail over and over again.

Read Vic's new, revised dream as follows:

I'm in my rig driving somewhere, but I don't know where. My brakes give out, and I start gaining speed going downhill. I hear the grinding as I force the rig into a lower gear to slow it down. I see my parents' old car in front of me and an uphill turnoff just ahead. I know that I can steer my truck right up into the turn off and come to a stop. I make the turn, and the truck stops. My parents see what's happened and turn around to follow me. We get out and hug.

Does something this simple work? Yes. Krakow and Neidhardt collaborated on a study and found that revising nightmares in this manner alleviated nightmare frequency and intensity for 70 percent of the participants. This result lasted even after a year and a half had passed. Try it and sleep well.

Part IV
Focusing on Feeling

In this part . . .

We point out that you can't feel anxious and relaxed at the same time. So we give you some quick, easy relaxation techniques for calming your mind and body. Address all your senses through breathing, muscle relaxation, aromatherapy, music, massage, and imagery.

Sometimes, you need a little more help to quell your anxiety. We review the various herbs and supplements that have been widely touted as anxiety cures — you'll see which ones work and which don't. We then help you decide if prescription medication looks like an approach for you to consider. You find out about the most commonly prescribed medications for anxiety — how they work and their most frequent side effects.

Finally, we offer you a guide for letting go of anxiety through *acceptance*. You'll see that acceptance involves finding out how to let go of ego, tolerate uncertainty, embrace imperfection, and connect with and experience the present moment.

Chapter 12

Relaxation: The Five-Minute Solution

"*I* don't have time to relax. My life is far too hectic. I barely see my friends as it is now. I can't remember the last time that I took a whole weekend off. I even neglect my own family. By the time the dinner dishes are put away, unable to think about anything else, I collapse in front of the television."

Does this sound like you or someone you care about? When contemplating making changes in their lives, people complain about having too little time more than anything else. Modern life moves at a faster pace. Beepers and cellphones follow you everywhere — at work, at home, in the car, and for some, into sleep.

We asked a wise Yogi master how long he practices everyday, fully expecting to hear the discouraging answer, "An hour or two." Imagine our surprise when he told us, "Five minutes." That's all he needs. He went on to explain that he usually takes more time, but he only commits to five minutes out of each day.

We listened to our teacher and we now ask a mere five minutes of ourselves daily. Five minutes has changed our lives. That's not much. Everyone can find five minutes. And if you do five minutes, it just might stretch into 10 or 20. But if it doesn't, that really is okay. Relaxation slowly infiltrates your life without you even knowing it, and when anxiety hits, you'll have a valuable tool for calming the storm within.

In this chapter, the relaxation procedures fall into any one of three major categories — various breathing techniques, ways for relaxing the body, and a few sensory experiences. Some of these can take a little longer to gain full mastery over, but they can all be done in five minutes once you get the hang of it. The key is daily practice. Like every other skill, the more you do it, the easier and faster it gets.

Blowing Anxiety Away

Breathing is what you've practiced, more than anything else in your life. In waking moments, you don't even think about your breathing. Yet, of all biological functions, breathing is critical to life. You can go days or weeks without food and a couple of days without water but only minutes without breathing. You need oxygen to purify the bloodstream, burn up waste products, and rejuvenate every part of the body and mind. If you're not getting enough oxygen, then your

- ✔ Thinking becomes sluggish
- ✔ Blood pressure goes up
- ✔ Heart rate increases

You'll also get dizzy, shaky, and depressed, and you'll eventually lose consciousness and die.

Many people react to stress with rapid, shallow breathing that throws off the desired ratio of oxygen to carbon dioxide in the blood. This phenomenon is called *hyperventilation,* and it causes a variety of distressing symptoms:

- ✔ Blurred vision
- ✔ Disorientation
- ✔ Jitteriness
- ✔ Loss of consciousness
- ✔ Muscle cramps
- ✔ Poor concentration
- ✔ Rapid pulse
- ✔ Tingling sensations in the extremities or face

Hyperventilation frequently accompanies panic attacks as well as chronic anxiety. Many of the symptoms of over-breathing feel like symptoms of anxiety, and many people with anxiety disorders tend to hyperventilate. Therefore, finding out how to breathe properly is considered to be an effective antidote to anxiety.

When you came into the world, unless you had a physical problem with your lungs, you probably breathed just fine. Look at most babies. Unless they're in distress from hunger or pain, they need no instruction in how to breathe or relax. Their little tummies rise and fall with each breath in a rhythmic, natural way. The stresses of everyday life, however, have since meddled with your inborn, natural breathing response.

Under stress, people usually breathe shallow and fast, or sometimes, they don't breathe at all. Some people hold their breath when they feel stressed and aren't even aware of doing it. Try noticing your breathing when you feel stressed, and see if you're a breath holder or a rapid, shallow breather.

You can also check out how you breathe when you're not stressed:

1. **Lie down on your back.**

2. **Put one hand on your stomach and the other on your chest.**

3. **Notice the movements of your hands as you breathe.**

   If you're breathing correctly, the hand on your stomach rises as you inhale and lowers as you exhale. The hand on your chest doesn't move so much, and to the extent that it does, it should do so in tandem with the other hand.

The odds are that if you have a problem with anxiety, your breathing could use a tune-up. That's especially so if you have trouble with panic attacks, which we discuss in Chapter 2. Breathing practice can start you on the way toward feeling calmer.

Anxiety and relaxation make for strange bedfellows

Have you ever known two people who couldn't be in the same room at the same time? If they show up at the same party, trouble is bound to brew. They're like oil and water — they just don't mix.

Anxiety and relaxation are a little like that. Think about it. How can you be anxious at the same time that you're relaxed? Not an easy accomplishment. Psychologists have a term for this phenomenon — *reciprocal inhibition*. Many psychologists believe that the techniques described in this chapter work because relaxation inhibits anxiety, and anxiety inhibits relaxation. Training yourself diligently in the use of relaxation skills should help you inhibit your anxiety.

The benefits of controlled breathing

Just in case you think that breathing better sounds like a rather unimaginative, inelegant way of reducing anxiety, you may want to consider its healthy effects. Studies show that training in breathing can contribute to the reduction of panic attacks within a matter of a few weeks. Other studies have indicated that controlled breathing can slightly reduce blood pressure, improve the heart's rhythm, reduce certain types of epileptic seizures, sharpen mental performance, increase blood circulation, quell worry, and possibly even improve the outcome of cardiac rehabilitation efforts following a heart attack. Not a bad list of benefits for such a simple skill.

Abdominal breathing — only five minutes a day

Figure out how to breathe with your *diaphragm* — the muscle that lies between your abdominal cavity and your lung cavity. Try this exercise to start breathing like a baby again. You might want to lie down or you can do this while sitting as long as you have a large comfortable chair that you can stretch out in.

1. **Check out your body for tension. Notice if certain muscles feel tight, if your breathing is shallow and rapid, if you're clenching your teeth, or if you have other distressing feelings.**

   You may rate your tension on a 1- to 10-point scale, with 1 representing complete relaxation and 10 meaning total tension.

2. **Place a hand on your stomach.**

3. **Breathe in slowly through your nose and fill the lower part of your lungs.**

   You'll know you're doing this correctly if your hand rises from your abdomen.

4. **Pause and hold your breath for a moment.**

5. **Exhale slowly.**

   As the air goes out, imagine your entire body is deflating like a balloon and let it go limp.

6. **Pause briefly again.**

7. **Inhale the same way slowly through your nose to a slow count of four.**

   Check to see that your hand rises from your abdomen. Your chest should move only slightly and in tandem with your stomach.

8. **Pause and hold your breath briefly.**

9. **Exhale to a slow count of six.**

   At first, if you find that hard to do, use a count of four. Later, you'll find that slowing down to a count of six is easier.

10. **Continue breathing in and out in this fashion for five minutes.**

11. **Check out your body again for tension and rate that tension on a scale of 1 to 10.**

We recommend that you do this exercise once a day for five minutes. You'll find it relaxing, and it won't add stress to your day by taking away valuable time. Five minutes for ten days in a row. After you do that, try noticing your breathing at various times during your regular routine. You'll quickly see whether you're breathing through the diaphragm or the upper chest like so many people do. Slowly but surely, abdominal breathing can become a new habit that decreases your stress.

Book breathing

Okay, just in case you're having trouble getting the hang of abdominal breathing, we have another way to help you discover the skill — *book breathing*. It sounds strange, but you'll find it easy to do.

1. Check out your body for tension and rate it on a 1- to 10-point scale, with 1 representing complete relaxation and 10 meaning total tension.

2. Find an average-size book and open it.

3. Lie down on your back on a bed, a couch, or the floor.

4. Place the open book on your stomach with the open pages on your stomach and the binding facing away from your stomach.

5. Take a moment to simply relax.

6. Inhale slowly through your nose so that the book rises.

7. Hold your breath briefly and exhale slowly.

8. Continue breathing this way. Allow your breathing to be slow, easy, and regular.

9. Inhale and allow the book to rise; then exhale and watch the book slowly drop.

10. Continue breathing this way for five minutes: Notice the feelings in your body as you do. Pay attention to how the air feels going in your nostrils, into your lungs, and out again.

11. Rate the tension in your body again on a 1- to 10-point scale.

All it takes is five minutes a day of breathing practice; everyone can find five minutes.

After you've practiced book or abdominal breathing for ten days, notice your breathing throughout the day. Allow your diaphragm to develop the habit of taking charge of your breathing. You'll feel better a little at a time.

Whenever you feel anxiety or panic coming on, try using one of these breathing exercises. You may head it off at the pass. On the other hand, anxiety and especially panic may rise to a level that makes these exercises more difficult. If that happens to you, try our panic-breathing technique.

Panic breathing

Now and then, you need a faster, more powerful technique. Perhaps you went to the mall and felt trapped, or maybe you were on your way to a job interview and felt overwhelmed. Whatever the situation, when stress hits you, like an unexpected punch in the stomach, try our panic-breathing technique.

1. **Inhale deeply and slowly through your nose.**

2. **Hold your breath for a slow count of six.**

3. **Slowly breathe out through your lips to a count of eight, making a slight hissing sound as you do.**

   That sound can be so soft that only you can hear it. You don't have to worry about anyone around you thinking that you're crazy.

4. **Repeat this type of breath five or ten times.**

You may think that panic breathing could be difficult to do when stress suddenly strikes like a lightning bolt. We won't deny it takes some practice. However, my colleagues and I (Charles Elliott, co-author) successfully taught children to use this technique when they had to face painful medical procedures. When the kids used the panic breathing technique, they felt a little calmer and reported feeling less distress and pain. The key is the slight hissing sound, which gives you a much easier way to slow down your breath.

If panic breathing doesn't help, and you feel like you might be having a full-blown panic attack that won't go away, try breathing in and out of a paper bag with the opening wrapped around your mouth. Breathing this way rebalances the ratio of oxygen to carbon dioxide and should cut the panic attack short. When you breathe too rapidly, your body accumulates an excess of oxygen, although it feels like you have too little of it. Breathing in the bag brings the level of carbon dioxide up to normal.

Mantra breathing

Mantras are often used for various types of meditation. For some people, a mantra is a word with some type of spiritual connotation. One of the off-shoots of the Hindu religion purportedly first developed the use of a mantra to be assigned by a Guru in a ceremony. This word was said to have special powers that could result in redemption.

However, mantras have also been chanted as a nonreligious technique, much as we suggest in this chapter. They've been employed to modulate breathing in addition to their use with meditation. Using a mantra to relax your breathing isn't hard to do.

1. **Choose a meaningless word or a string of letters that has a pleasing, smooth sound.** This word may have no particular meaning, but if it is suggestive of relaxation, all the better. Any word that you want to use is okay. You can also pick something neutral, such as *one,* or a word that does relate to relaxation, such as *relax, calm,* or *peace.* Some folks even use a short phrase, such as "let go . . . relax." The possibilities include:

   mmmmmm

   iiimmm

   aing

   ohhmmm

   shiam

   shaaaammm

   shalooom

2. **Find a comfortable place to sit.**

3. **Close your eyes.**

4. **Slowly begin repeating your mantra out loud.** Stretch one full pronunciation out to about ten seconds.

5. **Gradually allow your voice to get lower and lower as you say your mantra.**

6. **If thoughts come up, simply notice them and go back to your mantra.**

7. **Continue for 15 or 20 minutes.**

But wait; we said five minutes will do, and it will. At first, however, try it for a little longer time. Later, you can shorten it to five minutes anytime that you want. For that matter, you can do it for merely five minutes from the get go. Any amount is useful. Sometimes, you're likely to want to continue longer; at other times, that won't be the case, and that's okay.

The gentle inhale/exhale technique

You're likely to find that the gentle inhale/exhale breathing technique is the simplest. It just takes a few minutes and requires only a bit of your attention.

1. **Find a comfortable place to sit down.**

2. **Notice your breathing: Feel the air as it flows through your nostrils and into your lungs and feel your muscles pull the air in and out.**

3. **Let your breathing flow rhythmically, even, and smooth.**

4. **Imagine that you're holding a flower with dainty, delicate petals up to your nose.** Allow your breath to soften so that the petals remain undisturbed.

5. **Rhythmically breathe in and out in an even flow.**

6. **Continue to notice the air as it passes through your airways.**

7. **Notice how focusing on nothing but your breathing gently relaxes your mind and body.**

8. **Allow the air to refresh you.**

9. **Continue your gentle breathing and focus merely on all the sensations of smooth, even breathing.**

Work on the gentle inhale/exhale technique for five minutes a day for ten days. After that, you just may want to continue with one or more of our breathing techniques each day of your life. After all, you have to breathe anyway. You may as well do it in a relaxing, anxiety-reducing manner.

Chilling Out

Some of you may find that breathing techniques quell your anxiety quickly. Others may require a technique that directly aims at total body relaxation. Researchers have discovered a cornucopia of benefits from body relaxation training methods, which are now included in the vast majority of anxiety treatment programs. We describe three types of body relaxation: progressive muscle, autogenic, and applied.

Relaxing by tightening: Progressive muscle relaxation

Over a half century ago, Dr. Edmund Jacobsen, a Chicago physician, developed what has come to be the most widely used relaxation technique in the

United States, *progressive muscle relaxation.* You can find a wide variety of similar techniques, all described as progressive muscle relaxation, in various books and journals. Each of them may use slightly different muscle groups or go in a different order, but they all do essentially the same thing.

Progressive muscle relaxation involves going through various muscle groups in the body and tensing each one for a little while, followed by a quick letting go of the tension. You then attend to the sensation of release, noticing how the limp muscles feel in contrast to their previous tense state.

Getting ready to mellow

You'll find it useful to look for the right place to do your progressive muscle relaxation. You probably don't have a soundproof room, but find the quietest place that you can. Consider turning off the telephones.

Choose some comfortable clothing or at least loosen any clothing that you have on that's tight and constricting. You don't need shoes, belts, or anything uncomfortable.

Realize that when you begin tensing each muscle group, you shouldn't overexert; don't tighten using more than about two thirds of all your effort. You want strong, firm tension; you're not body building. When you tense, hold it for six to ten seconds and notice how the tension feels. Then let go of the tension all at the same time, as though a string holding the muscle up was cut loose.

After you release the muscle, focus on the relaxed feeling and allow it to deepen for ten or fifteen seconds. If you don't achieve a desired state of relaxation for that muscle group, you can do the procedure one or two more times if you want.

You should know that you can't *make* relaxation happen. You *allow* it to happen. Perfectionists struggle with this idea. Don't force it and rid your mind of the idea that you *must* do this exercise *perfectly.* This is a skill that you acquire slowly over time.

When you tighten one muscle group, try to keep all the other muscles in your body relaxed. Doing this takes a little practice, but you can figure out how to tense one body area at a time. Keep your face especially relaxed when you're tensing any area other than your face. Yoga instructors often say, "Soften your eyes." We're not exactly sure what that means, but it seems to help us relax when we try to soften our eyes — whatever it is that we're doing.

Occasionally, relaxation training makes people feel surprisingly uncomfortable. If this happens to you, simply stop. If it continues to occur with repeated practice, you may want to seek professional help. Also, don't tighten any body part that makes you feel uncomfortable. Avoid tightening any area that's suffered injury or has given you frequent trouble, such as a lower back.

Discovering the progressive muscle technique

Now, you're ready to start. Sit down in your chosen place and get comfortable.

1. **Take a deep breath, hold, imagine, and let the tension go.**

   Pulling the air in from your abdomen, breathe deeply. (See "Abdominal breathing — only five minutes a day" section, earlier in this chapter, if you're unclear about this.) Hold your breath for three or four seconds and slowly let the air out. Imagine your whole body is a balloon losing air as you exhale and let tension go out with the air. Take three more such breaths and feel your entire body getting more limp with each one.

2. **Squeeze your hands tight and then relax.**

   Squeeze your fingers into a fist. Feel the tension and hold it for six to ten seconds. Then, all at once, release your hands and let them go limp. Allow the tension in your hands to flow out. Let the relaxation deepen for 10 to 15 seconds.

3. **Tighten your arms and relax.**

   Bring your lower arms up almost to your shoulders and tighten the muscles. Make sure you tense the muscles on the inside and outside of both the upper and lower arms. If you're not sure you're doing that, use one hand to do a tension check on the other arm. Hold the tension a little while and then drop your arms as though you cut a string holding them up. Let the tension flow out and the relaxation flow in.

4. **Raise up your shoulders, tighten, and then relax.**

   Raise your shoulders up as though you were a turtle trying to get into its shell. Hold the tension and then let your shoulders drop. Feel the relaxation deepen for 10 to 15 seconds.

5. **Tighten and relax the muscles in your upper back.**

   Pull your shoulders back and bring your shoulder blades closer together. Hold that tension a little while . . . and let it go.

6. **Scrunch up your entire face and then relax.**

   Squeeze your forehead down, bring your jaws together, tighten your eyes and eyebrows, and contract your tongue and lips. Let the tension grow and hold it . . . then relax and let go.

7. **Tighten and relax your neck in the back of your head.**

   Avoid hurting anything and gently pull your head back toward your back and feel the muscles tighten in the back of your neck. Notice that tension and hold it, let go, and relax. Feel relaxation deepening and repeat it if you want.

8. **Contract the front neck muscles and then loosen.**

   Gently move your chin toward your chest. Tighten your neck muscles and let the tension increase and maintain it; then relax. Feel the tension melting away like candle wax.

9. **Tighten the muscles in your stomach and chest and maintain the tension. Then let it go.**

10. **Arch your back, hang on to the contraction, and then relax.**

    Be gentle with your lower back and skip it entirely if you've ever had trouble with this part of your body. Tighten these muscles by arching your lower back, pressing it back against the chair, or tensing the muscles any way you want. Gently increase and maintain the tension, but not too much. Now, relax and allow the waves to roll in.

11. **Contract and relax your buttocks muscles.**

    Tighten your buttocks so as to gently lift yourself up in your chair. Hold the tension. Then let tension melt and relaxation grow.

12. **Squeeze and relax your thigh muscles.**

    Tighten and hold these muscles. Then relax and feel the tension draining out; let the calm deepen and spread.

13. **Contract and relax your calves.**

    Tighten the muscles in your calves by pulling your toes toward your face. Take care; if you ever get muscle cramps, don't overdo. Hold the tension . . . let go. Let tension drain into the floor.

14. **Gently curl your toes, maintain the tension and then relax.**

15. **Take a little time to tour your entire body.**

    Notice if you feel different than when you began. If you find any areas of tension, allow the relaxed areas around it to come in and replace them. If that doesn't work, repeat the tense-and-relax procedure for the tense area.

16. **Spend a few minutes enjoying the relaxed feelings.**

    Let relaxation spread and penetrate every muscle fiber in your body. Notice any feelings you have. You may feel warmth, or you may feel a floating sensation. Perhaps you'll feel a sense of sinking down. Whatever it is, allow it to happen. When you wish, you can open your eyes and go on with your day, perhaps feeling like you just returned from a brief vacation.

Some people like to make a tape of the progressive muscle relaxation instructions to facilitate their efforts. If you do, be sure to make your tape in a slow, calming voice.

Extolling the virtues of progressive muscle relaxation

Many people believe that for a remedy to be truly effective, it must take plenty of work and possibly feel a little painful — the no pain, no gain philosophy. As you can see, progressive muscle relaxation isn't especially arduous, and it actually feels good, so can it really do anything for you? Well, for starters, progressive relaxation training is usually a component of most successful treatment programs for anxiety.

However, studies also show that progressive muscle relaxation can effectively reduce various types of chronic pain, such as the pain associated with ulcerative colitis, cancer, and headaches. It also works to reduce insomnia. A study published in the December 2001 issue of the *Journal of Clinical Psychology* found that in addition to inducing greater relaxation, progressive muscle relaxation also led to increased mental quiet and joy. Other studies have suggested that it may improve the functioning of your immune system. And *Neuropsychological Rehabilitation* (1999, Volume 9) reported that for patients with Alzheimer's disease, progressive muscle relaxation actually improved both their behavioral problems as well as their performance on verbal fluency and memory tasks.

We aren't suggesting that progressive muscle relaxation cures Alzheimer's; it won't cure cancer, and it won't whisk away all your pain or eradicate all your anxiety. However, many studies clearly show that it exerts benefits across a surprisingly wide range of problems. We recommend that you give it a try.

In the beginning, take a little longer than five minutes to go through the steps of progressive muscle relaxation. Usually, if you take 20 or 30 minutes several times at first, it works better. However, the more you practice, the more quickly you'll find that you can slide into serenity. So even if you listen to tapes, consider shortening the procedure on your own after a while. For example, you can tense all the muscles in your lower body at once, followed by all your upper body muscles. At other times, you may want to simply tense and relax a few body areas that carry most of your tension. Most often, that involves the neck, shoulder, and back muscles. Some folks tell us that they eventually discover how to relax in a single minute after they become proficient.

Hypnotizing yourself: Autogenic training

Autogenic (meaning "produced from within") training was also introduced well over a half-century ago, just a few years after Jacobson developed progressive muscle relaxation. Shulz, the German neuropsychiatrist who developed this strategy for reducing stress, based his technique on self-hypnosis and the power of suggestion.

Autogenic training is the most passive way of relaxing. All relaxation techniques work better if you approach them by allowing them to happen rather than forcing anything. However, autogenic training is based on not *doing* anything; it simply involves passive responses to suggestions. Other chapters discuss how thoughts can drive your anxiety up a wall. Fortunately, the opposite is true as well. Calm ideas elicit a sense of relaxation almost reflexively, if you let them.

That's because your mind automatically associates certain responses with different words and images. For example, imagine cutting a lemon with a sharp knife and seeing the juice squirting out as you slice. Imagine picking up half the lemon, smelling it, opening your mouth, and taking a large bite into the sour, juicy, pulpy flesh of the lemon. Now, back to reality. Are you salivating? If so, words alone created this response.

In fact, if you tried to salivate without any words or images, you're likely to fail. You just can't make some responses happen. The same goes for relaxation. Try it and see. Psychologist Steven Hayes, our colleague, explained how impossible it is to force relaxation: Imagine that you're hooked up to a machine that measures your tension levels by analyzing your muscle tension, heart rate, and other physical responses to stress. Then we offer you one million dollars if you do nothing but relax. That's right; one million dollars. Oh, and by the way, to give you even more motivation, we hold a gun to your head and tell you that if you fail to relax, we'll fire the gun. Now, RELAX! Do you suspect that you might have trouble?

Instead, realize that relaxation is accomplished by letting go. You allow it to happen as a natural response to calming suggestions. You can't force relaxation.

Autogenic relaxation involves thinking about your body in a state of cozy calm. Lie down, loosen your clothing or put on some more comfortable clothing, close your eyes, and spend time focusing on each of the autogenic concepts that follow and imagine that you feel heavy and warm, that your heart is quiet, and that your breathing is ever soooooo eeeeeeasy. Try focusing on each concept separately until you've seen what it can do for you. Then you can see what it feels like to combine them.

Just think about the words and images that autogenic training presents to you; do not try to make anything happen because, if you do, you'll ruin the effect.

> ✔ **Heavy:** My hands, arms, and legs feel heavy. . . . They are soooo heavy. I don't have to do anything at all because they're so heavy that I can't lift them if I wanted to. My hands and arms are heavy . . . very, very heavy. Gravity weighs down my arms and draws tension away. Tension is draining. . . . Hear these words over and over: Heavy like weights strapped around my arms . . . very heavy. My legs are heavy . . . very,

very heavy. Weights strapped around my legs . . . sinking . . . relaxed and calm . . . sinking into a state of calm and serenity . . . do nothing and no need to make anything happen. Worries and concerns are melting away, sinking out of sight quietly and peacefully.

✔ **Warm:** My arms and legs are warm and heavy. A desert sun shines its rays on my arms and legs. It penetrates the skin and muscles . . . tension melting . . . warm and serene . . . warm blankets wrapped around me . . . I'm submersed in a warm whirlpool of circulating water, sinking into calm and relaxation . . . feeling tension float away . . . dissolving . . . Hear these words over and over: warm, melting . . . no need to make anything happen. The sun warms my body, serene and placid . . . sinking . . . so warm and calm . . . peaceful and relaxed.

✔ **Quiet heart:** Place one hand over your heart. Remind yourself that your heart is beating strong and steady, evenly and calm . . . nothing to do . . . so steady and strong . . . heart rhythmically thumping . . . like a steady, slow drum beat . . . sinking into a river of relaxation . . . tension fading . . . Hearing these words echo in your head over and over: Heart regular, strong, steady . . . steady, drumming, beating, relaxation deepening, soothing and quiet . . . a time to let worries go . . . warm, calm, steady . . . peaceful and relaxed.

✔ **Easy breathing:** Sit in a comfortable position and remind yourself that your breathing is soooo rhythmic and eeeeasy . . . no need to breathe a certain way. Just let it happen. Allow your body to find its own rhythm and pace. Think about these words and phrases over and over again: no worries, tension easing away, relaxed, even, calm, serene, easy, flowing breath. My body just takes over and breathes how it wants . . . peaceful . . . air flowing easily in and out . . . in and out . . . so calm and relaxed . . . smooth and effortless . . . steady and rhythmic.

Is autogenic training worth its salt?

Can something as passive and effortless as autogenic training really do anything for you? Actually, the studies on its effectiveness haven't all been as sound from a scientific standpoint as the studies on progressive muscle relaxation. Nevertheless, autogenic training is the most popular relaxation training among European professionals. A number of reasonably sound studies suggest that it has stress-reducing value in addition to controlling various anxiety disorders, quelling motion sickness, and easing certain types of chronic muscle pain and the pain and distress that follows coronary bypass surgery. A study published in the journal *Complementary Therapies in Medicine* (2000, Volume 8) found that it's at least as effective as standard anti-anxiety medication for treating Generalized Anxiety Disorder. (See Chapter 2 for a description of Generalized Anxiety Disorder.)

The applied advantage

Afraid of the dentist? *Applied relaxation* (applying a relaxation technique to a stressful situation) can help you deal with your fears. A Scandinavian study found that applied relaxation decreased the fear of a trip to the dentist and helped people to get the needed treatment that they had been avoiding. Applied relaxation has also been used successfully to treat Generalized Anxiety Disorder. Furthermore, this approach appears to help people with Panic Disorder. (See Chapter 2 for a description of Generalized Anxiety Disorder and Panic Disorder.) One of the most common uses of applied relaxation is for relief from chronic pain.

Relaxing when it counts: Applied relaxation

Discovering how to relax using breathing techniques, progressive muscle relaxation, or autogenic training may help you reduce your anxiety. But if you just do these activities when you're lying around in your bed or spending a quiet day at home, you miss the opportunity to challenge your fears with a powerful tool. *Applied relaxation* means taking the techniques that you practiced and putting them to work when you're under the most stress.

The key to success lies in the mastery of the technique in nonstressful settings before taking the next step. For example, maybe you practiced the progressive relaxation technique many times, and you can tighten and loosen your muscles, achieving a state of relaxation in just a few minutes.

Now that you've mastered the technique in a nonstressful setting, think of a particular situation that frightens you, such as public speaking. For example, you've scheduled a speaking engagement for a large event with an audience of several hundred. Prior to your speech, you practice your favorite relaxation technique. You try to maintain that state as you walk up to give your speech, but you panic anyway. What happened?

That's pretty much what we would have expected because applied relaxation works best if you break the tasks into more manageable steps. For example, you could practice relaxation while preparing a talk for a small audience. Then you could practice relaxation while thinking about giving your talk. You continue your practice in graduated, small steps. (Discover more about how to take small, graduated steps in Chapter 8.)

Relaxing Via Your Senses

Your path to finding relaxation may lead you through a variety of experiences. We can't possibly know which direction will work best for you. You have to experiment with various approaches to discover your own relaxation remedy. In this section, we ask that you allow your senses to soothe you.

Sounds to soothe the savage beast

Ever since people populated the planet, they have turned to music for solace. From primitive drums to symphony orchestras, sound elicits emotion — patriotic fervor, love, excitement, and fear — and even relaxation. An entire profession of music therapists has capitalized on the power of music. Music therapists work in hospitals, schools, and nursing homes using sounds to soothe distress.

But you don't need to be a music therapist to make use of music's power. You probably already know what type of music calms you. Perhaps you love classical music or jazz. You may not have thought of trying out a tape or CD of ocean waves, babbling brooks, whispering wind, or other sounds of nature. Many find those sounds quite relaxing, and although it makes no sense to us, some teenagers tell us that they feel relaxed listening to heavy metal music. Go figure.

Visit any well-supplied music store or Web site and find an extensive array of possibilities. Experiment and try new sounds. Many of these recordings boast of containing specially mixed music for optimal relaxation.

Buyer beware! Don't buy just any tape that you see with the word *relaxation* on the label. Unfortunately, some of these products are rather inferior. Either get recommendations or listen to a sample — some Web sites have the capacity to let you listen.

Only the nose knows for sure

Ever walk through a mall and smell freshly baked cinnamon rolls? Perhaps you were tempted to buy one just because of the aroma. We suspect that the smell of the delicacies is no accident — we sometimes think that the bakers must pump the air up and out from around their ovens into the entire mall ventilation system, knowing the powerful effects of aroma.

In addition to making you hungry, the cinnamon roll scent may have also elicited pleasant emotions and memories. Perhaps it took you back to Sunday mornings when your mother baked fresh rolls or to a pleasant café. If so, the aroma automatically brought on your memories — no effort was required.

A huge perfume industry exploits the power of aromas to attract and seduce. Manufacturers of deodorants, lotions, powders, hair sprays, and air fresheners do the same, and you can explore the ability of aroma for calming your jangled nerves.

Aromatherapy makes use of various essential oils — natural substances extracted from plants. These substances ostensibly affect both physical and emotional health. We can't vouch for these claims because good studies on their effects are lacking. However, the theory behind aromatherapy isn't entirely wacky because the cranial nerve transmits messages from the nose into the parts of the brain that control mood, memories, and appetite.

If you're really physically sick, please consult a qualified doctor — aromatherapy isn't likely to cure you. No one knows if aromatherapy truly promotes good health. Also, do not use these substances when pregnant.

However, if you want to experiment with various aromas to see if any of them help you relax, go for it. Preliminary studies have suggested that certain aromas may alleviate anxiety, and decrease nicotine withdrawal symptoms and headaches. So giving aromatherapy a try probably wouldn't hurt.

Consider the following aromatherapy scent suggestions, but be sure to shop around because prices can vary substantially. A trusted local health food store may make a good place to start.

- Chamomile
- Eucalyptus
- Lavender
- Neroli (citrus aurantium)

These essential oils may help relieve anxiety and combat sleeplessness. Besides, they smell pretty good, so put a few drops in your warm bath or on your pillow. Have a good sleep.

Massaging away stress

About 15 times a day, one of our dogs sticks his nose under one of our arms to indicate that he's overdue for a rubdown. Dogs unabashedly beg for touching, petting, and rubbing. We found that they're pretty good at getting it, too.

People need to be touched, too. It's great to be hugged and stroked by the people we care about. However, one wonderful way to satisfy the need to be touched and relax at the same time is through a professional massage. If you've never indulged, consider treating yourself to a massage. In years past, only the elite sought massage therapy. Today, people flock to massage therapists to reduce stress, manage pain, and to just plain feel good.

Other than your lover, you should only go to a trained and licensed masseur or masseuse. Massage therapy is *not* a sexual encounter, although some in the sex trade masquerade as massage therapists in so-called lotion parlors.

Although long considered an alternative medical intervention with dubious value, new research has fueled interest in the benefits of massage. A study published in 2001 in the *International Journal of Neuroscience* found that massage increased work productivity and reduced work related injuries.

Another way of getting a massage is to sit in a whirlpool for five minutes. This can be really relaxing because, in addition to the massage that you get from the force of the water jets, the feel of the warm water that's forced into the whirlpool and the sound of the water rushing around, like ocean waves rolling onto the beach, also have a calming effect. Although some homes have whirlpools built into their bathtubs, most health spas and YM-YWCAs also have whirlpools that patrons can enjoy for a small fee in excess of the basic membership.

Everybody needs touching

In the 1940s, many European babies ended up in orphanages. A shocking number of these orphans failed to grow or interact with others, and some appeared to wilt away and die for no discernable reason. They had sufficient food, clothing, and shelter. A physician named Dr. Spitz investigated and found that their failure to thrive appeared to be due to a lack of human touch. In other words, the caregivers provided nutrients but not contact.

This early finding has been supported by numerous studies conducted by psychologist Tiffany Field and her colleagues. One of these studies found that premature infants who were given regular massages gained more weight than those who merely received standard medical care. Other studies by this research group have included normal babies, as well as infants born with HIV or cocaine addiction, and young children with diabetes, eating disorders, and asthma. Babies and children who receive a massage regularly have lower amounts of stress hormones and lower levels of anxiety than those who don't. Other benefits that were identified include pain reduction, increased attentiveness, and enhanced immune function. If it's this good for babies, we figure that it's pretty good for you. Indulge!

Chapter 13

Creating Calm in Your Imagination

*P*eople who have a vivid imagination (perhaps someone like you) can think themselves into all kinds of anxious situations. Just give them a moment to play with an idea, and they're off on another anxiety trip.

But the good news is that you can backtrack — rewind to a calmer place — if you know how to apply *guided imagery*.

That technique worked for **Shauna.** Tense thoughts fill Shauna's every waking moment. From the time that she springs out of bed in the morning to the last gripping thought before restless sleep mercifully overtakes her, Shauna thinks. She replays every anxious moment at her job and dwells on each imagined error that she's made during the day, turning it over and over in her mind. She visualizes every flaw in her makeup, dress, and complexion. Images of incompetence, inadequacy, and unattractiveness flood her mind's eye.

To reduce the stress and anxiety that saturate the scenes in her mind, she decides to seek the services of Cynthia Rose, a highly regarded counselor. The counselor teaches her several breathing techniques, but Shauna can't hold back the avalanche of anxious images. She then tries progressive muscle relaxation, later massage, and then music and aromatherapy to no avail. Finally, Cynthia has an insight. "Shauna thinks in pictures," Cynthia says to herself. "She needs guided imagery!"

Guided imagery uses your imagination to envision a pleasant, relaxing time, or space. The best images incorporate all your senses. When visualizing them, you see, hear, smell, feel, and possibly taste. In Shauna's case, her images were full of anxiety-arousing situations. When she tried other relaxation techniques, they failed because anxious images still filled her mind. With guided imagery, however, the richness of the peaceful experience pushes aside all other concerns.

In this chapter, we show you how to improve your imagination. Then we give you several scripts to play with in your mind. Feel free to revise them in any way you want. Finally, you can customize your own special mental images.

Letting Your Imagination Roam

Some people, thinking of themselves as rather unimaginative, struggle to create pictures in their minds. These people generally feel uncomfortable with their drawing skills and have a hard time recalling the details of events that they've witnessed. Perhaps you're one of them. If so, using your imagination to relax and reduce your anxiety may not be the approach for you.

On the other hand, it just might. Guided imagery encompasses more than the visual sense; it includes smell, taste, touch, and sound. We can help you sharpen your ability to use all these senses.

We encourage you to give these exercises a shot, but people all have different strengths and weaknesses, and you may find that one or more of these exercises just don't work for you. If you discover that guided imagery isn't for you, that's okay. This book discusses many other ways to relax.

Just before doing each series of numbered steps for the guided imagery exercises in this chapter:

1. Find a comfortable place to sit or lie down.

2. Make sure that you loosen any tight garments and shoes.

3. Close your eyes and take a few slow deep breaths.

Imagining touch

Imagery exercises work best if they incorporate more than one sense. Imagining bodily sensations enhances the overall experience of relaxing, guided imagery. Take the following steps to see how this works:

1. **Imagine an oversized, sunken bathtub.**

2. **Picture yourself turning the faucet on and feeling the water coming out.**

   You can feel that the water is cold and wet as it pours over your hand. Gradually, the temperature increases until it reaches your perfect range.

3. **The tub fills, and you can mentally see yourself pouring bath oil in and mixing it around.**

   You can feel how silky the water becomes.

4. **You imagine putting your foot in the water.**

   The water feels just a bit too hot at first, but you find that the warm temperature soothes you after lowering your body into the bathtub.

5. **You lie back and luxuriate in the slick, smooth, warm water.**

   You can feel it envelop you as the warmth loosens your muscles.

Were you able to feel the sensations: the wetness and the silky warmth? If not, don't despair. You can improve your awareness by spending just five minutes a day actively participating in a real experience and then committing that experience to your memory. Try one or more of the following exercises each day for five days straight, and you can experiment with other exercises, too. Just be sure to focus on touch.

- ✔ **Hold your hands under different temperatures of water.** Notice how they feel. Better yet, fill the basin and submerge your hands to conserve water.

- ✔ **Rub oil on the back of your hand and wrist.** Notice how the oil feels.

- ✔ **Take a warm bath and notice the sensations of wetness, warmth, and silkiness.** Focus on all your bodily sensations.

- ✔ **Put a washcloth in hot water, squeeze it out, and press it to your forehead.** Notice the warmth and the texture of the cloth.

- ✔ **Sit in front of the fireplace and notice where the heat hits your body.** Experience the warmth.

After participating in one of the preceding exercises, wait one minute. Then try to conjure up what the sensations felt like in your mind. The following day, do the exercise, wait five minutes, and then recall the sensations. Each day, make the length of time between the actual experience and your recollection of the experience a little longer.

Recalling sounds

You don't have to be a musician to appreciate music or to re-create it in your mind. Guided imagery often asks you to create the sounds of nature in your mind to enhance relaxation. Taking the following steps, try imagining what an ocean beach sounds like:

1. **Imagine that you're lying on a beach.**

   You can hear the ocean waves rolling in one after the other. In and out. The soft roar soothes and relaxes. In and out.

2. **In your mind, you hear each wave rolling in and coming to a crescendo as it breaks gently onto the beach.**

   A brief moment of quiet follows as the next wave prepares to roll in. A few seagulls cry out as they fly overhead.

Were you able to hear the ocean and the gulls? You can improve your ability to re-create sounds in your mind by actively experiencing the real McCoy beforehand. Try some of the following exercises for just five minutes a day for five days. You may think of some other ways to practice listening to sounds with your mind's eye, too.

✔ **Listen to a short passage from a favorite song.** Play it several times and listen to each note. Tune in and concentrate.

✔ **Sit in a chair in your living room and listen.** Turn off the phones, stereos, and anything else cranking out noise. Closing your eyes and listening carefully, notice every sound that you hear — perhaps the traffic outside, a dog barking, a little wind, or the house creaking.

✔ **Listen to the sound of yourself eating an apple, a celery stick, or a carrot.** Not only is it good for you, but you'll also hear interesting sounds. Eat slowly and hear each crunch. Notice the initial sharp sound of biting and the more muted chewing.

Following your experience, wait one minute. Then reproduce the sounds in your mind. Hear them again. Don't worry if you can't do it. With practice, you're likely to get better. Increase the wait a little each day between the actual experience and your recollection.

Conjuring up smells

Our dogs have a far better sense of smell than we do. They seem to know exactly which bush on their walking route needs re-marking. We're pretty sure that they know exactly which rival dog did what to which bush. Perhaps that we can't smell as well as they can is a good thing.

But smell has a powerful influence on people as well. Certain smells alert us to danger — such as the smell of smoke or spoiling food — while others inevitably conjure up pleasant memories and feelings — such as the aroma of your favorite baked delight or the perfumed scent of a loved one. See if this description brings a smell wafting into your mind:

1. **Imagine that you're sleeping on a screened porch in a country cottage nestled in the forest.**

   You've been aware of a slow, steady rainfall through the night. When you awaken, the sun is shining.

2. **In your mind, you can smell the sweet smell of freshly cleaned air, crisp and cool.**

   The earthy smell of the forest floor washed by nature reaches your awareness.

3. **You stretch and breathe deeply.**

   You detect the musty odor of fallen leaves. A pleasant, refreshing feeling engulfs you.

How did this scene smell in your mind? Smell is a primitive sense and may not be as easy to consciously produce with your imagination. That may be because a description of smell is more difficult to put into words. However, with practice, you're likely to improve. Try a few of these activities to help you develop your imagination's sense of smell:

- ✔ **Make a cup of hot chocolate.** Before drinking it, spend a minute taking in the aroma. Focus on the smell as you take each sip.

- ✔ **Bake dinner rolls.** Don't worry; you can buy the ready-made kind that you pop out onto a cookie sheet. Sit in the kitchen while they bake. Open the oven door a couple of times to intensify the experience.

- ✔ **Visit a department store, go to the perfume counter, and test several different scents.** Try to describe the differences.

Now try to remember what smell you experienced a minute later. Take a little longer each day before trying to recall the odors. Don't be concerned if you find this difficult; many people do.

Remembering tastes

Which foods do you associate with comfort and relaxation? Many people think of chicken soup or herbal tea. One of us spreads peanut butter on toast when really stressed, and the other occasionally indulges in ice cream — especially chocolate and caramel swirls threaded through rich vanilla. Are you salivating yet? If not, try playing out this imaginary scene:

1. **Imagine an exquisite chocolate truffle.**

   You're not sure what's inside, but you look forward to finding out.

2. **In your mind, you take the truffle to your lips and slowly bite off a corner of the truffle.**

   The rich, sweet chocolate coats your tongue.

3. **You can imagine taking another bite and detect a creamy, fruity center.**

   You never tasted anything so rich and delectable yet not overpowering. The sweet but slightly tangy cherry flavor fills your body with satisfaction.

Could you taste the truffle with your imagination? Perhaps you found it easier than the smell. Either way, you can improve your ability to recall tastes with practice. Try one or more of these exercises:

✔ **Bake some fresh iced brownies.** Okay, you can pick some up from a bakery if you must. First, taste the brownie with the tip of your tongue. Hold it in your mouth and move it to different spots on your tongue. Then chew it and notice the icing and the cake flavors mixing together.

✔ **Open and heat up a can of your favorite soup to eat.** Pour a little into a cup or bowl. Put a small spoonful into your mouth. Be sure it's not too hot. Notice how the soup tastes on every part of your tongue.

You can do this taste-focusing activity with any food that you want. The key is to take some time and focus. Savor the flavors and pay attention to the nuances — sweet, sour, bitter, or salty. Again, try to call the tastes to mind after about a minute. Then stretch the period between the actual experience and the recall out a little longer each time that you practice.

Painting pictures in your mind

Many of our clients report that scenes of anticipated disasters and doom invade their imagination. These scenes cause them more anxiety than actual disastrous events usually do. Visual imagery can fuel your anxiety, or you can enlist your visual imagination to help you drown the fires of anxiety. Try painting this picture in your mind:

1. **Imagine that you're at a mountain resort in late spring.**

2. **In your mind, you spent the day trekking through a forest. Now, you're relaxing on the deck of your cabin overlooking a valley lake ringed by mountain peaks.**

   The water on the lake is still; the dark blue surface reflects surprisingly clear images of the trees and mountains. The sun sinks behind a mountain peak, painting the clouds above in brilliant hues of red, orange, and pink. The mountains remain capped with snow from the winter. Dark green fir trees stand proudly above a carpet of pine cones and needles.

Mindfulness: Finding peace in the present

Our sense-sharpening exercises actually form part of a more powerful approach to overcoming anxiety — *mindfulness,* discussed in greater depth in Chapter 16. A technique that has been used for several thousands of years in both the secular and religious settings of the East, mindfulness involves immersing yourself in the present with full awareness. When you fully attend to your immediate surroundings, catastrophic predictions about the future fade and anxiety drops. Mindfulness has only recently found its way into Western psychology. However, in the past few years, researchers have discovered that training in mindfulness can substantially supplement other approaches to anxiety reduction. We recommend that you work on sharpening your awareness of your experiences and then read Chapter 16 to discover more.

How did this scene look in your mind? If you practice sharpening your visual imagery, you'll become an expert eyewitness. Wherever you are, take one minute to inspect the view in front of you. It doesn't matter what that is. Scrutinize the image from every angle. Notice colors, textures, shapes, proportions, and positions. Then close your eyes. Try to recollect the images in your mind. Focus on every detail. You can practice this anywhere and at any time. It just takes a few minutes. Each day, delay your imagery retrieval a little longer after turning away from the scene that you just studied.

Full Sensory Imaging

The best and most effective guided imagery incorporates multiple senses — not necessarily every one, every time, but for the most part, the more the better. If you aren't as adept at using one or two senses, try to focus on using your more-developed senses. We have a couple of imaginary scenes in the upcoming sections for you to try that use most of your senses to recall an experience.

If you like our scenes, use them. Perhaps you'll want to make a tape recording of one or both of them. If you do, feel free to modify the scene in any way that helps you to imagine it more vividly or feel more at peace. Make an audiotape recording of yourself reading the following sections and then listen to the tapes to help you relax. Perhaps you can play a recording of ocean sounds in the background as you read and record the "Relaxing at the beach" exercise. Similarly, you may play a recording of forest sounds as you tape yourself reading "A forest fantasy." Commercial tapes are also available (see the Appendix).

Relaxing at the beach

1. **Imagine that you're walking barefoot through a sandy beach on a warm, sunny day.**

   The sand feels warm between your toes. Reaching the ocean shore and feeling the cool, refreshing water lap over your feet, you smell the crisp, salty air and take a deep breath; calmness comes over you.

2. **You walk further and reach an area where rocks jut out into the surf.**

   A wave crashes onto the rocks and sends a fine mist high into the air; small droplets spray on your face and feel delightfully refreshing.

3. **Seagulls glide effortlessly high above and then dive, skimming the surface of the water.**

   They look like acrobats of the sky, gracefully soaring in and out of sight. The surf and the seagulls orchestrate a soothing sound track. A wooden Adirondack chair beckons you farther down the beach.

4. **You stroll over to the chair and stretch out on it when you get there.**

   The wood warmed by the sun is smooth against your skin.

5. **Magically, a frosted glass of your favorite beverage is placed on a small side table.**

6. **Sipping and feeling the cold liquid fill your mouth and slide down your throat, you feel refreshed and satisfied, serene and content.**

7. **You take a look out at the horizon, and a couple of sailboats float lazily in the distance.**

   You feel the warm sun bathe your skin; at the same time, a gentle breeze cools your skin to a perfect balance. You've never felt so relaxed in your life.

8. **You lie back and close your eyes.**

   You can feel all the muscles in your body let go. You feel sleepy, but alert at the same time. Nature's beauty fills you with awe, melting your worries away.

A forest fantasy

1. **Imagine that you're walking through pine trees and brush.**

   The sap of the trees gives off a sweet, pungent aroma. You hear the branches rustle in the breeze. Sunlight filters through the branches of the trees, making shadows dance across the ground.

2. **Your feet can feel the spring in the path covered with years of fallen leaves.**

   You hear a brook babbling in the distance.

3. **You reach into your backpack, take out a container of cold water, and sip.**

   As you sip, you feel at peace and start to relax. You hear birds overhead.

4. **As you climb, the trees begin to thin.**

   You reach the stream, clear with water flowing swiftly over and around the small rocks in its bed.

5. **You bend down to touch the water; it's cold, clean, and pure.**

6. **You splash a bit of the brisk water over your face and feel cleansed.**

   Just ahead, you notice a grassy meadow, filled with wild flowers. The flowers' fragrance gently fills the air with sweetness.

7. **You reach a grassy, soft spot and sit down.**

   From here, you can see for many miles in the distance. The air is pure and clean. The sun feels warm on your skin. The sky is a brilliant blue backdrop to a few white, billowy clouds.

8. **Sleepiness overtakes you and you lie down.**

   You can feel your entire body relaxing. Your everyday concerns seem trivial. All that matters is the moment. You cherish the experience of connection to the earth.

Customizing Your Own Images

You may want to create your own imaginary journey. It can be somewhere that you've been before or somewhere you've never seen. Try a few out to see how they work for you. Many people use guided imagery to help them go to sleep. Others use these images to help them relax before a stressful event, such as taking a test. We have a few helpful hints for designing your own guided imagery for relaxation:

- ✔ The most important hint is to enjoy yourself.
- ✔ Be creative; let your mind go wild, coming up with any scene that might feel good to you.
- ✔ Use multiple senses — the more the better.
- ✔ Add descriptive details. Consider using a thesaurus for rich adjectives.

✔ Make your scene long enough that it lasts a little while. It takes some time to let your body relax.

✔ Perhaps you could play soothing music or sounds in the background as you make the tape.

✔ Be sure to include relaxing suggestions such as "I'm feeling calmer," "My worries are melting away," or "My body feels loose and relaxed."

✔ Realize that designing an image has no right or wrong way. Don't judge your scene.

✔ If it doesn't work for you, don't sweat it. You can find many other ways to relax.

Imagining a positive outcome

Athletes commonly use images to reduce their performance anxiety. In addition, many of them create images of success. For example, a gymnast might envision himself making a perfect dismount off the balance beam over and over. Or a runner might see herself pushing through pain, stretching her legs out for a first-place finish again and again. Various studies indicate that imagery can give an athlete an extra boost.

Another way to use imagery is to face your fears in a less stressful way than meeting them head on in real life. You do this by repeatedly imagining yourself conquering your fears. We tell you more about exactly how to imagine yourself conquering your fears in Chapter 8.

Chapter 14

Relieving Anxiety with Herbs and Dietary Supplements

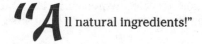

"*A*ll natural ingredients!"

"Nature's way!"

Advertising slogans like those sound healthy and appealing — especially appealing to people who think that ingesting synthetic chemicals to alleviate anxiety is a little creepy, and that supplements and herbs grown naturally in the wild can safely decrease anxiety without distressing side effects. No wonder vitamin, herb, and supplement sales have soared in recent years.

In this chapter, we tell you about herbs and supplements for anxiety. But more importantly, we share the latest information about the effectiveness of these strategies including warnings about their possible dangers and downsides.

Tell your doctor about any so-called natural products that you consume for any purpose whatsoever. Your physician needs to know this information in order to help you avoid unintentionally mixing up a dangerous concoction.

Searching for Supplements

Dietary supplements include vitamins, amino acids, minerals, enzymes, metabolites, or botanicals that reputedly enhance your health and/or your body's functions. Such supplements appear in many different forms — capsules, powders, tablets, teas, liquids, and granules. You can buy supplements from the Internet, your local drugstore, grocery store, or health food store. Claimed benefits of supplements include improved immune systems, enhanced sleep, stronger bones, revved-up sexual response, cancer cures, and overcoming anxiety.

People seek supplements often because they assume that they're safer than prescription drugs. That's not necessarily true. Supplements are not considered drugs in the United States and therefore are not subjected to the same level of scrutiny as most medications. Before a prescription drug can come to market, the manufacturer must conduct clinical studies to establish the safety, effectiveness, dosage, and possible deleterious interactions with other medications. The U.S. Food and Drug Administration doesn't require clinical trials to establish the safety of herbs. Instead, after a supplement makes it to market, the only way it will be removed is if enough consumers suffer serious side effects and complain to the right agencies, which can trigger an FDA investigation and possible decision to withdraw the herb from store shelves.

Another serious problem with supplements is that untrained sales people often make recommendations for their use. Fortunately, healthcare professionals who are also interested and trained in the safe and effective use of supplements can help. By contrast, sales clerks vary widely in the usefulness of their advice. Dolores' story isn't all that unusual.

A young, fit salesperson smiles at **Dolores** as she enters the health food store. Dolores tells him that she would like to find a natural remedy to help her calm down. She reports difficulty concentrating, poor sleep, and always feeling on edge. The young man nods and suggests a regimen of vitamins and supplements to build up her resistance to stress, improve her concentration, and ease her symptoms of anxiety.

Pulling bottles off the shelves, he tells her, "Some B vitamins to build you up, C to fight infections. Here's some amino acids, L-lysine and tyrosine, and a compound, 5-HTP. Minerals: calcium, zinc, potassium, and magnesium. Kelp nourishes. Melatonin for sleep. Oh yes, maybe some SAM-e to improve your mood. Then the herbs: hops, passion flower, valerian, lemon balm, chamomile, and kava kava. Now, take these at least an hour before you eat. Eat carbohydrates with these, not protein. And this one needs to be taken just before bed."

Hector mixes a potent brew

It's payday, and **Hector's** buddies invite him to hoist a few beers. "Sure," he says. "I can't stay too long, but I could use a couple of beers; it's been a tough week." Munching on spicy bar mix, Hector finishes off two beers over the course of an hour and a half. He stumbles a bit as he gets off the bar stool, and the bartender asks if he's okay. Hector reassures the bartender that he's sober. After all, he only had two beers.

Driving home, Hector drifts into the left lane for a moment but swerves back into line. Just then, he hears a car behind him honking. A few moments later, he sees police lights flashing. Puzzled, he pulls over. Hector fails a field sobriety test, but a breathalyzer test registers Hector's blood alcohol level at .03, well below the legal limit. What's going on?

Hector recently complained to his physician about feeling stressed at his job. His doctor prescribed a low dose of anti-anxiety medication and warned Hector not to take too much — it could be addictive if he wasn't careful. Hector found the medication useful, and it calmed him a bit, but the medication didn't quite do the trick. A friend recommended two herbs to try. Hector figured that would be a great, natural way to enhance the prescribed drug and that herbs certainly couldn't hurt him. To add up Hector's scorecard, he had combined two anxiety-alleviating herbs, a prescription, drug, and alcohol — and was lucky that the police pulled him over. Hector could have ended up in a serious accident, harming himself or others.

Don't forget — even moderate alcohol consumption, combined with anti-anxiety agents, can intensify sedative effects to the point of substantial impairment and even death. *Be careful!*

The bill comes to $214, and Dolores goes home feeling a bit overwhelmed. One day at work, after ingesting a dozen pills, Dolores runs to the bathroom to throw-up. A concerned friend asks her what's making her sick. Dolores tells her about all the supplements that she's taking. Her friend suggests that Dolores seek the advice of a naturopathic practitioner; she explains that these professionals attend a four-year, full-time training program and must pass a rigorous exam.

Dolores visits a naturopathic practitioner who advises her to dump the majority of her purchases in favor of a multiple vitamin and one herbal supplement. He also discusses several relaxation strategies, exercise routines, and self-help books. Within a few weeks, Dolores feels like a new person.

Viva vitamins!

Chronic stress taxes the body. The results of several studies link mood disorders to vitamin deficiencies, and especially severe deficiencies may make your anxiety worse. Therefore, many experts recommend a good multi-vitamin supplement. Make sure that it includes all the B-complex vitamins, particularly B1, B2, B6, and B12. In addition, experts recommend increasing your vitamins C and E intake. Low levels of the mineral selenium have been linked to anxiety and a depressed mood. Finally, calcium is often suggested for its reputed calming effect. Most believe that including magnesium with calcium is best because the minerals work synergistically.

Can vitamins and minerals cure your anxiety? That's not likely. However, they may just help to keep your body in better shape for handling the stresses that come your way. Just take care and don't take huge quantities. Even vitamins can produce toxic effects at megadoses.

Sifting through the slew of supplements

If you search the Internet and your local health food stores, you can probably find over a hundred supplements advertised as antidotes for anxiety. But do they work? Only a few that we know of. The following have at least garnered a smidge of evidence in support of their value as possible anxiety axes.

✔ **Melatonin:** Reaching a peak around midnight, this hormone helps to regulate sleep rhythms in the body, in particular, the problem of falling asleep at the right time (known as sleep onset) as opposed to problems of awakening in the early morning and being unable to go back to sleep. Synthetic melatonin taken in the early evening, a few hours before bedtime may alleviate this particular type of insomnia, a common problem among those who have excessive anxiety. Some people claim it helps them alleviate jet-lag-related sleep problems when traveling across a number of time zones. People who work varying time shifts also report that melatonin helps them adjust to new sleep schedules.

Side effects such as dizziness, irritability, fatigue, headache, and low-level depression are all possible, but all long-term side effects aren't really known at this time. Also, avoid driving or drinking alcohol when you take melatonin.

If you have an autoimmune disease or if you are depressed, you should probably avoid melatonin.

✔ **SAM-e:** Claimed to relieve the pain and stiffness of osteoarthritis and fibromyalgia, this amino acid occurs naturally in the body. It may also help treat depression and anxiety. However, research on this supplement remains scant. SAM-e appears to increase levels of serotonin and dopamine in the brain, which could theoretically alleviate anxiety.

The possible side effects such as gastrointestinal upset, nervousness, insomnia, headache, and agitation may result, but again, little is known about the possible long-term effects.

Don't take SAM-e if you have bipolar disorder or severe depression. SAM-e may contribute to mania, which is a dangerous, euphoric state that often includes poor judgment and risky behaviors.

✔ **5-HTP:** This popular supplement is a compound that increases the levels of serotonin in the brain. Serotonin plays a critical role in regulating mood and anxiety. Some evidence also exists that 5-HTP may increase the brain's natural pain-relievers, *endorphins*. (See Chapter 10 for more on endorphins.) Unfortunately, only limited research has been conducted on this supplement. These studies suggest that 5-HTP may reduce anxiety somewhat.

The most widely reported side effects of 5-HTP include nausea, drowsiness, and dry mouth. Other side effects are relatively rare, but these include headache, dizziness, and constipation.

Do not take 5-HTP if you are also taking another antidepressant. Also, avoid it if you have tumors or cardiovascular disease.

A number of practitioners of alternative medicine also frequently recommend the supplement gamma-amino butyric acid (GABA). This supplement may have a mild tranquilizing effect, but little data is available to substantiate that claim. In addition, some suggest that magnesium may improve circulation and muscular relaxation, but again, not much evidence backs up this claim.

Hunting for Helpful Herbs

In the past decade or so, people have flocked to health food stores, grocery stores, and drugstores in search of safe, natural remedies to their anxiety. Herbs promise to decrease symptoms of stress without potential side effects. Unfortunately, sincere, well-meaning clerks who know little about their product, other than what's on the label or the manufacturer's flyers, sell the vast majority of herbs today. However, a few people do have extensive training in the safe use of herbal therapy, but even those with such training often have precious little data to draw from.

Two herbs — kava kava and valerian — appear to effectively reduce anxiety-related symptoms. In the following two sections, "Kava Kava" and "Valerian," we tell you about important cautions, safety data or the lack thereof, and the latest findings concerning kava kava and valerian. Most of this research was conducted in Europe where interest is particularly high.

Kava kava

The islanders in the South Pacific consumed kava kava for both pleasure and healing. They used it to treat a host of ailments including obesity, syphilis, and gonorrhea, but we don't recommend it for those problems. The islanders also used it for relaxation, insomnia, and anxiety reduction. Kava kava is used extensively in Europe for anxiety. It appears to act on the central nervous system including the limbic system, which regulates emotion.

Effectiveness

Studies on the effectiveness of kava kava appear to support the islanders' impressions about its ability to quell anxiety and possibly alleviate insomnia. A few reasonably good studies have pitted kava kava against prescription anti-anxiety drugs and found it to compare favorably.

Dosages

Those who appear to benefit from kava kava in research studies generally take about 300 milligrams (mg) of standardized extract containing 70 percent kavalactones (considered the active ingredient of kava kava), (yielding 210 mg of pure kavalactones) divided into two or three doses through the day.

You should know that kava kava sold off the shelf may contain a much lower percentage of kavalactones. In that case, you need to calculate the total milligrams from the percentage of kavalactones contained in the extract. Unfortunately, the percentage sometimes doesn't appear on the label. Be sure to buy a kava kava product with that information. Teas and beverages containing kava kava rarely give you this information and not surprisingly, they usually contain so little of the product that they wouldn't likely do anything for your anxiety.

Cautions!

Don't use kava kava if you're pregnant or breast-feeding or if you have Parkinson's or liver disease. The herb can interact with alcohol or other anti-anxiety medications. You might feel a little drowsy, so be careful about driving or operating machinery. Don't take kava kava in large doses or for prolonged periods of time (over four to eight weeks). Chronic kava kava use may cause discoloration of the skin or nails and dry, scaly skin.

Recently, the German government reported a few cases of high doses of kava kava being associated with liver problems. If you take kava kava and drink alcohol regularly, stop! If you notice dark urine or yellowing of the eyes, stop! If you take other drugs that can adversely affect your liver, don't take kava kava!

Valerian

Valerian is an herb native to Europe and Asia. The word comes from the Latin term meaning *well-being.* It has been suggested for digestive problems, insomnia, and anxiety. Like many herbs, valerian is used extensively in Europe but is gaining in popularity in the United States.

Effectiveness

A number of studies with placebo control groups suggest that valerian enhances the quality of sleep for insomniacs. One study reviewed in *The Desktop Guide to Complementary & Alternative Medicine* (Mosby 2001 New York), compared valerian with a prescription sleep aid (oxazepam) and found it equally effective. A few controlled studies support valerian's use for the treatment of anxiety. However, these are relatively few in number, so its value for sleep is clearer than for anxiety.

Dosages

Specific recommended doses for the use of valerian with anxiety reduction aren't available as yet. However, for the treatment of insomnia, taking between 400 and 900 mg is generally recommended. You should know that the quality and purity of valerian products varies widely. Products with valerenic acid are considered to be somewhat superior.

Cautions!

Valerian appears to be a relatively safe herb. However, you shouldn't take valerian if you have liver problems or are pregnant or nursing. Side effects can include stomach upset, headaches, and infrequently, liver damage. If you take too much, you may experience confusion, hypersensitivity, insomnia, or even hallucinations. It may interact with other drugs at high dosages, so take care when combining valerian and medications.

Waiting for the verdict on other herbal remedies

Many other herbal remedies for anxiety appear in books, magazines, and stores. Peddlers promote these as safe, effective methods. But beware; many of these herbs haven't been subjected to scrutiny for effectiveness or safety. We suggest that you avoid these because so many other anxiety-reducing agents and strategies work without dangerous side effects.

Research on the use of herbs taken by pregnant or breast-feeding mothers has almost never been conducted. That's because no one wants to take any chances of harming the fetus or newborn. You should probably avoid all herbal products if you are pregnant or breast-feeding. At the very least, consult your physician before taking any herbs or supplements. We just don't have enough information to justify the risk.

On the other hand, we don't think that you need to be overly alarmed about drinking a little herbal tea from time to time. Most of these brews contain relatively small amounts of the active ingredients and likely pose little threat. But if you really want to overcome your anxiety with herbs or supplements, use the ones with the most research backing their claims. You may be curious about other herbs often recommended for anxiety reduction. Table 14-1 presents a quick overview of the most popular herbs.

Table 14-1	Herbs with more hype than hope	
Herb	*Research*	*Dangers*
Chamomile	Insufficient research to make reasonable conclusions about its effectiveness for anxiety reduction.	Rare, severe allergic reactions possible. Should not be taken by those who have severe allergies to ragweed.
Ginkgo biloba	Research is insufficient to make reasonable conclusions about its effectiveness for anxiety reduction. Limited data suggests that it may improve short-term memory and/or your thinking ability. It may have limited usefulness for those with mild Alzheimer's or dementia.	Side effects can include stomach upset, anxiety, insomnia, and bleeding complications. Do not take with other blood thinning medications or before or after surgery.
Lemon balm	Widely touted for the relief of anxiety and bodily tension. However, research supporting its efficacy is scarce.	Appears to be relatively harmless.
Hops	Used for restlessness and insomnia. Insufficient research to support these assertions.	Don't use if you're depressed.

Herb	Research	Dangers
Ginseng	Often suggested for stress and fatigue. Although many consumers swear by it, research has generally failed to support its effectiveness. A few studies suggest it creates a sense of well-being.	Among chronic, heavy consumers, hypertension, excitation, and insomnia have been reported. It may interact with a variety of other drugs. Consult your physician if you take any other medications.
St. John's Wort	Usually promoted for use with depression, but also recommended for alleviating anxiety. A number of studies on depression indicate it may have some value. Its use for anxiety isn't supported as yet, although most antidepressants decrease anxiety to some extent.	Don't take it if you're taking another antidepressant medication. Side effects include oversensitivity to sun, stomach upset, restlessness, and headache. May interact badly with wine or cheese.

People have used herbal remedies for thousands of years. Some of them work. In fact, a significant number of prescription medications are derived from herbs. You may want to try out an herb or two for your anxiety. We recommend that you read the literature about each herb carefully to make an informed choice before purchasing them from a reputable dealer.

If you have severe anxiety, don't rely exclusively on herbs. You should consult a professional for therapy and/or medications. Inadequately treated anxiety is a serious problem.

Chapter 15

Prescribing Peacefulness

· ·

· ·

The last several decades have witnessed an explosion in new knowledge about emotions, mental illness, and brain chemistry. Scientists recognize changes in the brain that accompany many psychological disorders. New and old drugs address these chemical imbalances, and using these drugs has both advantages and disadvantages.

This chapter helps you make an informed decision about whether to use medication for your anxiety. We give you information about the most widely prescribed drugs and some of their more common side effects. Only you, in consultation with your healthcare provider, can determine what's best for helping you.

Making Up Your Mind About Medications

Deciding whether to medicate your anxiety brings up a number of issues to consider. This decision isn't one to take lightly. You should consult with your therapist if you have one, as well as your physician. Before you decide on medication, what have you done to alleviate your anxiety? Have you read this book and tried to follow the recommendations? Have you

✔ Cleared out your roadblocks to change? (See Chapter 3.)

✔ Tracked your worries over time? (See Chapter 4.)

✔ Challenged your anxious thoughts, assumptions, and words? (See Chapters 5, 6, and 7.)

   ✔ Confronted your fears head on? (See Chapter 8.)

   ✔ Simplified your life? (See Chapter 9.)

   ✔ Exercised? (See Chapter 10.)

   ✔ Tried improving your sleep? (See Chapter 11.)

   ✔ Tried using relaxation? (See Chapters 12 and 13.)

   ✔ Practiced mindfulness? (See Chapter 16.)

With a few important exceptions, which we review in this chapter, we recommend that you go through the preceding list in this section prior to adding medication. Why? First, some research suggests that certain medications may actually interfere with the long-term effectiveness of the most successful treatments for anxiety. That's especially true of the techniques designed to confront phobias and fears directly through exposure (see Chapter 8). Second, if you try the strategies above, you very well may discover that you don't need medication. Many of our recommended anxiety axes have the potential to cement change for the long haul as well as positively affect your entire life.

The downside of medications

You need to reflect on both sides of any important decision. Medications certainly have an upside and they have a downside. The negative side of the argument includes:

   ✔ **Addiction:** Some medications can lead to physical and/or mental dependency. Getting off of those medications can be difficult, even dangerous if not done properly. (However, contrary to what some people think, many medications are available that do *not* have addictive potential.)

   ✔ **Long-term effects:** We don't really have good information on possible long-term effects with some of the newest medications.

   ✔ **Philosophy:** Some people just feel strongly that they don't like to take medications. And that's okay but only to a point.

   ✔ **Pregnancy and breast-feeding:** Only a few drugs are recommended for women who are pregnant or breast-feeding. The potential effects on the baby or fetus are just too risky.

   ✔ **Side effects:** Most medications have various side effects, such as gastrointestinal upset, headaches, dizziness, dry mouth, and sexual dysfunction. Working with your physician to find the right medication — a drug that alleviates your anxiety and doesn't cause you overly troublesome side effects — may take some time.

The upside of medications

Sometimes medications make good sense. In weighing the pros and cons, we suggest that you take a good look at the benefits that medications can offer:

- When serious depression accompanies anxiety, medication can sometimes provide faster relief, especially when the tendency toward suicide is present.

- When anxiety severely interferes with your life, medication sometimes can provide relief more quickly than therapy or lifestyle changes. Such interferences include:

  - **Panic attacks** that occur frequently and cause expensive trips to the emergency room.

  - **Anxiety** that feels so severe that you stop going to work or miss out on important life events.

  - **Compulsions** and **obsessions** (see Chapter 2) that take control of your life and consume large blocks of time.

- When you've tried the recommendations in this book, consulted a qualified therapist (see Chapter 22 for advice on finding a good therapist), and you still suffer from excessive anxiety.

- If your physician tells you that your stress level must be controlled quickly due to a physical condition, such as dangerously high blood pressure, medication to control your high blood pressure may also in a few cases reduce your stress in addition to adding a few years to your life.

- When you experience a sudden, traumatic event, a brief regimen of the right medication may help you get through it. Traumas that happen to most people at one time or another include:

  - The sudden death of a loved one

  - An unexpected accident

  - Severe illness

  - An unexpected financial disaster

  - A natural disaster, such as a hurricane or earthquake

  - Being the victim of a serious crime

  - Being the victim of terrorism

Kenneth's story is a good example of how medication can help some people get through a difficult but temporary period in their lives.

Kenneth worked a few blocks from the World Trade Center in New York. On September 11, he heard the first explosion and left his office to see what was going on. He saw the huge billows of smoke heading his way and watched with terror as people fell from the tower. He joined the crowds running to escape the oncoming blanket of smoke and debris and escaped without serious physical injury.

Through the weeks and then months that followed the event, Kenneth had trouble sleeping. He couldn't get his mind off the horrific images. He felt jumpy and on edge, and had trouble going back to work. He went to his doctor because everything felt unreal. His doctor told him that he was suffering from an acute stress disorder and that if the symptoms continued for another couple of months, then therapy would be a good idea. However, he said that for now, a prescription of an antidepressant medication would probably give him some quick relief and possibly prevent a chronic condition from developing.

Understanding Medication Options

Today, physicians have a wide range of medications for the treatment of anxiety disorders. New drugs and applications appear all the time. Do not expect our list to cover every possible medication for anxiety. In addition, our review does not intend to replace professional medical advice.

If you decide to ask your doctor about medication, don't forget to discuss the following critical issues if they apply to you. Communicating with your doctor about these considerations can help avert a disastrous outcome. Be sure to tell your doctor if you

- ✔ Are pregnant or plan to become pregnant
- ✔ Are breast-feeding
- ✔ Drink alcohol
- ✔ Take any other prescription drugs
- ✔ Take any over-the-counter medications
- ✔ Take herbs or supplements
- ✔ Have any physical conditions, such as high blood pressure, liver disease, diabetes, or kidney disease
- ✔ Have had any bad reactions to medications in the past
- ✔ Have any allergies
- ✔ Take birth control pills (some medications for anxiety reduce their effectiveness)

Most drugs prescribed for anxiety belong to one of the following categories. We'll discuss these in addition to a few miscellaneous medications:

- Antidepressants.
  - Tricyclic
  - MAO Inhibitors
  - Selective Serotonin Reuptake Inhibitors (SSRIs)
  - "Designer" or atypical antidepressants
- Benzodiazepines (minor tranquilizers)
- Miscellaneous tranquilizers
- Beta blockers
- Atypical antipsychotics
- Mood stabilizers and miscellaneous

You may notice that some of these categories sound a little strange. For example, antidepressants used to treat depression and beta blockers, used for hypertension, don't sound like a group of medications for the treatment of anxiety. But we show you that they have an important role to play with certain types of anxiety.

Antidepressants

Antidepressant medications have been used to treat anxiety for many decades. That's interesting because anxiety and depression often occur together. And both problems appear to have some similarity in terms of their biological underpinnings.

MAO inhibitors

MAO inhibitors are the oldest type of antidepressant medication. They inhibit a substance that oxidizes critical neurotransmitters in the brain. Thus, more of these neurotransmitters remain available to effectively regulate mood. MAO inhibitors are used infrequently because they have serious side effects. The most serious of these side effects occurs when those who take this medication consume food containing the tyramine, which can trigger a hypertensive crisis. The side effect involves a spike in blood pressure that could lead to a stroke or even death.

Unfortunately, many foods, such as those that follow, contain tyramine:

- Avocados
- Beer

- Cheese
- Salami
- Soy
- Tomatoes
- Wine

Nevertheless, MAO inhibitors can be effective when other antidepressants haven't worked. If your doctor prescribes one of them to you, he probably has a good reason for doing so. However, watch what you eat and avoid the foods in the preceding list. MAO inhibitors include Nardil, Parnate, and Marplan.

Tricyclic antidepressants

Tricyclic antidepressants increase the length of time that the neurotransmitter norepinephrine is available to the nerve synapses and can take anywhere from two to twelve weeks to exert maximum effectiveness. Some people temporarily experience *increased* anxiety with tricyclic medications. In large part due to side effects that can increase anxiety and agitation, nearly 30 percent of patients discontinue taking them.

That's why many physicians prescribe medication for anxiety disorders by starting low on the dosage and going slow with increases. In other words, they will prescribe a very low dose initially in order for your body to adjust to it with minimal side effects. They gradually increase the dosage in order to minimize negative reactions. It can take a while to reach an effective dose this way, but you'll probably find yourself able to tolerate the medication more easily.

Even with careful dosing, tricyclic medications can cause considerable side effects, including dizziness, weight gain, dry mouth, blurred vision, and constipation. Some of these effects resolve over time, but many of them persist even after several weeks. Tricyclics have lost some of their popularity to the newer SSRIs described below because the SSRIs have fewer of these annoying side effects. Common tricyclic medications include Tofranil, Elavil, Adapin, Pamelor, and Anafranil (prescribed especially for Obsessive-Compulsive Disorder and Panic Disorder, because it has a different mechanism of action on the brain than the other tricyclic medications.).

Selective Serotonin Reuptake Inhibitors (SSRIs)

SSRIs didn't come onto the scene until the tricyclics had been around for 30 years or so. Psychiatrists were frustrated with the side effects from the tricyclics and MAO inhibitors, but reasonable alternatives were still unavailable. The pharmaceutical industry worked prodigiously to develop better options.

The first prize in this pursuit was Prozac, which was followed by a slew of imitators. The SSRIs increase the levels of the critical neurotransmitter serotonin at the nerve synapses by inhibiting the reabsorption of serotonin into the nerve cells. You should know that SSRIs still have significant side effects, though these tend to be milder and some abate with time.

Like other antidepressants, SSRIs are effective treatments for various anxiety disorders. See Chapter 2 for a description of anxiety disorders. See Table 15-1, later in this chapter, for a listing of the popular SSRIs. Doctors prescribe SSRIs for

- Agoraphobia
- Generalized Anxiety Disorder
- Obsessive-Compulsive Disorder
- Panic attacks and Panic Disorder
- Post-Traumatic Stress Disorder
- Specific Phobias
- Social Phobias

Among the medication options, SSRIs are considered the first line of defense for Post-Traumatic Stress Disorder.

Table 15-1	Popular SSRIs	
Trade Name	*Most Frequent Side Effects*	*Precautions*
Celexa	Headache, tremor, sedation, abnormal dreams, nausea, sweating, dry mouth, and problems with ejaculation.	Do not take Celexa with another antidepressant or St. John's Wort, which could cause death.
Luvox	Headache, drowsiness, dizziness, convulsions, nausea, hepatotoxicity, decreased libido, and sweating.	Fatal reactions have been reported when taken with MAO inhibitors. Do not take with other antidepressants or St. John's Wort. Luvox increases the effects of kava kava. Smoking and drinking reduce its effectiveness.

(continued)

Table 15-1 *(continued)*

Trade Name	Most Frequent Side Effects	Precautions
Paxil	Headache, sedation, tremor, nausea, sweating, and decreased libido.	Fatal reactions have been reported when taken with MAO inhibitors. Do not take with other antidepressants or St. John's Wort. When taken with Warfarin, can increase bleeding.
Prozac	Headache, nervousness, insomnia, tremor, nausea, diarrhea, dry mouth, sweating, and decreased libido.	Do not take with other antidepressants or St. John's Wort. Can cause a paradoxical increase in Obsessive-Compulsive Disorder when taken with Buspirone.
Zoloft	Headache, insomnia, agitation, male sexual dysfunction, diarrhea, nausea, constipation, tremor, and fatigue.	Fatal reactions have been reported when taken with MAO inhibitors. Do not take with other antidepressants or St. John's Wort.

Designer antidepressants

This new class of antidepressants targets other important neurotransmitters by themselves or in conjunction with serotonin. They are starting to look fairly promising for the treatment of various anxiety disorders.

As with most of the medications for anxiety, these should generally be avoided when pregnant or breast-feeding. Consult your physician for the best alternatives.

Saving your sex life?

Many medications for the treatment of anxiety, as well as depression, interfere with arousal and the ability to achieve an orgasm. The worst offenders in this group of medications are the Selective Serotonin Reuptake Inhibitors (SSRIs). Many folks taking these medications are so pleased with their reduced anxiety that they hesitate to complain to their doctors about this side effect. Others are just too embarrassed to bring it up. You should know that this side effect is extremely common, and your doctor has no doubt heard many patients report this problem. So go ahead and talk with your doctor — no need for embarrassment. Certain medications have a lower tendency to cause this side effect than others so your doctor may recommend a switch. Or alternatively, there are medications such as Viagra that can be used to treat the sexual side effects directly. If you talk to your doctor, you can explore the best options.

Currently, some of the more widely prescribed designer antidepressants include:

- ✔ **Effexor:** The FDA recently approved this drug for the treatment of Generalized Anxiety Disorder (GAD). However, it also appears likely that it can treat other anxiety disorders, such as Panic Disorder, Post-Traumatic Stress Disorder, and so on.

  - **Common side effects:** These include sweating, insomnia, weakness, dizziness, dry mouth, sexual dysfunction, dry mouth, abnormal vision, migraine, swelling, and weight loss or gain.

  - **Precautions:** Those with hypertension should generally avoid this medication, and special care should be taken with children and/or the elderly. Those with bipolar disorder run the risk of inducing a euphoric, manic phase. It can increase the effects of alcohol, opioids, sedatives, and antihistamines.

- ✔ **Serzone:** This medication is also reported as effective for Generalized Anxiety Disorder and Social Phobias. A particular advantage of this drug is that it works more rapidly than most antidepressants.

  - **Side Effects:** Headache, weakness, dry mouth, nausea, hypotension, constipation, drowsiness, insomnia, confusion, blurred vision, urinary retention, and cough. However, it has fewer disagreeable side effects than the SSRIs, including sexual problems.

  - **Precautions:** Caution should be taken with children, the elderly, those with cardiovascular disease, or seizure disorders. It can increase the effects of alcohol and other central nervous system depressants.

- ✔ **Remeron:** This medication has shown some effectiveness with Panic Disorder, Generalized Anxiety Disorder, Obsessive-Compulsive Disorder, and Post-Traumatic Stress Disorder. Like Serzone, it works more rapidly than the SSRIs and causes relatively few sexual problems.

  - **Side Effects:** Weakness, dizziness, drowsiness, diarrhea, dry mouth, increased appetite, urinary retention, blurry vision, abnormal dreams, and possibly weight gain.

  - **Precautions:** Those who've had hypersensitivity to tricyclic anti-depressants and those with convulsive disorders or in recovery from a myocardial infarction shouldn't use this Remeron. It can increase the effects of alcohol, barbiturates, and benzodiazepines. A few fatal reactions were reported when taken with antihistamines. Reports also indicate the possibility of hypertensive crisis when taken with MAO inhibitors.

- ✔ **Welbutrin:** This medication has relatively less support for its effectiveness with anxiety disorders. More commonly, Welbutrin is prescribed for depression or as an aid to smoking cessation. However, scattered reports indicate it may be useful for social anxiety and other anxiety related problems.

- **Side Effects:** Headache, seizures, agitation, palpitations, nausea, vomiting, and insomnia.

  A common side effect of Welbutrin is agitation and anxiety. Be sure to let your doctor know if you experience increased distress with this medication.

- **Precautions:** People with seizure disorders should never take Welbutrin. Those with eating disorders or liver disease should generally avoid this medication. It may add to the effects of alcohol and other central nervous system depressants.

Benzodiazepines

Better known as tranquilizers, the benzodiazepines were first introduced over 40 years ago. At first blush, these seemed like perfect medications for a host of anxiety problems. Unlike the antidepressants, they work rapidly, often quelling symptoms within 15 to 20 minutes. Not only that, they can be taken merely on an as-needed basis, when having to deal with an especially anxiety-arousing situation, such as confronting a phobia, giving a speech, or going to a job interview. The side effects tend to be less disturbing than those associated with antidepressants as well. And for 20 years or so after their introduction, they were seen as safer than barbiturates with a lower risk of overdose. They rapidly became the standard treatment for most of the anxiety disorders. They appear to work by reinforcing a substance in the brain that inhibits the excitability of nerve cells. What could be better?

Well, it turns out that the benzodiazepines do have some problems. Nothing's perfect after all. Dependency or addiction is a significant risk. As with many addictions, the withdrawal from benzodiazepines can be difficult and even dangerous. Furthermore, if you stop taking them, your anxiety is almost bound to return. Experiencing a rebound anxiety upon withdrawal that's more severe than that experienced before taking the drug is possible.

Benzodiazepines are also associated with increasing the risk of falling among the elderly. And falls among the elderly too often result in hip fractures. In addition, a recent report suggested that benzodiazepines may double the risk of getting into a motor vehicle accident.

That risk rapidly escalates when benzodiazepines are taken in combination with alcohol. In fact, benzodiazepines are particularly problematic for those who have a history of substance abuse. They readily become addicted to these medications and are at greater risk for combining alcohol with their medication.

It would seem logical and humane to prescribe benzodiazepines to those who have suffered a recent trauma. Indeed, these medications have the potential to improve sleep and reduce both arousal and anxiety. However, one recent study published in the 1998 *Journal of Clinical Psychopharmacology* found that the early and prolonged administration of benzodiazepines after a trauma actually appeared to increase the rate of full-blown Post-Traumatic Stress Disorder later. (See Chapter 2 for more information about Post-Traumatic Stress Disorder.)

It would also seem compellingly logical that combining benzodiazepines with some of the various changes in behavior or thinking that can reduce anxiety (see Chapters 5, 6, 7, and 8) would make for a useful, synergistic combination that could yield better outcomes than with either approach by itself. Yet studies conducted by psychologist Dr. Michael Otto at Massachusetts General Hospital have found that the risk of relapse is increased when these medications are combined with changes in thinking and behaving. In the long run, it appears that for most people, learning coping strategies to deal with their anxiety seems better than merely seeking pharmacological solutions — especially with respect to the benzodiazepines.

Nevertheless, the benzodiazepines remain one of the most popular approaches to the treatment of anxiety disorders, especially among general practitioners who have no special training in psychiatry. In part, that may be due to the popularity and low side effect profile of the drugs. And these medications can sometimes have an important role to play, especially for short-term, acute stress and anxiety, as well as for those whom other medications haven't helped. We simply urge caution with the use of these agents. Table 15-2 lists the more popular tranquilizers.

Table 15-2	The Ever Popular Benzodiazepines (Tranquilizers)	
Trade Name	*Most Frequent Side Effects*	*Precautions*
Ativan	Dizziness, drowsiness, confusion, blurred vision, and unsteadiness	Avoid if you have a history of drug abuse or narrow-angle glaucoma. Can increase the effects of alcohol and other central nervous system depressants.
Klonopin	Drowsiness, nausea, constipation, increased salivation, abnormal eye movements, confusion, and chest congestion	Same as for Ativan.

(continued)

Table 15-2 *(continued)*

Trade Name	Most Frequent Side Effects	Precautions
Librium	Drowsiness, confusion, blurred vision, dizziness, loss of coordination, and nausea	Avoid with history of drug abuse (but often used to facilitate alcohol withdrawal) or narrow-angle glaucoma. Can increase the effects of alcohol and other central nervous system depressants.
Serax	Nausea, vomiting, diarrhea, lethargy, and drowsiness	Should be avoided among those with hypersensitivity to penicillin. May decrease the effect of oral contraceptives and tetracyclines.
Tranxene	Dizziness, drowsiness, confusion, blurred vision, fatigue, and confusion	Same as for Librium.
Valium	Dizziness, drowsiness, blurred vision, fatigue, and confusion	Same as for Librium.
Xanax	Dizziness, drowsiness, confusion, headache, tremors, blurred vision, and unsteadiness	Same as for Ativan.

Miscellaneous tranquilizers

A few miscellaneous tranquilizers are chemically unrelated to the benzodiazepines and thus appear to work rather differently.

You should know that in addition to our miscellaneous list, other types of tranquilizers are available. Furthermore, exciting new types of anti-anxiety drugs are under development, and some are undergoing clinical trials. Some of these are fast acting, yet may have few of the undesirable side effects that have been found with the benzodiazepines.

For the time being, we list three anti-anxiety medications that your doctor might prescribe.

✔ **Buspar:** This medication belongs to a class of chemical compounds referred to as *azaspirodecanediones,* (which are actually far less intimidating than their name). Exactly how buspar works is unknown, but it appears to affect the dopamine and the 5-HT(1A) receptors in the brain. It has been studied the most for the treatment of Generalized Anxiety Disorder, but may have value for treating various other anxiety related problems, such as Social Phobia and Post-Traumatic Stress Disorder, among others. It may not be as useful for panic attacks as other medications. Although extensive evidence would be necessary to rule out addictive potential, the current belief is that Buspar's likelihood for producing dependence is quite low.

- **Side Effects:** The most common side effects are usually mild and include headache, dizziness, drowsiness, and nausea.

- **Precautions:** Buspar shouldn't be taken in conjunction with MAO inhibitors as it may elevate blood pressure. Although it appears to interact less with alcohol than the benzodiazepines, combining them is probably best avoided. Before operating a motor vehicle, be certain that it doesn't have an adverse affect on performance, judgment, and coordination. Care should be taken for those who have impaired liver or kidney function.

✔ **Vistaril (also marketed as Atarax and Rezine):** This medication is a tranquilizer and also an antihistamine that's used to treat various kinds of anxiety and tension-related problems as well as allergic reactions, such as hives and itching. Fast acting, this drug takes effect within 30 minutes.

- **Side Effects:** The most common side effects include dizziness, drowsiness, dry mouth, sleepiness, and confusion.

- **Precautions:** It may increase the effects of alcohol and other central nervous system depressants. Considerable caution should be taken when driving or operating machinery. Generally not considered for long-term use. Special care needs to be taken when prescribed for the elderly.

Beta blockers

Because anxiety can increase blood pressure, perhaps it's not surprising that a few medications for the treatment of hypertension also reduce anxiety. Chief among these are the so-called beta blockers that block the effects of norepinephrine. Thus, they control much of the physical symptoms of anxiety, such as shaking, trembling, rapid heartbeat, and blushing. In the treatment of anxiety, their usefulness is primarily limited to Specific Phobias, such as social anxiety and performance anxiety. They're highly popular among professional musicians who often use them to reduce their performance anxiety prior to an important concert or audition. Two beta blockers, Inderal and Tenormin, are most frequently prescribed for these purposes:

✔ **Inderal:** Generally, Inderal is used for the short-term alleviation of stage fright, public speaking, test anxiety, and social anxiety. It's often given as a single dose prior to a performance.

- **Side Effects:** Usually, people report few side effects. However, some feel drowsy, light-headed, and lethargic. Sometimes it can cause blood pressure to drop excessively.

- **Precautions:** People who suffer from asthma, chronic lung disease, diabetes, certain heart diseases, those with low blood pressure, and anyone who is severely depressed shouldn't take this drug.

✔ **Tenormin:** This medication usually has fewer side effects than Inderal and is longer acting. Tenormin is also often given as a single dose prior to a performance.

- **Side Effects:** Generally mild but can include insomnia, fatigue, dizziness, mental changes, nausea, diarrhea, and excessively low blood pressure.

- **Precautions:** It can cause excessively high blood pressure if taken regularly and then suddenly stopped. Alcohol can increase sedation and lead to excessively low blood pressure. May have less wheezing effects but those with low blood pressure, asthma, other chronic lung conditions, diabetes, kidney disease, thyroid disease, and serious depression should generally avoid this medication.

Atypical antipsychotics

In recent years, a new class of antipsychotic medication arrived on the scene called *atypical antipsychotic medications.* They are atypical in the sense that, unlike earlier medications, they have a much lower risk of certain serious side effects, and they can be used to treat a far broader range of problems than simply psychosis. The atypical antipsychotics target a different neurotransmitter than the SSRIs and sometimes are used in combination with SSRIs. When used to treat anxiety related problems, these medications are usually prescribed at far lower doses than when used for psychotic disorders.

Upon seeing this category, you could have easily thought, "Hey, I'm anxious; I'm not crazy!" And in fact, psychosis is a serious mental disorder that often involves disordered thinking, hallucinations, delusions, and other serious distortions of reality. So you might wonder why medications designed to treat psychosis would have anything to do with treating anxiety. Those who merely suffer from anxiety, rarely if ever, experience the kind of substantially confused thinking that psychotics do.

The primary use of these medications to date has been for the treatment of serious cases of Post-Traumatic Stress Disorder in addition to Obsessive-Compulsive Disorder (see Chapter 2). Evidence to date suggests that they can substantially improve outcomes for people who haven't done well on other medications for these problems. Studies haven't been conducted on the use of these medications for other anxiety disorders, such as Generalized Anxiety Disorder, Agoraphobia, and Panic Disorder (see Chapter 2). However, case reports are rolling in that suggest they may be beneficial for these problems as well. Soon, studies may back those reports up with stronger evidence.

So with all the exciting potential of these medications, you may think they would quickly become the treatment of choice for most anxiety disorders. Well, hold the phone. That's not likely to happen anytime soon because they occasionally have some especially distressing side effects. Possibly the most feared are known as extrapyramidal side effects (EPS), which can include a wide range of problems, such as

- Abnormal, uncontrollable irregular muscle movements in the face, mouth, and sometimes, other body parts
- An intense feeling of restlessness
- Muscle stiffness
- Prolonged spasms or muscle contractions
- Shuffling gait

The good news is that these EPS effects appear to occur much less often with the newer atypical antipsychotic medications as opposed to the older, traditional antipsychotic medications. Because the risk of EPS is relatively low, those with severe anxiety disorders for whom changes in behavior or thinking (see Chapters 5, 6, 7, and 8) or other medications haven't helped sufficiently, may wish to consider using these new anti-anxiety tools.

However, because the risk exists, those whose relatively milder anxiety problems would probably want to avoid them. We discuss four of the new antipsychotic medications in this chapter. Others are under development.

As with most of the medications for anxiety, these should generally be avoided when pregnant or breast-feeding. Consult your physician for the best alternatives.

- **Risperdal:** This medication has received the most attention from researchers in regard to the treatment of severe Post-Traumatic Stress Disorder and Obsessive-Compulsive Disorder. Many consider it likely that Risperdal may effectively treat other severe anxiety disorders as well. It has been shown to further reduce symptoms of anxiety, depression, and anger when added to SSRI medications.

  - **Side Effects:** Most common side effects include drowsiness, dizziness, weight gain, nausea, and constipation. However, it can also lead to extrapyramidal symptoms, such as muscle stiffness, involuntary movements, shuffling gait, and so on.

- **Precautions:** Those with seizure disorders should avoid this medication. You should also avoid rapidly standing up as well as hot tubs and hot baths as these could cause hypotension to occur. Various serious drug interactions can occur with over-the-counter medications. May increase the sedative effects of alcohol and other central nervous system depressants.

✔ **Zyprexa:** This medication doesn't have much research demonstrating its effectiveness for anxiety disorders. However, a few studies and a number of reports suggest that it may be effective for the treatment of severe Post-Traumatic Stress Disorder, as well as for reducing the anxiety experienced among Alzheimer's patients. Effectiveness with other anxiety disorders is promising but remains to be demonstrated with certainty.

  - **Side Effects:** Common side effects include dry mouth, constipation, weight gain, and drowsiness. May have somewhat less likelihood of developing EPS effects, such as muscle stiffness, involuntary movements, shuffling gait, and so on, than Risperdal.

  - **Precautions:** Can lead to excessive sedation when mixed with alcohol or other central nervous system depressants. Should also avoid rapidly standing up as well as hot tubs and hot baths as these could cause hypotension to occur. May interact with various over-the-counter medications.

✔ **Seroquel:** Almost no research backs this medication in terms of treatment for anxiety problems. However, it well may have significant potential.

  - **Side Effects:** Common side effects include dizziness, dry mouth, headache, back pain, weight gain, nausea, constipation, and headache. May have the lowest risk of extrapyramidal side effects of all atypical antipsychotics.

  - **Precautions:** Those with liver disease or seizure disorders should take special care with this drug. It can cause hypotension upon standing rapidly.

✔ **Geodon:** Like Seroquel, Geodon is new on the market and almost no research backs it in terms of treatment for anxiety problems. Again, it may have significant potential, which future studies will determine.

  - **Side Effects:** Common side effects include nausea, constipation, anorexia, insomnia, agitation, and headache. It may have a lower risk of extrapyramidal symptoms, such as muscle stiffness, involuntary movements, shuffling gait, and so on, than risperdal. It appears to also have a reduced tendency to cause weight gain.

  - **Precautions:** Special care should be taken for those with kidney or liver disease. May increase the sedative effects of alcohol and other central nervous system depressants.

Mood stabilizers and miscellaneous

These medications are usually prescribed for other conditions. However, when standard treatments haven't worked, doctors sometimes find them useful for their patients' anxiety. One such type of medication is generally employed for the treatment of seizures. Specific drugs in this category include Depakote and Neurontin.

Finally, Clonidine is a medication usually used to treat hypertension by relaxing the blood vessels. It seems to ease some symptoms of Post-Traumatic Stress Disorder, especially in children. Serious side effects have been reported, however.

Who's who in the prescribing world?

Physicians, psychiatrists, and psychologists — who's who? Most people find the distinctions between these healthcare professionals confusing.

- Physicians graduate from college and then complete four years of medical school followed by a minimum of one year of postgraduate training, often followed by a multi-year residency in their specialty. They receive relatively little training in the diagnosis of emotional and mental disorders, such as anxiety.

- Psychiatrists are trained as physicians first. They usually follow medical school with an additional four years of residency training in psychiatry, where they study the diagnosis and treatment of emotional and mental disorders. Psychiatrists are also highly trained experts in psychotropic medications.

- Psychologists graduate from college and usually complete a minimum of five years of psychology graduate school with training in the science of human behavior and the treatment and diagnosis of emotional and mental disorders. Following graduate school, psychologists complete a minimum of one to two years of post-doctoral fellowship training prior to eligibility for licensure.

Although family physicians prescribe the majority of psychotropic medications, many of them are uncomfortable doing so when dealing with complex emotional issues. Psychiatrists spend most of their time studying and prescribing psychotropic medications and should probably be consulted if medication issues are at all complicated. Psychologists generally provide psychotherapy and use psychological tests to aid in diagnosis and treatment planning.

A current controversy brews over prescription privileges. In New Mexico and the armed services, psychologists who choose to take additional training are allowed to prescribe psychotropic medication. Legislation is pending in a variety of other states to give prescription privileges to psychologists who undertake additional training.

Chapter 16

Mindful Acceptance

● ●

● ●

Has your car ever been stuck on a muddy road? What happens if you gun the accelerator harder when the wheels start to spin? They spin even harder, the mud flies everywhere, and the rut gets deeper. Anxiety can be like that: The harder that you try to break free, the tighter it seems to grip.

Then you have a flash of insight. You allow the car to rock back into the rut, and you gently accelerate at the right moment. You may feel the wheels start to spin again, but when they do, you back off once more. Eventually, you find a rhythm that lifts your wheels onto more solid ground — until the next rut down the road. But at least you get somewhere, and you do it by *accepting* the idea of going backward for a while.

In this chapter, we explain how to use *acceptance* as one way to get out of your anxiety trap. Threads of what we call *mindful* acceptance show up throughout this book. In this chapter, we weave the threads together to form a tapestry. We show you that acceptance helps you to stop spinning your wheels so that you can calmly consider productive alternatives. We discuss how too much concern with ego and self-esteem can make seeing the way out difficult, and we explain how living in the present provides a stairway to a more balanced life.

Accepting Anxiety? Hey, That's a Switch!

So how come after showing you how to get rid of your anxiety, we tell you to mindfully accept it? Have *we* lost our minds? Isn't this book supposed to be about *overcoming* anxiety?

Well, yes of course, we want you to overcome your anxiety. But the paradox of anxiety is that the more you feel that you must rid yourself of it, the more anxious you feel. The more that your anxiety disturbs you, the more it will ensnare you.

Perhaps you went to a carnival or birthday party where someone gave you a Chinese handcuff — a little, decorative, woven straw tube. You put both index fingers into the tube. Then you try to extract your fingers. The tube closes tightly around your fingers. The harder you pull, the tighter the handcuffs squeeze; a way out doesn't seem to exist. So you pull even harder Eventually, you realize that the only way out is to quit trying.

Anxiety mimics the squeezing of Chinese handcuffs. The more that you struggle, the more trapped you feel. Insisting that your anxiety go away this second is a sure-fire way of increasing it!

Taking a dispassionate view

Anthropologists study the behavior and culture of human beings. They make their observations objectively from a dispassionate, scientific perspective. We want you to view your anxiety like an anthropologist — coolly detached.

Wait for the next time that you feel anxious. Study your anxiety and all that goes with it and prepare a report that conveys what anxiety feels like in your body, how it affects your thoughts, and what it does to your actions. Don't judge the anxiety — just observe it. Then, being as objective as possible, answer the following questions for your report:

✔ Where in my body do I feel tension? In my shoulders, back, jaw, hands, or neck? Study it and describe how the tension feels.

✔ Are my hands sweating?

✔ Is my heart racing? If so, how fast?

✔ Do I feel tightness in my chest or throat?

✔ Do I feel dizzy? Study the dizziness and describe it.

✔ What am I thinking? Am I . . .

- Making negative predictions about the future?

- Making a mountain out of a molehill?

- Turning an unpleasant event into a catastrophe?

- Upset about something that's outside of my control?

✔ What is my anxiety telling me to do?

- To avoid doing something that I want to do?

- That I need to be perfect?

- That I have to cover up my anxiety?

Mel's story that follows provides a good example of how your powers of observation may help you to get a handle on your anxious feelings:

Mel, a 38-year-old hospital administrator, experienced his first panic attack three years ago. Over those three years, his attacks increased in frequency and intensity, and he even started to miss work on days when he feared having to lead staff meetings.

Now, he works with a therapist to decrease his panic. The therapist notices that Mel's perfectionism drives him to demand instant improvement. He reads everything assigned and tries to do every task — perfectly. The therapist, realizing that Mel needs to slow down and back up, gives him an assignment. Thus, Mel, pretending that he's an anthropologist on a mission, writes a report about anxiety as follows:

I started noticing a little shortness of breath. I thought: It's starting again! Then my heart began to race. I noticed it was fast but not quite as fast as when I exercise. I wondered how long it would last. Then I noticed that my hands were sweating. I felt a little nauseous. I didn't want to go to work. I could almost hear the anxiety telling me that I would feel much better if I stayed home because if I went to work, I'd have to talk to a room full of upset surgeons. I have to tell them about the new call procedures. They're not going to like it. They'll probably rip me to shreds. What an interesting image. I've never really been ripped into shreds, but my image is amazing! If I get too anxious, my words will turn into nonsense, and I'll look like a total fool. This is interesting, too. I'm making incredibly negative predictions about the future. It's funny, as I say that, I feel just a tiny bit less anxious.

Mel discovered that letting go and merely observing his anxiety helped. Rather than attack his anxious feelings and thoughts, he watched and pondered about his experience by really trying to emulate the sense of scientific curiosity of anthropologists.

Oh, mercy, mercy, me!

Tune into your mind's internal chatter. If you're like most people with anxiety, your chatter too often consists of a slew of negative verbiage, such as some examples of mind chatter that follow:

- ✔ I'll never get it done on time.
- ✔ I'll look like a fool.
- ✔ I can't stay in control.
- ✔ I'm going to screw up.
- ✔ I might vomit.
- ✔ What if I have to run out of the room screaming?
- ✔ I hate myself.
- ✔ I'm a terrible parent.
- ✔ Nobody will like me.
- ✔ I think I'm stupid.
- ✔ Any minute now, they'll all find out what a phony I am.
- ✔ If people really knew me, they wouldn't like me.

Now, look at those statements and try changing the word *I* or *me* to *you* and change *I'll* to *you'll.* Say them out loud as though you're talking to someone whom you know well, perhaps a friend. Can you really imagine telling a friend?

- ✔ You'll look like a fool.
- ✔ You're a terrible parent.
- ✔ Nobody will like you.
- ✔ I hate you.

It's doubtful. The odds are that you'd never say anything like this to a friend or, for that matter, to a mere acquaintance, and yet that's what many people say to themselves time and time again.

It's as though a judge is sitting in your mind, but this judge has no mercy and no compassion. This judge evaluates every flaw or shortcoming and ignores mitigating circumstances.

Listen to your mind chattering away. When you hear the judge, try substituting with a more compassionate, self-forgiving approach. Be a friend to yourself.

Tolerating uncertainty

Anxious people usually detest uncertainty. If only they could control everything around them, they might not worry so much, and that's probably true; if you could control everything, you wouldn't have much cause for worry, would you?

The rather obvious flaw in this approach lies in the fact that life consists of constant uncertainty and a degree of chaos. In fact, a fundamental law of physics states that, even in so-called hard sciences, absolute certainty is nonexistent. Accidents and unforeseen events happen.

For example, you don't know the day and time that your car will break down on the way to work. You can't predict the stock market although many try. Bad things happen to good people all the time. Even if you spent every moment of your waking life trying to prevent illness, financial difficulties, and loss of loved ones, you couldn't do it.

Not only is the task of preventing calamities impossible, you can easily ruin most of your present moments if you try. Think about it. If you check your car's engine before leaving for work each day, if you scrimp and save every possible penny for retirement, if you never eat ice cream because of the fat content, if you overprotect your children because you worry that they'll get into trouble, if you wash your hands every time that you touch a door knob, if you never take a risk, then what would your life be like? Probably not much fun.

And worry doesn't change what will happen. Some people think that if they worry enough, bad things won't occur. Because bad things don't happen to them on most of those worry days, they feel like their worrying has paid off. But worry by itself has never in the history of humans prevented anything from happening. Not once.

Find out how to embrace uncertainty, which can make life both interesting and exciting. Discover how to appreciate adversity as well as a little suffering. Without some suffering and adversity, you fail to value the good moments.

When you find yourself feeling anxious, ask yourself if your worry concerns an attempt to control the unpredictable. For example, many people worry about their retirement funds in the stock market. They watch how their stocks are doing every single day. They scan the newspaper for financial information that might possibly help them know when to sell at just the right moment.

Now, we're certainly not trying to give you financial advice. Others far more knowledgeable than us can do that for you. However, we do know that most studies indicate that precise attempts to predict the stock market are doomed to fail. Yes, put enough money away for retirement and put a portion of that in the stock market if you can tolerate a little risk, but the stress and anxiety that you sustain if you obsess on a daily basis about your money can harm your health and do little to increase your wealth.

Let go of your need to predict and control. Of course, take reasonable precautions about your health, family, finances, and well-being, but when worry about the future invades the present enjoyment of your life, it has gone too far. Appreciate uncertainty and live well today.

Patience is a virtue

When you think about patience, what comes to mind? Calm, acceptance, and tolerance. When you become anxious, try to be patient and kind with yourself and say to yourself

- ✔ Okay, I'm feeling anxious. That's my experience.
- ✔ Like other feelings, anxiety comes and goes.
- ✔ Let me be present with my anxiety.

In the story of Jeanine that follows, Jeanine's contrasting reactions, first with impatience and then with patience, provides an example of how you too can turn your impatience into patience.

Jeanine begins to feel anxious during the morning commute. She leaves home at 7:15 a.m. and usually can count on being to work on time at 8 a.m. Frequently, she arrives about five minutes early, but once a month or so, traffic backs up, and she's a few minutes late. This morning appears to be one of those.

- ✔ **The impatient Jeanine:** Traffic is at a standstill, and anxiety churns in Jeanine's stomach and builds up like a musical crescendo. Sweating and clutching the steering wheel, she begins tracking the ways that she can change lanes and get through a bit faster. She hates starting her day out like this. She can't stand the anxiety and tries to get rid of it, but she fails. She visualizes her boss noticing her tardiness and the others at her office looking up at her. Anxiety turns to anger as she berates herself for not leaving earlier.

> ✔ **The patient Jeanine:** Traffic is at a standstill, and anxiety churns in Jeanine's stomach. Clutching the steering wheel, she fights the urge to change lanes. She notices and accepts the anxiety in her body, thinking, "I may be late, but most every morning, I am on time or early. My boss and coworkers know that. I can feel my anxiety, but that's my experience. How interesting. I'll arrive a few minutes late this morning, and that's okay."

In the second scenario, the anxiety dissipates because Jeanine allowed herself to feel it without judgment or intolerance. She connected to her present situation with patience.

Like everything else, making patience a habit takes practice. You build your tolerance for patience over time. Like building muscles by lifting weights, you can build the patience muscles in your mind a little at a time.

Reaching serenity or at least getting closer

Accepting anxiety involves a variety of related attitudes — being nonjudgmental, tolerating uncertainty, letting go of the need for absolute control, and patience. Realize that acceptance isn't the same as resignation — total surrender.

On the other hand, acceptance simply means appreciating that you, as well as all humans have strengths and limitations. You realize that you'll never completely rid yourself of anxiety. Rather, over time, you figure out how to deal with it and give up being anxious about your anxiety. Only then, will it stop overwhelming and dominating your life. The Serenity Prayer captures the spirit of acceptance nicely:

> God, grant me the serenity
>
> to accept the things I cannot change,
>
> courage to change the things I can,
>
> and the wisdom to know the difference.
>
> Living one day at a time;
>
> enjoying one moment at a time;
>
> accepting hardship as the pathway to peace.
>
> Taking, as He did, this sinful world as it is,
>
> not as I would have it.

Trusting that He will make all things right

if I surrender to His Will;

that I may be reasonably happy in this life,

and supremely happy with Him forever in the next.

— Reinhold Neibuhr, 1926

Letting Go of Ego

Everyone wants to have high self-esteem. Bookstores and libraries display hundreds of books about how to pump up your self-esteem. You may think that having high self-esteem would decrease your anxiety. It seems logical anyway.

However, self-esteem doesn't work that way. In fact, overly positive self-esteem causes more anxiety, as well as a host of other ills. Similarly, most positive human characteristics and qualities turn into negatives when they reach extreme levels. For example, courage, generosity, hardworking, and trust all are wonderful traits. But, excessive courage can make a person reckless, excessive generosity can make a person an easy mark for the unscrupulous, excessive focus on work can leave insufficient room for pleasure, and excessive trust can turn someone into a dupe. Perhaps our description of self-esteem as similar to a balloon may help you understand the shocking dangers of too much investment in ego and self-esteem.

Inflating and deflating the self-esteem balloon

We think of self-esteem like a balloon. Too little self-esteem is like an empty balloon. It has no air; it's flat, deflated, and can't float. Therefore, a deflated balloon isn't especially fun or useful. If your self-esteem is quite low, you probably spend time judging yourself harshly and negatively. Your energy probably suffers, and you may feel quite anxious about your perceived deficiencies.

Too much ego and self-esteem, however, is like a balloon that's tightly stretched and so full of air that it's about to explode. One tiny scrape, and the balloon bursts. People with too much self-esteem worry constantly about those scrapes. Any threat to their self-esteem causes considerable anxiety and sometimes anger. You can't do much in life without running into at least some threat to your ego. If your self-esteem balloon is too full of itself, those threats can appear especially ominous.

On the other hand, a balloon with just the right amount of air is pretty tough to break. It can bounce around easily, joyfully, and playfully. The balloon with the right amount of air doesn't worry so much about crashing or bursting.

In a sense, both the deflated balloon and the one close to the bursting point, worry plenty about their own state — their condition, worth, and vulnerability. The key to having just the right amount of ego — air in the balloon — is to have *less* concern with yourself (along with more concern for others) and less worry about how you stack up against others. When you can accept both your positive and negative qualities without being overly concerned for either, you'll have the right amount of air in your ego balloon, but that isn't always so easy to do. It takes a solid focus on learning, striving, and working hard, though not to excess.

It's not easy being green

All too often, anxious people feel that they must be perfect in order for others to like and accept them. No wonder they feel anxious. Nobody's perfect, and no one ever will be.

The seductive power of positive thinking

Since the 1950's, self-help gurus began a movement by encouraging everyone to pump up their self-esteem. Before 1950, less than a hundred articles were written on the topic of self-esteem in professional journals, however, in the past ten years alone, over 8,000 such articles appeared in social science journals. In addition, literally thousands of self-help books have promoted the unquestioned value of nurturing self-esteem. The self-esteem movement now permeates parenting magazines, school curriculums, and bookshelves. It seduced a generation of parents, teachers, and mental health workers into believing that the best thing that they could do for kids is to pump up their self-esteem.

So has more than a half-century of promoting self-esteem (also known as *ego*) paid off?

Hardly. Today, school achievement lags significantly behind where it was in 1960. School grades, however, are up. School violence is much higher than 50 years ago, and the rates of depression and anxiety among today's youth are higher than ever.

Why? An incredible number of recent research studies show a strong link between the over-abundant focus on the self and violence, poor school achievement, and emotional problems of all sorts. Deflated self-esteem also appears to be bad for you, and studies suggest that an overly inflated self-esteem is even worse. The answer appears to lie in having less focus on the almighty self.

Imagine a perfect woman. **Kelly** is perhaps as close to perfect as you can find. Kelly always wears exactly the right clothes — in fashion, the right colors, and her accessories match. She takes classes in interior design so that her house has just the right look. She exercises four times a week and eats only healthy foods. Her makeup, which she applies with punctilious care, appears flawless. She always knows just what to say, never stumbling over a single word or swearing. She always exhibits kindness and has a positive outlook.

Would you like to go out and have a beer with Kelly? Does she seem like someone you'd like to hang out at a pool with on a summer weekend? Would you feel easy and natural around Kelly? Frankly, we'd probably pass on the idea of having her as one of our best friends.

Think about one of your good friends — you like to spend time with, someone you enjoy and value, and someone you've known for a while. Picture that person in your mind and recall some of the good times that you spent together. Let yourself enjoy those images. Think about how much you appreciate this person and how your life has been enriched by the relationship.

Realize that you've always known about your friend's negative qualities and imperfections, yet you've continued to appreciate your friend. Perhaps you even find some of the flaws amusing or interesting. Maybe they give your friend color. Thinking about the flaws isn't likely to change your opinion or feelings either.

Try applying the same perspective to yourself. Appreciate your little flaws, foibles, and quirks. They make you interesting and unique.

Be a friend to yourself. Notice your gifts and your imperfections. Figure out how to acknowledge it all as one package. Don't disown your flaws.

Curtis tried an exercise that helped him to see that flaws don't cause people to disown you and walk away. Curtis filled in the Appreciating Flawed Friends exercise in Table 16-1when he thought about his buddy Jack. In each column, he wrote about Jack's qualities and imperfections.

Table 16-1	**Appreciating Flawed Friends**	
Positive Qualities	*Negative Qualities*	*Imperfections*
Jack is one of the funniest guys I know.		
He's always there for me.		
Jack will help me anytime I need it, no matter what.		

Positive Qualities	Negative Qualities	Imperfections
I like going to sporting events with him.		
I like the fact that Jack is really smart.	Sometimes Jack talks too much.	
	Even though he's smart, sometimes Jack makes stupid decisions, especially about money.	
		Jack's a little overweight.
		Sometimes Jack drinks a little too much.
		He doesn't always listen to me.
		Jack has terrible taste in clothes.

Curtis accepts Jack, flaws and all. There's no one that Curtis would rather spend time with, and Jack is the first person he would turn to in a crisis. Can Curtis accept himself like he does Jack? That's the task at hand.

Pull out some paper and do what Curtis did. Think of a good friend you've known a while and write down what you like and enjoy about her. Then list what about that person can put you off. Finally, write down her flaws.

If your friend filled out the same form on you, no doubt she would write about both wonderful qualities and some less-than-wonderful traits. And yet, your friend wouldn't suddenly give up the friendship because of your imperfection. Of course not; nobody is perfect. If we all gave up on our imperfect friends, we would have no friends at all.

Did you ever get a speeding ticket in your life? Six months ago, one of us came home with a speeding ticket. Just two months later, the other co-author came home with one too. Both of us started to get down on ourselves at first, but we were perfectly forgiving of the other. We quickly realized the importance of giving ourselves the same compassion that we gave to each other.

Self-forgiveness is difficult. Perhaps even more difficult is finding out how to drop defensive barriers in response to criticism from others. Figure out how to listen to criticism. Consider the fact that it may at least have an element of truth. Appreciate that portion of truth. If your spouse says that you don't listen, it's rather likely that your spouse's criticism is absolutely true, at least at times!

Try acknowledging any sliver of truth that criticism contains. Perhaps it's true *sometimes*. Perhaps the criticism is partially applicable. Instead of putting up barriers to communication and problem solving, admitting to some flaws brings people closer.

Some criticism that comes your way could be abusive. If the tone conveys hostility, you don't need to put up with it. If someone is constantly haranguing you with criticism, ask a trusted friend for a reality check. You may be the victim of verbal abuse. That's a different matter entirely.

Connecting with the Real Thing

In some ways, language represents the pinnacle of evolutionary development. Language makes us human, gives us art, allows us to express complex ideas, and provides us with the tools for creating solutions to problems. At the same time, language lays the foundation for much of our emotional distress. How could that be?

You may think that dogs don't get anxious, but they do. But only when in direct contact with experiences that cause them pain or discomfort. For example, dogs rarely enjoy going to the vet. More than a few dog owners have had to drag their dogs into the veterinarian's door by pulling on the leash with all their might.

However, humans do what dogs would never do. Humans wake up dreading the events of the day that lie ahead. Dogs don't wake up at 3:00 a.m. and think, "Oh no! Is today the day that I have to go to the vet? What will happen to me there?"

And dogs have few regrets. Oh sure, they sometimes look pretty guilty when caught chewing on their master's shoe. But one kind word and a pat on the head, and they've forgotten all about it. Some anxious people still remember the thank you note that they forgot to write to Aunt Betty six years ago.

Generally speaking, dogs seem much happier than most of us humans. Unless a dog has been horribly abused, it usually carries on with contentment, joy, and of course, quite a bit of sleeping. By contrast, humans worry a lot; they obsess over imagined horrors down the road, and they dwell on their past transgressions.

When you bring possible future catastrophes as well as past regrets into the present, you're essentially using language to disconnect you from real-life experience. Doing so can absolutely ruin your *present moments* — the time that you actually *live* your entire life! Consider the following example of Reggie, who dreaded the amount of work that he believed that he had to finish within five days down the road.

Reggie, a criminal defense attorney, has a solo practice. An important trial is coming up in five days. The amount of work in front of him almost chokes him with fear. Of course, he agonizes over the possibility of putting on a less-than-stellar performance, but most of all, he is concerned about the heavy preparation of papers, briefs, depositions, and petitions that must be completed, and soon. He knows that he'll be working from dawn to dusk with barely enough time to breathe. The funny thing about it though is that after the ordeal was over, he realized that most of those five days turned out to be fairly enjoyable. He worried over the possibility of not completing his tasks, which had nothing to do with any of the actual work that he performed. Most of that felt pretty good. Not a single, individual moment felt *horrible* by itself.

The next time that you obsess over future or past events, tasks, or outcomes, consider trying to do the following:

✔ Stay focused on each moment at a time as it comes to you.

✔ Spend a few minutes noticing all the sensations in your body at the moment — touch, smell, sights, and sounds.

✔ When thoughts about the tasks ahead enter your mind, simply acknowledge the presence of those thoughts and move your attention back to the present.

✔ If thoughts about past failures or regrets enter your mind, notice the presence of those thoughts and move your attention back to the present.

✔ Remind yourself that *thoughts* don't reflect reality and experience; they're only *thoughts.*

✔ When you notice disturbing thoughts about the future or the past, try just observing them, notice how interesting it is that your mind spins thoughts like these out, and return to the present moment.

✔ Remember: Few present moments truly feel unbearable. It's simply our ability to ruin the present with thoughts about the future or past that disturbs us.

✔ Consider re-reading Chapter 5 about how distorted thoughts can be and work on making them more realistic. Then go back to the present again.

In Chapter 5, we explained how to carefully analyze the way that anxiety can cause you to make negative, distorted predictions. Then we showed you ways of making more accurate predictions. Nevertheless, that approach can only take you so far. No matter how hard you work at it, you're likely to find negative predictions spinning out of your head every now and then. When they do in spite of your best efforts to rethink them with more accurate predictions, try to go over our preceding list. It can help you tune the negative chatter out.

We have another idea for you to quit listening to that occasional stream of worries about future events.

1. Think about how many times you've made negative forecasts in the past about some pending event.

2. Then ask yourself how often those forecasts have proven true. If you're not sure, keep a log on your negative predictions and see what percentage pans out.

3. Of those forecasts that do come true, how often is it as bad as you anticipated? If you're not sure how often, keep a log for a while.

Most people tell us that at least 90 percent of what they worry about never happens. Of those worrisome events that do occur, less than 10 percent are as bad as they anticipated. That's an overabundance of worry and ruined present moments just to anticipate a few unpleasant occurrences.

Taking these predictions seriously is rather like listening to a weather reporter on the television who tells you that blizzards, severe cold, and ice storms are forecasted for each day. So you dutifully don a heavy coat, gloves, and boots. Just one problem nags you, however. Ninety percent of the time, the reporter is absolutely wrong, and the weather is sunny and warm. When the reporter gets it almost right, rarely are conditions as bad as described. Perhaps it's time to stop listening to the weather reporter in your head. You can't turn the station off, but you can at least take the reports less seriously!

Making contact with the present

At this very moment, consider coming into direct contact with experience. This is something many people have rarely done. Have no expectations about what this exercise is *supposed* to do. Just study what happens.

1. Notice how this book feels in your hands. Feel the smooth cover and the edges of the pages.

2. Notice how your body feels — whether you're sitting, standing in a subway, riding a bus, or lying in bed. Feel the sensations in your skin

as it makes contact with the chair, the bed, the floor if you're standing, and so on.

3. Feel the muscles in your legs, your back, and your hands and arms as you hold the book.

4. Notice your breathing. Feel the air go in and out of your nostrils.

5. Notice any smells — whether pleasant or unpleasant. Think about how you could write a report about these smells.

6. If thoughts invade your mind, notice those also. Do not judge them. Then return to noticing all your present sensations.

7. Hear any sounds around you. If you hear loud, obnoxious sounds, try *not* to judge them. Instead of thinking about how jarring they sound, study the nuances in the sounds. Imagine how you would describe these sounds to a friend.

8. Again, if judgments enter your mind, observe how your mind spins these out like a reflex. Make no judgments about these thoughts or yourself.

9. Go back to focusing on the entire array of present-moment sensations.

Now, notice how you feel at the end of this exercise. Did you experience the sensations fully? What happened to your anxiety? Many people report that they feel little, if any anxiety during this experience. Others say their anxiety escalates.

If your anxiety increases during your first few attempts to connect with present-moment experience, don't worry. It happens for various reasons. Increased anxiety doesn't mean that you're doing something wrong. More than likely:

✔ You may have little experience connecting to the present. Therefore, it feels strange.

✔ Anxious thoughts may interrupt you frequently. If so, more practice may help to reduce their potency.

✔ You may be facing such an overwhelming stressor right now that putting this strategy into effect is unrealistic. If so, you may want to try other strategies in the book first.

Whatever the case, we recommend practicing frequent connection with present-moment experience.

Most anxiety and distress come from thoughts about the future or the past, not what's happening at this moment.

Mindfully noticing and enjoying life

Above and beyond reducing anxiety, mindful acceptance can improve the quality of your life. When you're anxious, so much of your mental energy focuses on negative sensations, thoughts, and images, that you miss much of life's simple pleasures.

Mindful eating

How many times have you eaten a meal and barely tasted it? Of course, if it tastes like microwaved cardboard, perhaps that's a good thing. However, most of the foods that we eat taste pretty good. What a shame to miss out on the full experience.

Choose a time to practice mindful eating. Be sure it's not a ten-minute lunch. But it doesn't require hours either. Worrisome thoughts may sometimes distract you. That's fine and normal. However, try merely noticing them. Rather than judge those thoughts or yourself, return your focus to your eating when you can as in the following exercise:

1. Slow down and focus before taking a bite.

2. Look at your food.

3. Notice how it's displayed on your plate or bowl.

4. Observe the food's colors, textures, and shapes.

5. Take time to smell the aroma.

6. Put a small portion on your fork or spoon.

7. Before you take a bite, hold it briefly under your nose.

8. Briefly put the food on your lips and then on the tip of your tongue.

9. Put the food in your mouth, but don't bite down for a moment or two.

10. Chew very slowly.

11. Notice how the taste and texture change with each bite.

12. Notice how the food tastes on different parts of your tongue.

13. Swallow the bite and notice how it feels sliding down your throat.

14. Follow this procedure throughout your meal.

15. Stay seated at the table with your meal for at least 20 minutes. If you finish eating before the 20 minutes is up, continue sitting until the full 20 minutes has elapsed and notice your surroundings and the sensations in your body.

Consider making mindful eating a regular part of your life. You'll feel calmer, enjoy your food more, and possibly even lose a little weight. Many weight loss programs suggest slowing your eating down. However, this approach does more — it enables you to fully experience your food. When your mind totally focuses on the present pleasure of eating, anxiety fades away.

Mindful walking

Look around at people walking to their various destinations. So often they rush frenziedly about like hamsters on an exercise wheel, not even aware of their surroundings. Rushing people, unlike hamsters, don't enjoy the exercise — rather, their minds fill with anxious anticipations and worries. It's a small wonder that we have an epidemic of high blood pressure these days.

We have an alternative for you to consider. Mindful walking. You've probably tried taking a walk sometime when you felt especially stressed. It probably helped. However, mindful walking can help you more. Do it this way:

1. Pause before you start.

2. Notice the feeling of air going in and out of your nose and lungs. Breathe quietly for five breaths.

3. Begin walking.

4. Notice the sensations in your leg muscles — your ankles, calves, and thighs. Spend a minute or two focusing only on these muscles and how they feel.

5. If troubling thoughts intrude, simply notice them. Watch them like clouds floating overhead. Do not judge them. When you can, refocus on your muscles.

6. Now, feel the bottom of your feet as they strike the ground. Try to notice how the heel hits first, then the foot rolls, and then you push off with the ball of your foot and toes. Concentrate on the bottom of your feet for a minute or two.

7. Bring yourself back to the present if troubling thoughts intrude.

8. Now, focus on the rhythm of your walking. Feel the pace of your legs and the swing of your arms. Stay with the rhythm for a minute or two and enjoy it.

9. Feel the air flowing into your nose and lungs. Then exhaling the air, take notice of the rhythm of your breathing. Focus on nothing else for a minute or two.

10. Now take heed of your feet, muscles, rhythm, and your breathing, shifting your attention from one to the other as you wish.

11. Practice meditation while walking for five minutes, five days in a row. Then consider if you want to make it a regular part of your life.

Enthusiasts extol the virtues of mindful walking. They claim it helps them reduce stress and become more serene. You can experiment with mindful walking in various ways. For example, try focusing on sights and sounds or focus on the smells as you encounter them. Play with this strategy and develop your own approach. Being mindful doesn't have a right or a wrong way.

Accepting Mindfulness into Your Life

Some people read about mindfulness and worry about the time it can consume. They say that it sounds like living life in slow motion and complain that nothing can ever get done if they try living that way. As much as we think that living a little slower isn't a bad idea for many people, mindful acceptance doesn't require significant chunks of time.

More than time, mindfulness entails a shift in philosophy that decreases the focus on ego, pride, and control, while emphasizing accepting the present with all its gifts and challenges. Being mindful requires humility because it acknowledges the uncertainty that's inherent within life.

Making mindful acceptance a habit doesn't happen overnight. With practice, allow it to evolve slowly into your life. Accept that you won't always stay in the present. Don't judge your attempts to live mindfully. When you see yourself living in the guilt-ridden past or anxious future, gently remind yourself to come back to the present.

Part V
Helping Others with Anxiety

The 5th Wave   By Rich Tennant

"I've tried thought remedies, meditation and breathing techniques, but nothing seems to work. I'm still feeling anxious and disoriented all day long."

In this part . . .

We reveal that today's kids appear more anxious than ever before. Kids are anxious about both real and imagined fears. We help you distinguish between normal and abnormal childhood fears. Then you discover how to prevent your children from developing abnormal fears and what you need to do if they already have too much anxiety.

The final chapter in this part details what you can do when someone you care about has anxiety and worry. First, we help you find out if your loved one suffers from anxiety, and then we show you how to talk about it. Finally, we provide strategies for working together on the problem.

Chapter 17

Helping Your Kids Fight Anxiety

• •

In This Chapter

▶ When to worry about your kids' anxiety

▶ Uncovering the usual anxieties of childhood

▶ Discovering the risk factors for childhood anxiety

▶ Alleviating your child's anxiety

• •

Childhood anxiety has grown to epidemic proportions during the past 40 to 50 years. Numerous studies confirm this alarming development, but one in particular is a shocker. Psychologist Jean Twenge compared symptoms of anxiety in today's kids with symptoms in seriously disturbed kids receiving hospital treatment in 1957. She reported in the *Journal of Personality and Social Psychology* (December 2000) that boys and girls today report a greater number of anxiety symptoms than psychiatric inpatient children in 1957.

Should these findings cause alarm? We think so. The statistics are bad enough in their own right, but when you consider the fact that anxiety disorders often precede the development of depression later on, it raises concerns that the consequences of childhood anxiety could worsen in the years to come.

In this chapter, you discover the difference between normal and problematic anxiety in kids. We explain that some childhood fears are completely normal, while others require intervention. In some cases, that means getting professional help. Whether you need a professional or not, we show you a number of procedures and activities that you can engage your children in to help them deal more effectively with their anxieties. Doing so may prevent more serious, long-term problems.

Separating Normal from Abnormal

So what's going on? Why do our children experience emotional turmoil? Of course, we all know the complexities and tensions of the world today — longer work hours, rapidly developing technologies, violence on television, and even terrorism. We also suspect that certain types of parenting hold partial responsibility, as we discuss in the "Parenting precautions" section, later in this chapter.

For the moment, what you as a parent need to know is how to distinguish the normal anxieties of childhood from abnormal suffering. Realize that the vast majority of kids feel anxious at various times to one degree or another. After all, one of the primary tasks of childhood is to figure out how to overcome the fears that life creates for everyone. Successful resolution of those fears usually results in good emotional adjustment. You just need to know whether your children's fears represent normal development or a more sinister frame of mind that requires help. Look at Table 17-1 to get an idea of the anxiety that you can expect your children to experience at one time or another during their youth.

Table 17-1	Does Your Child Have an Anxiety Problem?	
Anxiety Problem	*When Anxiety is Normal*	*When Anxiety Should Go Away*
Fear of separation from mother, father, or caregiver.	Common at ages 6–24 months. Don't worry!	If this continues with no improvement after 36–48 months, then you have some cause for concern.
Fear of unfamiliar adults.	Common from 6–10 months.	Don't be too concerned unless you see this after 2–3 years of age. And don't worry about a little shyness after that.
Fear of unfamiliar peers.	Common at ages 2–30 months.	If this continues without showing signs of reducing after 36 months, you have some cause for concern.
Fear of animals, darkness, and imaginary creatures.	Common between ages 2–6 years.	If these fears don't start to decline by 6 years of age, you have cause for concern. Many kids want a nightlight for a while; don't worry unless it's excessive.
School phobia.	Mild to moderate school or day care phobia is common from ages 3–6; it can briefly reappear when moving from elementary to middle school.	This should decline and cause no more than minimal problems after age 6. A brief reemergence at middle school is okay, but it should quell quickly. If not, it's a concern.

Anxiety Problem	When Anxiety is Normal	When Anxiety Should Go Away
Fear of evaluation by others.	This fear almost defines adolescence. Most teens worry a fair amount about what others think of them.	It should gradually reduce as adolescence unfolds.

Table 17-1 gives you some general guidelines about so-called normal childhood fears. However, independent of age, if fears seem especially serious and/or interfere with your child's life or schoolwork in a major way, they may be problematic and warrant attention. In addition, other anxiety problems in the "Inspecting the Most Common Childhood Anxiety Disorders" section, later in this chapter, such as Obsessive-Compulsive Disorder, panic attack, or generalized, excessive worrying about a wide variety of fears, are not particularly *normal* at any age.

If you have any doubts about the seriousness of your children's anxiety, you should consider a professional consultation. A mental health counselor or your pediatrician should be well equipped to handle your questions, quite possibly in a single visit. Anxiety problems sometimes predate other emotional difficulties, so you shouldn't wait to get them checked out.

Tyler's troubles

Julie doesn't know what to do about her 7-year-old son, **Tyler.** Every day, she battles with him about going to school. At first, she thinks he's really sick, so she takes him to the pediatrician. After a complete physical, the doctor reassures her that Tyler is healthy. The doctor encourages Julie to send Tyler to school and warns that if she doesn't, Tyler's behavior is likely to escalate.

"My stomach hurts," whines Tyler, "I don't want to go to school."

"Now sweetie, you've missed so many days," soothes Julie, "you really should go today; you're not that sick."

"But my stomach really hurts; it really, really does Mommy." Tyler begins to sob.

"You will go to school today," Julie says firmly, grabbing Tyler by the hand. Tyler plants his feet and pulls away, screaming. Julie can't believe what he's doing. He actually seems terrified; Julie's never seen him behave this way. Frantically, Tyler runs to his bedroom and hides in his closet. Julie finds him huddled, sobbing.

Tyler suffers from school phobia, a common but serious childhood anxiety disorder. Wisely, Julie decides to seek further professional help.

Inspecting the Most Common Childhood Anxiety Disorders

Some fear and anxiety are normal for kids. You can probably remember being afraid of the dark, monsters, or ghosts. However, other types of anxiety, while not always rare, do indicate a problem that you should address. We briefly review the more common types of problematic anxiety in kids in the following sections. Then we tell you about the primary risk factors lying behind these anxieties and most importantly, what you can do about them.

Leaving parents: Separation Anxiety Disorder

As we showed in Table 17-1 in the preceding section, kids frequently worry about separations from their parents when they're as young as 6 months to perhaps as old as 4 years of age. However, significant fear of separation past about the age of 4, accompanied by the following, warrants intervention:

- ✔ Excessive distress when separated from caregivers or anticipating such separation

- ✔ Exorbitant worry about harm to parents or caregivers

- ✔ Obstinate avoidance of school or other activities due to worries about separation

- ✔ Refusal to go to bed without being near a parent or caregiver

- ✔ Frequent nightmares about separation

- ✔ Frequent physical complaints, such as headaches, stomachaches, and so on, when separated from parents

Among the various anxiety disorders, Separation Anxiety Disorder (SAD) is relatively common in kids, but that doesn't mean it's normal. The average age it seems to start is around 7 to 8 years of age. The good news is that a large percentage of those with Separation Anxiety Disorder no longer fulfill the diagnostic criteria for the disorder after three or four years.

The bad news is that quite a few of these kids go on to develop other problems, especially depression. It's for that reason that we suggest prompt intervention if it persists longer than a month or two and interferes with normal life.

Getting back to school

School phobia is a relatively common separation anxiety in childhood. The treatment for School Phobia involves getting the child back to school as soon as possible. Children with school phobia often have parents who are slightly anxious themselves and care deeply about their kids. The first step is to convince the parents that they must be firm in their commitment to return the child to school.

A good way to calm the child and get him back to school is to give the child just enough change to place a phone call to the parent. The parent carries a pager. With agreement from the child's teacher, the child receives a get-out-of-class pass that allows one page to the parent per day. The parent then returns the phone call and speaks to the child for a few minutes. The child is encouraged to save the pass for times of great distress and praised when he does not use the pass at all during a day. This pass, allowing a parental phone call, gradually fades to one call for every other day, one call a week, and so on. After the first few days, if the parents' remain supportive and firm, the problem usually vanishes.

Worrying all the time: Generalized Anxiety Disorder

Based on what we know today, Generalize Anxiety Disorder (GAD) is probably fairly common among kids and more common among older kids than younger. It most often occurs on or after puberty and is characterized by

- Excessive anxiety and worry about school or family problems
- The worry causes physical symptoms, such as stomachaches, headaches, or loss of appetite
- The child has difficulty concentrating and/or may be irritable

Focusing on phobias: Specific Phobias

Most young kids at one time or another exhibit fear of the dark or monsters in the closet. So don't worry if your child has these fears unless the fear becomes so intense that it disrupts daily living in a significant way. The typical age of onset of a *real* phobia (as opposed to the earlier, minor fears) is about age 8 or 9.

Specific Phobias are exaggerated, intense fears that cause a child to avoid a particular object or situation. See Chapter 2 if you want more information on this type of anxiety.

Connecting with others: Social Phobia

Some kids are just plain shy. They're born that way, and relatives often make comments like, "He's just like his dad was at that age." Sometimes, shyness decreases with age, but when shyness swells and causes a child to fearfully avoid social encounters in everyday life, your little one may have a problem.

Social Phobia usually doesn't manage to get diagnosed until around 10 years of age. Signs generally appear at a younger age, but parents often have trouble distinguishing it from shyness until then. You can pick it up sooner if you observe your children carefully. If their fears of unfamiliar peers or adults show no improvement whatsoever by age 3 or so, you may want to check with a professional to determine if the problem is serious. See Chapter 2 for more information about Social Phobia.

Anxious repetition: Obsessive-Compulsive Disorder

This type of anxiety is somewhat less common than Separation Anxiety Disorder, GAD, Specific Phobias, and Social Phobias. Nevertheless, almost 1 in 50 teens has Obsessive-Compulsive Disorder (OCD). Often beginning in childhood, OCD develops on an average at around age 10. However, it can occur as early as 4 or 5 years of age.

Obsessions are recurring, unwanted thoughts that your child can't stop. See Chapter 2 for more details. Some of the most common obsessions among children include:

✔ Excessive fear of intruders

✔ Fear of germs

✔ Fear of illness

✔ Fixation on certain numbers

Compulsions involve rituals or various behaviors that your child feels compelled to repeat over and over. Common childhood compulsions include the following:

✔ Arranging objects in a precise manner

✔ Excessive hand washing

✔ Hoarding items of dubious value

✔ Repeatedly counting stairs, ceiling tiles, and steps taken while walking

Many children perform a few harmless rituals that involve magical thinking, such as not stepping on sidewalk cracks. However, any child that exhibits serious signs of Obsessive-Compulsive Disorder should be evaluated. It doesn't matter what age it shows up at because OCD tends not to improve without treatment.

Rare anxieties among children

A few anxiety disorders that occur in adults show up infrequently in children.

✔ **Agoraphobia** is often a response to panic and involves avoidance of places or situations in which you feel no escape is readily available.

✔ **Panic Disorder** involves a sudden onset of intense fearfulness, terror, and physical symptoms. It usually doesn't appear until late adolescence or after.

✔ **Post-Traumatic Stress Disorder** is a response to some traumatic event in which the person develops hyper-arousal, intrusive thoughts about the event, and avoidance of any reminders of the event.

See Chapter 2 for more details on all these anxiety disorders. If any of these anxieties show up in your children, we recommend a professional consultation.

Post-Traumatic Stress Disorder among children

Although thankfully rather rare in children, PTSD symptoms are slightly different among kids than adults. Like adults, children can get PTSD from abuse or other directly experienced trauma. (PTSD among New York City kids spiked after the September 11 terrorist attacks. Fourth and fifth graders were particularly affected.) Also, similar to adults, kids can develop PTSD from witnessing trauma happening to others, such as seeing a parent beaten. Children with PTSD become restless, agitated, irritable, and scattered. Instead of nightmares and intrusive thoughts, children may act out their terror in play. They may have bad dreams, but these usually don't have content specifically relevant to the trauma. Like adults, they become anxious and alert to any possible sign of danger. They also tend to overreact to trivial incidents, such as being bumped into or criticized.

Nipping Anxiety in the Bud

How does anxiety begin? The risk for developing anxiety begins at conception. That's right, studies of twins have demonstrated that almost half of what causes anxiety lies in your genes. However, that's just the beginning. Many other factors come into play, and you can do much about these factors, as we explain.

Early mastery experiences

When a hungry or uncomfortable baby cries out and parents respond by feeding or comforting, the baby has experienced a beginning sense of mastery. In other words, what the baby does results in a predictable outcome. This early opportunity can be repeated thousands of times over the next few years in various ways. For example, the toddler discovers how to use language to make requests that then get rewarded. If parents respond unpredictably and chaotically to an infant's attempts to control, anxiety is likely to increase.

So in order to decrease the probability of anxiety, responding predictably to young children is imperative. For young infants, parents should respond with reasonable consistency to most of their distress. Later, predictability is still important but should occur only to age-appropriate distress or requests. In other words, you wouldn't want to reinforce a 2-year-old's temper tantrums by caving in.

Anxiety's brain chemistry

Recent research at Columbia University explores the effect of the brain chemical serotonin, which is produced naturally in the human body, on the development of anxiety. Experimenters bred mice that lacked important receptors for serotonin, which left them unable to utilize this important neurotransmitter. They found that mice between 5 and 20 days old without the ability to process serotonin developed *mouse anxiety* as adults. But when they raised mice with normal serotonin receptors and later depleted the mice of serotonin when they had reached adulthood, the mice didn't develop anxiety.

What does this research have to do with anxious kids? It points to the importance of biological factors in the development of anxiety. Even prenatal and early infantile experiences may affect emotional well-being long into the future. Perhaps treating childhood anxiety early can help to prevent future problems.

More research is needed to understand how all this works. However, we know that not only do biological interventions (such as medications) affect serotonin levels, but it appears that behavioral strategies, such as those described in this book, also alter brain chemistry in productive ways.

As your children grow older, you should provide as many opportunities as possible for them to experience a feeling of mastery. You can do this by

- Involving them in sports
- Interesting them in hobbies that require some skill
- Playing games of skill, such as puzzles or scrabble
- Making sure that they have the chance to experience success at school and getting immediate help if they start struggling with their studies
- Training them to have good manners and social skills

Fine-tuning emotions

One of the most important tasks of childhood consists of learning how to control emotions, tolerate frustration, and delay gratification. Again, young infants need prompt gratification. However, with increasing age, the world tends to look unfavorably upon those who demand instant gratification and rejects those who are unable to keep a reasonable lid on their emotional outbursts.

You can help your child learn these crucial skills of emotional regulation. Helping children express emotions without letting them run out of control involves a few basic steps:

- **Validate your child's emotions.** When your child feels distressed, anxious, or worried, validate her emotion. You do that by saying,

    "I see that you are a little afraid of . . . "

    "You seem worried about . . . "

  As you can see, this validating statement should also try to help your child connect the feeling to what's going on.

- **Don't deny your children's feelings.** To the greatest degree possible, don't deny the feeling or try to take it away. In other words, you don't want to say, "You shouldn't be scared," or worse, "You're not really afraid."

- **Don't overprotect.** No one likes to see children feel fearful or anxious. However, they need to figure out how to deal with most fears on their own. If you try to solve all their problems or keep them from all worries and danger, you're doing more harm than good.

- **Help your kids learn to calm down.** You can teach them to take a few slow, deep breaths or count to ten slowly. You can also explain that extreme anxiety and fear will reduce eventually.

- **Praise your children.** When they make efforts to overcome anxieties, praise your kids. However, don't punish them for failing to do so.

✔ **Don't provide unnecessary reassurance.** Making comments such as, "There's nothing to be afraid of," is unnecessary. Kids need to find out how to handle a little stress and anxiety on their own. Don't constantly reassure them, or you'll create a sure-fire path to anxiety.

Inoculating against anxiety

Certain situations, activities, animals, and objects commonly turn into phobias. The following list of children's fears shows that children experience fears that are often similar to those that adults experience.

✔ Airplanes

✔ Being alone

✔ Dogs

✔ Heights

✔ Rodents

✔ Snakes

✔ Spiders and insects

✔ Thunder and lightning

If you want to prevent your children from acquiring one of these common phobias, you can inoculate them. You do that by providing safe interactions with the potentially feared event or object — prior to any fear developing.

Try the following activities:

✔ Take your kids to a museum or zoo that offers hands-on experiences with snakes and insects.

✔ Climb a mountain together.

✔ Watch a storm from the safety of your living room couch. Discuss how lightning and thunder work.

✔ If you don't have a dog or cat of your own, go to the pound and visit puppies and kittens.

Research has proven that this method works. For example, studies have shown that children bitten by dogs don't develop a phobia as readily if they have had past, positive experiences with dogs. Children who fly at an early age rarely develop a phobia to flying. The more experiences that you provide to your child, the better your child's chances are of growing up without phobias.

For all of you somewhat phobic parents, try not to make faces or get too squeamish when you inoculate your kids against phobias. Don't say, "Oooh, how gross!" Even if you feel nervous, try not to show it.

Parenting precautions

A parent can set children up to develop an anxiety disorder, or a parent can help to prevent anxiety.

- **Permissive parents** engage with their kids and show concern and caring. But permissive parents hate confrontation, and they abhor seeing their kids feel bad. Therefore, they set low expectations for their children, and they don't push them to act mature or try new things.

- **Authoritarian parents** represent the opposite extreme. They demand, direct, and expect instant obedience from their children. They control every detail of their children's lives and tend to be overly structured and hostile.

The permissive parent and authoritarian parent

Both the permissive and the authoritarian types of parents fuel anxiety in children. The following story is about both types. The mother demonstrates permissive parenting, and the father is an authoritarian.

Four-year-old **Nancy** screams with terror. Her parents rush into her room to see what's wrong. "There's a bad man in my room; I saw him," she cries. Nancy's mother hugs her, strokes her hair, and tells her, "Everything will be okay now that mommy's here."

Her dad turns on the light. He checks her closet and under her bed and snaps, "There's nobody here. Just stay in your bed and go to sleep. Don't be such a baby."

When this scene reenacts itself night after night for six weeks straight, Nancy's dad becomes increasingly annoyed and speaks harshly to her about what he calls her silly fears. At the same time, her mother overprotects Nancy. Her mom even starts to sleep in her room to make her feel safe. Her fears only intensify. Poor Nancy receives mixed messages from her parents, and neither message helps.

Authoritative parenting

A different kind of parenting can help your kids deal with anxiety better. It's called *authoritative* parenting (as opposed to authoritarian). Authoritative parents provide clear expectations for their children. They encourage their kids to face challenges. They validate their children's feelings of anxiety, but urge them to deal with it. They aren't harsh or punitive, but they don't over-protect. Using Nancy's story again, the following demonstrates how authoritative parents would deal with Nancy's anxieties.

Four-year-old **Nancy** screams with terror. Her parents rush into her room to see what's wrong. "There's a bad man in my room; I saw him," she cries.

Nancy's mom gives her a quick hug and says, "You sound afraid, sweetie."

Her dad turns on the light, checks the closet, and under the bed, and says, "Nobody's here, honey. But if you'd like, we can leave a nightlight on."

Nancy says, "No, can't mommy just stay here with me tonight?"

Nancy's mom tells her, "No, you need to handle this yourself. I know you're worried, but it will be okay." They turn the night light on, and tell her, "Here's your bear; he'll keep you company. We'll see you in the morning."

Nancy cries softly for a few minutes and falls back to sleep.

"But, but, but," you protest, "I tried that, and it didn't work for me!"

Perhaps your child kept on crying and wouldn't stop. Well, sometimes that happens. Occasionally, you may need to hang in there for an hour or two. Eventually, the vast majority of kids start falling asleep sooner. If that doesn't happen after four or five nights in a row, you may need to consult a professional.

Helping Already Anxious Children

Perhaps you have some anxious children. Don't make yourself anxious by blaming yourself for the problem. Multiple factors probably went into making your kids anxious. And you probably weren't able to read this book prior to their developing anxiety, so you didn't know what you could do to prevent it. So now what do you do?

Helping yourself first

Most of you have probably heard airline flight attendants instruct you about how to deal with the oxygen masks should they drop down. They tell you to put the mask on yourself prior to assisting your child. That's because if you don't help yourself first, you won't be in any condition to help your child.

The same principle applies to anxiety in your kids. You need to tackle your own anxiety prior to trying to help your children. Children learn much of their emotional responses by observing their parents; it makes sense that anxious parents end up more often with anxious children. The nice part of getting rid of your own anxiety first is that this is likely to help your children, as well as give you the resources for assisting with their worries.

You can do this by reading this book for yourself. Pick and choose the strategies that best fit your problem and personality. However, if the ideas you choose first don't seem to work, don't despair. The vast majority of the time, one or more of the techniques that we describe does help.

Modeling mellow

If you don't have a problem with anxiety or if you overcame your excessive worries for the most part, you're ready to teach by example. Children learn a great deal by watching the people they care about. You may recall a time when your child surprised you by repeating words you thought or wished he hadn't heard. Trust us, kids see and hear everything.

Therefore, take advantage of every opportunity to model relatively calm behavior and thinking. Don't invalidate your child's anxiety by saying it's a stupid or silly fear. Furthermore, demonstrating complete calm is not as useful as showing how you handle the concern yourself. Table 17-2 shows some common childhood fears and how you may model an effective response.

Table 17-2	Modeling a Better Way
Fear	*Parental Modeling*
Thunderstorms	I understand a thunderstorm is coming tonight. Sometimes, I get a little nervous about them, but I know that we are safe at home. I'm always careful to seek shelter during a thunderstorm. But I know that thunderstorms can't really hurt you when you're inside.
Insects	I used to think that insects were gross, awful, and scary, but now I realize that they're more afraid of me than I am of them. Insects run away from people when they can. Sometimes, they're so scared that they freeze. I admit that I still use plenty of tissue to pick them up, and that's okay. Let me show you how I do it.

(continued)

Table 17-2 *(continued)*	
Fear	*Parental Modeling*
Heights	I sometimes feel a little nervous looking down from high places. Here we are on the top of the Washington Monument. Let's hold hands and go to the window together. You can't fall off, and it can't hurt you. Looking down from heights is kind of fun. The scariness is kind of exciting after you get used to it.
Being alone (Don't do unless your child expressed anxiety about feeling safe alone.)	Your father's going on a trip tomorrow. I used to feel pretty afraid staying at home by myself, but I realize that I can take pretty good care of myself and of you. We have a security door, and if anyone tried to get in, we can always call the police. Our dogs are pretty good protection, too. Do you ever get scared? If you do, we can talk about it.

Leading children through anxiety

As we discuss in Chapter 8, gradual exposure to whatever causes anxiety is one of the most effective ways of overcoming fear. Whether the anxious person is a child or an adult, the strategy is much the same. Therefore, if you want to help your children who already have anxiety, first model coping as we described in Table 17-2 in this chapter. Then, consider using *exposure,* which involves breaking the feared situation or object into small steps. You gradually confront and stay with each step until anxiety reduces by 50 percent or more.

Read Chapter 8 for important, additional details about exposure. However, keep a few things in mind when doing this as a guide for your child:

✔ **Break the steps down as small as you possibly can.** Don't expect your child to master a fear overnight. It takes time. And children need smaller steps than adults. For example, if you're dealing with a fear of dogs, don't expect your child to immediately walk up and pet a dog on the first attempt. You may instead start with pictures and storybooks about dogs. Then you could progress to seeing dogs at a distance, behind an enclosed fence. You gradually work up to direct contact, perhaps at a pet store.

✔ **Expect to see some distress.** This is the hard part for parents. No one likes to see their kids get upset. But you can't avoid having your kids feel modest distress if you want them to get over their anxiety. Sometimes, this part is more than some parents can handle. In those cases, a close friend or relative may be willing to pitch in and help. At the same time, if your child exhibits extreme anxiety and upset, you need to break the task down further or get professional help.

✔ **Praise your child for any successes.** Pay attention to any improvement and compliment your child. However, don't pressure your child by saying that this shows what a big boy or girl he or she is.

✔ **Show patience.** Don't get so worked up that your own emotions spill over and frighten your child further. Again, if that starts to happen, stop for a while, enlist a friend's assistance, or seek a professional's advice.

Penny and Stan plan a Mexico vacation at a resort right on the beach. The brochure describes a family-friendly atmosphere. They purchase a snorkel and diving mask for their 3-year-old, **Benjamin,** who enjoys the plane ride and looks forward to snorkeling.

When they arrive, the hotel appears as beautiful as promised. The beach beckons, and the ocean water promises to be clear. Penny, Stan, and Benjamin quickly unpack and make their way down to the beach. They walk into the water slowly, delighted by the warm temperature. Suddenly, a large wave breaks in front of them and knocks Benjamin over. Benjamin opens his mouth in surprise, and saltwater gags him. He cries and runs back to the shore, screaming.

They spend the rest of the vacation with Benjamin, begging him to go into the ocean again to no avail. The parents end up taking turns baby-sitting with Benjamin, and their vacation dream fades.

At home, Benjamin's fear grows, as untreated fears often do. He fusses in the bath, not wanting any water to splash on his face. He won't even consider getting into a swimming pool.

Benjamin's parents take the lead and guide him through exposure. First, on a hot day, they put a rubber, inflated wading pool into the backyard. They fill it and model getting in. Eventually, Benjamin shows a little interest and joins them in the pool. After he gets more comfortable, the parents do a little playful splashing with each other and encourage Benjamin to splash them. He doesn't notice that his own face gets a little water on it.

Then his parents suggest that Benjamin put just a part of his face into the water. He resists at first, but they encourage him. When he puts his chin into the water, they applaud. Stan bets Benjamin that he can't put his whole face in. Benjamin proves him wrong.

The parents provide a wide range of gradually increasing challenges, including using the mask and snorkel in pools of various sizes. Then they go to a freshwater lake and do the same. Eventually, they take another vacation to the ocean and gradually expose Benjamin to the water there as well.

Relaxing reduces anxiety

Children benefit from learning to relax, much in the same way that adults do. We discussed relaxation methods for adults in Chapters 12 and 13, but kids need some slightly different strategies. That's because they don't have the same attention span as adults.

Usually, we suggest teaching kids relaxation on an individual basis rather than in groups. Kids in groups tend to get embarrassed. They deal with their embarrassment by acting silly and then fail to derive much benefit from the procedure. Individual training doesn't usually create as much embarrassment, and keeping their attention is easier.

Breathing relaxation

The following directives are intended to teach kids abdominal breathing that's been shown to effectively reduce anxiety. Feel free to use your own creativity to design similar instructions.

1. Lie down on the floor and put your hands on your tummy.

2. Pretend that your stomach is a big balloon and that you want to fill it as full as you can.

3. Breathe in and see how big you can make your stomach. Make a whooshing sound like a balloon losing air as you slowly let the air out. Excellent.

4. Let's do it again. Breathe in and fill the balloon. Hold it for a moment and then let the air out of your balloon ever so slowly as you make whooshing sounds.

Repeat this instruction for eight or ten breaths. Tell your kids to practice it daily.

Relaxing muscles

An especially effective way of achieving relaxation is through muscle relaxation. The following series of directives may help a child relax. Again, feel free to use your creativity. Have your child work each muscle group for about ten seconds before relaxing. Then relax for about ten seconds.

1. **Sit down in this chair, close your eyes, and relax.**

2. **Pretend the floor is trying to rise up and that you have to push it back down with your legs and feet. Push, push, push.**

   Okay, now relax your legs and feet. Notice how nice they feel.

3. **Oh, oh. The floor is starting to rise again. Push it back down.**

   Good job; now relax.

4. **Now tighten your stomach muscles. Make your stomach into a shield of armor; strong like Superman. Hold the muscles in.**

   Good, now relax.

5. **One more time; tighten those stomach muscles into steel. Hold it.**

   Great, now relax and see how nice, warm, and relaxed your stomach feels.

6. **Now, spread your fingers and put your hands together in front of your chest. Squeeze your hands together. Pretend you're squeezing play dough between your hands and make it as squished as you can. Push hard and use your arm muscles, too.**

   Okay, now relax. Take a deep breath. Hold it. Now let the air out slowly.

7. **Again, spread your fingers wide, and squish play dough between your hands. Hold it.**

   Great. Now relax.

8. **Pretend you're a turtle. You want to go into your shell. To do that, bring your shoulders way up high and try to touch your ears with your shoulders. Feel your head go down into your shell. Hold it.**

   Okay. Now relax. See how nice, warm, and relaxed your shoulders and neck feel.

9. **One more time now. Be a turtle and go into your shell. Hold it.**

   Good. Now relax.

10. **Finally, squish your face up like it does when you eat something that tastes really, really bad. Squish it up tight. Hold it.**

    Okay; now relax. Take a deep breath. Hold it; now let the air out slowly.

11. **One more time. Squish your face up real tight. Hold it.**

    Relax. Good job! See how limp and relaxed your body feels. When you feel upset or worried, you can do this all by yourself to feel better. You don't have to do all the muscles like we did. You can just do what you want to.

Imagining your way to relaxation

One way to help your child relax is through reading books. Before bed, kids find stories very relaxing. Reading rids their minds of worries and concerns from the day. You can also find various books and tapes specifically designed for helping kids relax. Unfortunately, some of the tapes use imagery of beautiful, relaxing scenes that kids may find rather boring.

Rather than idyllic scenes of beaches and lakes, kids can relax quite nicely to more fanciful scenes. The scenes don't need be about relaxation per se; they just need to be entertaining and pleasant. Again, the point is to provide engaging alternatives to worries and fears. One great idea comes from one of our clients and that client's mother. You can design your own book with your child. The client wrote and illustrated each page of her own relaxation book as in the following excerpt, titled "Imagine Unicorns and Smiling Stars":

Close your eyes and relax.

> Imagine unicorns dancing.
>
> Imagine outer space. Look at the planets spinning and floating.
>
> Imagine smiling stars. See how happy they are.
>
> Imagine blue moons. See the moons smiling.
>
> Imagine nice aliens. They like you.
>
> Imagine spaceships soaring.
>
> Imagine unicorns dancing in outer space with smiling stars, blue moons, and friendly aliens in their spaceship soaring.
>
> Now, relax. Dream wonderful dreams.

Exorcizing anxiety through exercise

Exercise burns off excess adrenaline, which fuels anxiety. All kids obviously need regular exercise, and studies show that most don't exercise enough. Anxious kids may be reluctant to engage in organized sports. They may feel inadequate or even afraid of negative evaluation by others.

Yet it may be more important for anxious kids to participate in sports for two reasons. First, sports can provide them with important mastery experiences. Although they may feel frustrated and upset at first, they usually experience considerable pride and a sense of accomplishment as their skills improve. Second, aerobic activity directly decreases anxiety.

The challenge is to find a sport that provides your child with the greatest possible chance of at least modest success. Consider the following activities for your child:

✔ **Swim teams:** This is an individual sport that doesn't involve balls thrown at your head or collisions with other players. Swimmers compete against themselves, and many swim teams reward most participants with ribbons, whether they come in first or sixth.

- ✔ **Track and Field:** This also is an individual sport that has a wide variety of different skill possibilities. Some kids are fast and can run short dashes. Others discover that they can develop the endurance to run long distances. Still others can shot put.

- ✔ **Tennis:** A low contact and relatively safe sport. Good instruction can make most normal kids adequate tennis players.

- ✔ **Martial arts:** Good for enhancing a sense of competence and confidence. Many martial arts instructors have great skill for working with uncoordinated, fearful kids. Almost all kids can experience improvements and success with martial arts.

- ✔ **Dance:** This sport includes many different types of dance from ballet to square dancing. Musically inclined kids often do quite well with dance classes.

In other words, find something for your kids to do that involves physical activity. They can benefit in terms of decreased anxiety, increased confidence, and greater connections with others. Don't forget to include family bikes, hikes, or walks. Model the benefits of lifelong activity and exercise.

Chapter 18

When Someone You Love Suffers from Anxiety

*E*ven people who live together sometimes don't know each other as well as they think. That's because most people try to look and act as well adjusted as they can — revealing weaknesses, limitations, and vulnerabilities isn't easy.

This chapter helps you communicate with your partner in the event that he experiences anxiety. With the right communication style, instead of provoking feelings of anger and resentment, you can negotiate a new role — that of a helpful coach. You can also team up to tackle anxiety by finding ways to simplify life, have fun, and relax together. Finally, find out how simply accepting your partner's anxiety and limitations can lead to a better relationship and paradoxically, less anxiety.

Discovering if Your Partner Suffers With Anxiety

Why do people hide their anxious feelings? Upbringing and fear are two big reasons:

✔ Revealing negative feelings can be embarrassing, especially to someone with an anxiety disorder. Although self-disclosure usually works out well and brings people closer together, people often fear rejection or ridicule.

✔ Children may have been taught to repress or deny feelings by their parents. They may have been told, "Don't be such a baby," or "Boys don't cry." Whatever the case, when that happens, they grow up keeping concerns to themselves.

So how do you really know if your partner has a problem with anxiety? And does it matter if you know or not? We think it does. Knowing whether your partner experiences anxiety can promote better understanding and communication.

The following list of indications may help you to discern whether your partner suffers from anxiety. Ask yourself if your partner

✔ Seems restless and keyed up?

✔ Avoids situations for seemingly silly reasons?

✔ Ruminates about future catastrophes?

✔ Is reluctant to leave the house?

✔ Has trouble sleeping?

✔ Has trouble concentrating?

✔ Is plagued with self-doubts?

✔ Is constantly vigilant and on the alert for dangers?

✔ Is overly worried about germs, contamination, or dirt?

✔ Frequently rechecks whether the doors are locked or the coffee pot is turned off?

✔ Seems terrified by anything specific such as insects, dogs, thunderstorms, and so on?

✔ Responds with irritation when pushed to attend social functions, such as parties, weddings, meetings, neighborhood functions, or anywhere you might encounter strangers?

Note: The resistance could be due to simple dislike of the activity, but carefully consider whether anxiety may lie at the bottom of the problem.

A couple of the symptoms in the preceding list (especially irritability, poor concentration, poor sleep, and self-doubts) could also indicate depression. Depression is a serious condition that usually also includes loss of interest in activities previously considered pleasurable, change in appetite, and depressed mood. See Chapter 2 for more information about depression. If your partner seems depressed, talk with your partner and then consult with a mental health practitioner or your family physician.

Now, if you answered yes to any of the questions in the preceding list (and your partner doesn't seem particularly depressed), we don't recommend that you approach your partner and say, "Look at this list — you're a nut case! I knew it." This would be a really bad idea.

Instead, consider asking your partner a few questions. This should definitely not occur immediately following a conflict or argument. Possible questions to ask include:

- ✔ What's the biggest stress in your life lately?

- ✔ What worries you the most?

- ✔ Sometimes, when I go to events like this, I feel anxious. I'm wondering how you're feeling about going?

- ✔ I noticed you've had trouble sleeping lately. What's been on your mind?

Try to make your questions as nonthreatening and safe to answer as possible. In addition, think about asking questions that don't have a simple yes or no answer. For example, if you ask your partner if she is anxious, then she may reply with a simple, "No," and the discussion is over.

Our list of questions for you about your partner's anxiety and our list of questions to ask your partner open the door to communicating about anxiety. After you broach the subject and confirm that your partner struggles with anxiety, you can build a plan from there. But you need to know how to keep the conversation going.

Talking Together About Anxiety

Talking about a partner's vulnerability isn't always easy. Keeping a few ideas in mind may help. For example, if you find the conversation turning into an argument, then it's not helpful. Back off. Your partner may not be ready to face the problem. If so, you might check out the "Accepting Anxiety with Love" section, later in this chapter.

Not every couple can communicate easily about difficult subjects without arguing. If that's the case for the two of you, we suggest relationship counseling because reading a few pages about talking together won't solve fundamental communication problems. However, as a couple, if you're able to talk about anxiety without experiencing a communication breakdown, we have some general guidelines for you.

Sometimes, one person in a relationship actually prefers to take care of the other or even feels more powerful knowing that her partner has a problem. Such a partner may sabotage her partner's efforts more than provide help. If your partner starts to sabotage your efforts, again, seek relationship counseling or individual therapy.

Helping without owning the albatross

The first order of business in a discussion of your partner's anxiety is to show empathic concern. That means putting yourself in your partner's shoes and seeing the world through his eyes. Then you can try to understand the source of the worry.

However, expressing empathy and concern doesn't mean that you need to solve the problem. You can't. You may be able to help, as we show in the "Guiding the Way" section, later in this chapter, but you don't control the emotions of other people — they do.

Realizing that helpers don't own the responsibility for making change happen is important. Otherwise, you're likely to become frustrated and angry if and when efforts to change stall. Frustration and anger only make overcoming anxiety more difficult.

Avoiding blame

Just as you don't want to blame yourself by owning the problem when your partner becomes anxious, it's equally important to avoid blaming your partner. Your partner developed anxiety for all the reasons we list in Chapter 3. Nobody asks for an anxiety disorder. Nobody wants one, and change is difficult.

People are particularly tempted to blame their partners when they make great efforts to help, yet their partners seem ungrateful and resistant. You must understand that anxiety's tentacles tenaciously tighten their grip when threatened. That's because anxiety's like an old habit. It may not feel good, but at least it's familiar. When you start to work on reducing anxiety, anxiety typically increases before it gets better.

Therefore, make every effort to avoid blame and be patient. Success and failure aren't up to you. You want to help, but if change doesn't happen, it means nothing about your helpfulness.

When help turns into harm

People with anxiety desperately seek ways to alleviate their distress. One common way is to ask for reassurance. If it's your partner who has anxiety, of course you want to help by giving that reassurance. For example, people who have a great fear of illness often ask their spouses if they look okay or if they're running a temperature. Reassuring your partner presents one problem — it makes matters worse.

How can something designed to alleviate anxiety create more anxiety? Well, the immediate reduction in anxiety reinforces or rewards the act of seeking assistance. Thus, rather than learning to depend on one's own good sense, giving reassurance teaches the recipient to look for answers elsewhere. Both dependency and anxiety thereby increase. The following anecdote demonstrates how reassurance can aggravate anxiety.

James and **Roberto** have lived together for the past three years. Both graduate students, they lead busy lives. Lately though, James stops attending social events, complaining of fatigue. Roberto finds himself going alone and misses James' company.

Roberto receives an announcement that he is the recipient of this year's Departmental Dissertation of the Year Award. Of course, he wants James to attend, but James fears sitting alone and feeling trapped. Roberto reassures James that the auditorium is safe and that he could get out if he needed to by sitting on the aisle. James still resists; Roberto suggests they get a friend to attend with him.

Finally, after considerable cajoling, reassurance, and extra measures to ensure his comfort, his concerns about feeling trapped dissipate; James agrees to go to the event. However, as each new event comes up, it seems that James requires more reassurance and attention. James withdraws more and his anxiety increases.

Roberto fell into the trap of not only being empathetic but also owning James's problem. Unfortunately, when you own your partner's problem by giving too much reassurance and excessive help, it usually just makes things worse. Dependency, avoidance, and anxiousness all deepen. It's a matter of balance. Give truly needed help, show real concern, but avoid going too far.

If you've been in the habit of giving your partner frequent, large doses of reassurance, don't suddenly stop without discussing the issue first. Otherwise, your partner is likely to think you've stopped caring. You need to let your partner know and come to an agreement that eliminating unnecessary reassurance is a good idea. Then, agree that you will reassure once on any given concern, but when asked repeatedly, you will simply smile and say, "We agreed that I can't answer that."

Guiding the Way

Assuming you've had a healthy discussion with your partner about her anxiety problem, you may be able to help further. But first, take a look at yourself. If you also wrestle with anxiety, do all that you can for yourself before trying to tackle your partner's anxiety.

Only after you take care of your own anxiety should you consider coaching your partner to overcome her anxiety. A coach is a guide who encourages, plans, corrects, and supports. Part of the job of a coach requires modeling how to handle stress and worry. You can't do a good job of modeling if you're quaking in your boots.

Coaches can help plan and direct one of the most effective ways of overcoming anxiety, gradual exposure. *Exposure* involves taking any given fear into small steps and facing it. Most importantly, exposure asks the person to stay with each step until the anxiety has reduced by at least 50 percent. If any given step creates too much anxiety, the coach can help devise ways of breaking the task into smaller pieces.

Be sure to read Chapter 8 for important details about exposure prior to attempting to help your partner develop an exposure plan. If you run into any difficulty in terms of your partner resisting or arguing with you, consult a professional. Of course you want to help, but it isn't worth harming your relationship to do so. Consider the story of Doug and Rosie.

Doug and **Rosie** have dated for over a year. In all that time, they've never gone to a movie together because Rosie wrestles with a mild case of agoraphobia. Although she's able to go most places and do what she needs to in life, she dreads going anywhere that makes her feel trapped, especially movie theaters. She fantasizes that she'll need to get out, but she won't find her way to an exit because of the crowd and the darkness. She imagines that she would trip over people, fall on her face, and desperately crawl through the darkened theater.

Doug realizes that Rosie makes one excuse after another to avoid going to movies even though she enjoys watching them on television. Gently, he asks Rosie, "Some things make me a little anxious — heavy traffic or big crowds — what makes you anxious?" Rosie confesses that crowded movie theaters make her feel closed in and trapped.

Several days later, Doug sees a copy of this book in a bookstore and buys it with Rosie in mind. He starts reading, paying particular attention to Chapter 8 about exposure. Doug and Rosie have a productive discussion about her concerns and decide to face them. Doug volunteers to coach.

First, together they devise a tower of fear, which breaks down the feared situation into small steps. (See more on the tower of fear in Chapter 8.) Rosie's tower of fear consists of ten blocks. Figure 18-1, later in this chapter, shows five of Rosie's blocks.

Figure 18-1:
Rosie's
tower
of fear.

Going to a
crowded
theater alone
and sitting in
a middle row.

Sitting with
Doug in the
middle row of
a crowded
theater.

Sitting in a
crowded
theater on
an aisle seat
with Doug.

Going to an
uncrowded
movie and
sitting in a
middle row seat.

Sitting by the
exit door with
Doug in an
almost empty
theater.

Doug plays a role in most of Rosie's tasks. Not only does he accompany her, he celebrates her successes and encourages her when she starts to falter. He holds her hand on the easier items and gives less support toward the end. It takes attending a number of movies with Doug before she agrees to her final task of going by herself.

Rosie and Doug go to the theater together on her last item, but he chooses a movie playing on a different screen. Although Rosie feels frightened, she sticks it out. She feels good about her accomplishment, and the two of them become closer.

So just exactly how does a coach help a partner?

✔ Begin only if your partner clearly expresses an interest and a desire for your assistance. It won't work if your partner doesn't want to change or to have your involvement.

✔ Define your role. In other words, come to a clear understanding of how much and what input of yours that your partner wants. Would your partner like you to be involved in the planning? How so? Does your partner want you to coach her through the execution of that plan?

　　• Ask if your partner wants you to simply observe or actively encourage.

　　• Ask if you should stand next to your partner, hold a hand, or stand a few feet away.

✔ Help your partner develop the plan but don't take on the full responsibility for designing the exposure hierarchy. (See Chapter 8 for details.)

✔ Keep your own emotions in check. Don't let your desire to help overwhelm you and cause you to help excessively.

✔ Don't let your emotions cause you to push your partner too much. Respect your partner's decisions to move ahead or not. Give encouragement but do so gently.

✔ After the plan is in place, expect your partner to have ups and downs. Some days go better than others. Remember, determining how the plan plays itself out isn't up to you.

✔ Before asking your partner to carry out a step, see if she wants you to model the task first. If you model, showing a small amount of anxiety yourself if you really feel it is fine. Just don't try to model actions that you personally can't do.

✔ Practice going through the steps with imagery first. Don't carry it out in real life until your partner feels more comfortable with the imagery. You can consult Chapter 8 for details about using your imagination through exposure as well.

✔ Set up some rewards for success at a few intervals along the hierarchy. Do something you both can enjoy together. You can also give some honest praise for success; just be sure not to sound patronizing.

✔ If your partner appears anxious at any step but not overwhelmed, encourage staying with that step until the anxiety comes down 50 percent. Obviously, don't absolutely insist, just encourage. Remind your partner that anxiety comes down with enough time.

Teaming Up Against Anxiety

One other way that you can help your partner overcome anxiety is to collaborate on ways to decrease stress in both your lives. With a little ingenuity, you can explore a variety of solutions that are likely to feel good to you even if you personally don't suffer from anxiety at all. For example:

✔ **Take a stress management class at a local center for adult continuing education.** These classes help people make lifestyle changes and set goals. Many of the ideas make life more fun and interesting in addition to reducing stress.

✔ **Take regular walks with your partner.** It's a great way to reduce stress, but even if you don't have much stress, strolling under the sky together is a wonderful time to talk and great for your health.

✔ **Take a yoga class together.** Again, even if you don't have anxiety, yoga is terrific for balance, muscle strength, flexibility, and overall health.

✔ **Explore spirituality together.** You may choose to attend a church, a synagogue, a mosque, or scope out a less traditional method of communing with a higher power, such as immersing yourselves in nature. Thinking about things bigger than yourselves or the mundane events of the world provides a peaceful perspective.

✔ **Look for creative ways to simplify your joint lives.** Consider looking for help with household chores if you both work. Carefully analyze the way that you spend time. Make sure that your time reflects your priorities. See Chapter 9 for more ideas.

✔ **Get away.** Take a vacation. You don't have to spend much money. And if you don't have the time for a long vacation, go away for an occasional evening at a local hotel. Getting away from the telephone, computer, doorbell, and other endless tasks and demands, even for a night, can help rejuvenate both of you.

Accepting Anxiety with Love

It may seem rather counterintuitive, but accepting your partner's battle with anxiety is one of the most useful attitudes that you can take. Acceptance paradoxically forms the foundation for change. In other words, whenever you discuss your partner's anxiety or engage in any effort to help, you need to appreciate and love all your partner's strengths and weaknesses.

You fell in love with the whole package — not just the good stuff. After all, you're not perfect nor is your partner. You wouldn't want perfection if you had it. If perfect people even existed, we can only imagine that they would be quite boring. Besides, studies show that people who try to be perfect more often become depressed, anxious, and distressed.

Therefore, rather than expecting perfection, accept your loved one "as is." You need to accept and embrace both the possibility of productive change as well as the chance that your partner may remain stuck. Accepting your partner is especially important when your efforts to help

- ✔ Result in an argument
- ✔ Seem ineffective
- ✔ Are not well received by your partner
- ✔ Seem merely to increase your partner's anxiety even after multiple exposure trials

What does acceptance do? More than you may think. Acceptance allows the partners to join together and grow closer because acceptance avoids putting pressure onto your partner. Intense expectations only serve to increase anxiety and resistance to change.

Acceptance conveys the message that you will love your partner no matter what. You will care if your partner stays the same or if your partner succeeds in making changes. This message frees your partner to

- ✔ Take risks
- ✔ Make mistakes
- ✔ Feel vulnerable
- ✔ Feel loved

Change requires risk-taking, vulnerability, and mistakes. When people feel that they can safely goof up, look silly, cry, or fail miserably, they can take those risks. Think about it. When do you take risks or try new things? Probably not around an especially critical audience.

Giving up anxiety and fear takes tremendous courage in order to face the risks involved. Letting go of your need to see your partner change helps bolster the courage needed. Letting go of your need includes giving up ego. In other words, this is not about you.

When you take on the role of a helper, it doesn't mean that your worth is at stake. Of course, you want to do the best you can, but you can't force others to change. Your partner ultimately must own the responsibility.

Part VI
The Part of Tens

The 5th Wave   By Rich Tennant

"This readout shows your heart rate, blood pressure, bone density, anxiety level, plaque buildup, liver function, and expected lifetime."

In this part . . .

*W*e offer ten quick ways to defeat anxious feelings on the spot. Discover ten strategies that may look like ways to deal with anxiety but that just don't work. If anxiety comes back, we review ten ways of dealing with such relapses. Also, be sure to take a look at the ten indications that you may need professional help.

Chapter 19

Ten Ways to Stop Anxiety Quickly

Sometimes you need quick, temporary relief from anxiety. With that in mind, this chapter describes ten assorted therapies from the first-aid kit. Select one or more when worry and stress start to get out of hand.

Breathing Out Your Anxiety

Anxiety tends to make breathing shallow and rapid. And rapid, shallow breathing has a way of increasing anxiety — not a useful cycle. Try this quick, easy to learn, breathing technique to restore a calming pattern of breathing. You can do this anytime, anywhere. It really works. Give it a try.

1. Inhale deeply through your nose.

2. Hold your breath for a few seconds.

3. Slowly let your breath out through your lips while making a slight sound — hissing, sighing, or whatever.

4. Repeat Steps 1 through 3 for a minimum of ten breaths.

Talking with a Friend

Anxiety is a lonely feeling, and loneliness increases anxiety. Research shows that social support helps people deal with almost any type of emotional distress. So don't hesitate to reach out to friends and family. Find a trusted person to confide in. You may think that no one would want to hear about your troubles, but we're not talking about whining and complaining. We're talking about sharing what's going on with you.

No doubt you would do the same for someone else. People probably exist who want you to call them in troubled times. If you find yourself without friends, call upon a minister, priest, or rabbi. If you have no religious connections, call a crisis line. You can also see Chapter 22 for signs that you may need professional help.

Exercising Aerobically

Anxiety usually floods the body with adrenaline. Adrenaline makes your heart beat faster, your muscles tighten, and various other body sensations that feel distressing. Nothing burns off adrenaline faster than aerobic exercise. See Chapter 10 for more information about this type of exercise. Good examples include jogging; a long, fast walk; dancing; rope jumping; and tennis.

Soothing the Body

The most distressing aspect of anxiety is the way that it makes your body feel — tense, queasy, racy, and tight. Quick ways to temporarily break through the tension include the following:

- Soaking in a hot bath for a good while.
- Taking a long, hot shower.
- Enjoying a 15-minute massage, such as in a chair or mat with an electronic heating and vibrating massager.

Taking Kava Kava

Kava Kava stands out among all the herbal remedies as the most likely to alleviate your anxiety. You probably have less chance of becoming addicted to it than certain medications such as the benzodiazepines (see Chapter 15) and for some people, it seems to work almost as well. Be sure to buy your Kava Kava from a reputable health food store and check to see that the label provides information concerning the percentage of lactones it contains. You can read about Kava Kava in Chapter 14, including information about lactones. Also, be sure to check with your physician prior to taking any herbal remedies because of possible interactions with other drugs.

Challenging Your Anxious Thinking

The way you think strongly influences the way you feel. Anxious people inevitably think about things in ways that increase their anxiety. One of the best ways of dealing with anxiety is to examine the evidence for your anxious thoughts.

First, write down what you're worried about. Afterwards, ask yourself some questions about those thoughts, such as

> ✔ Is this worry truly as awful as I'm thinking it is?
>
> ✔ Could some evidence contradict my anxious thoughts?
>
> ✔ In a year, how important will this event be to me?
>
> ✔ Am I making a dire prediction without any real basis?

After answering these questions, try to write down a more realistic perspective. See Chapter 5 for discovering more about how to write out your anxious thoughts, analyze them for distortions, and replace them with more realistic, calmer thoughts.

Listening to Music

Sounds influence the way that you feel. Think about it. If you listen to fingernails scraping across a blackboard, how do you feel? Most people report that it gives them a creepy, anxious feeling. Just as noxious sounds jangle the nerves, soothing sounds can calm you.

Select music that you find relaxing. Get comfortable and close your eyes. Turn the volume to a comforting level. Relax. Listen.

Finding Distractions

In general, avoiding your anxiety isn't a good idea. But until you discover better ways of dealing with it, sometimes, distractions can help. And remember, they're just a temporary bandage and won't last. However, once in a while, distraction helps. Consider the following:

- A good book
- A movie
- Television, mindless as it may be
- Video games

Having Sex

If you have an available, willing partner, sex is a wonderful way to relax. It can certainly take your mind off anxiety! And, like aerobic exercise, it burns off adrenaline. What a perfect combination.

On the other hand, some anxious people get anxious about their sexual performance. If that's you, don't try this strategy — at least until you overcome your anxiety about this issue. And, if you don't have an available, willing partner, we don't recommend hiring one.

Staying with the Moment

What are you worried about? Chances are, it's something that hasn't even happened yet and may never occur. The fact is, almost 90 percent of what people worry about never actually happens. And if it does occur, it rarely ends up as catastrophic as the worriers predict.

Therefore, we suggest that you focus on the here and now. What are you doing? Look around you. Notice how the air feels as it goes in and out your nose. Feel your feet and the muscles in your legs as you sit. If you still feel anxiety, study it. Notice the various sensations in your body and realize that they won't kill you. They pass eventually as you observe them. If you accept feeling just a bit anxious, the feelings abate more quickly than if you tell yourself that you must get rid of them at once. Read Chapter 16 for more ideas about mindful acceptance.

Enjoy the moment.

Chapter 20

Ten Anxiety Busters That Just Don't Work

Most of this book gives you ideas for how to deal with anxiety. This chapter tells you what not to do. Don't feel bad if you tried one or more of these ways of coping with your anxiety — some are tempting. But a whole host of research studies and clinical experience tells us that they just don't work and may even make anxiety worse.

Avoiding What Scares You

Why not? If you're afraid of snakes, it's perfectly natural to stay away from snakes. Or if you worry about driving on highways, why not take the local streets? The problem with avoidance is that it feels too good. Staying away becomes a pattern. *Avoidance fertilizes anxiety.*

That's because people with problematic anxiety feel nervous about many things. After they avoid one thing, another fear blooms. Avoidance worked for the first one, so why not avoid this one too? Eventually, fears, like weeds, choke and crowd out a healthy life. Furthermore, behavior tells your brain what to believe. Avoidance behavior also increases fear because it increases your brain's belief that what you're avoiding is truly fearful. For example, **Allen** felt uncomfortable in crowds. He worried about being able to escape from stadiums if he felt the need. So he avoided sporting events. That worked pretty well, but then he noticed he was uptight in crowded shopping malls. So he let his wife do most of the shopping. No big deal. But then, he started to feel uncomfortable in restaurants. And so on. . . .

Whining and Complaining

"Why me?"

"It isn't fair."

"I hate being anxious. I can't stand it."

People with these attitudes hope for deliverance from their discomfort. They complain constantly and do little to help themselves. Some seem to just enjoy griping. Others hope for sympathy.

But that doesn't work. People don't like listening to a bombardment of grumbling and discontent. It only turns people off. Overcoming anxiety takes work and commitment. Not whining and complaining.

 We're not talking about merely discussing and sharing your problems with a friend or loved one here. Sharing your concerns can be a useful way to reduce your anxiety and obtain a little support. What's the difference between sharing and complaining? Whiners usually drone on and on and have little interest in exploring productive solutions.

Seeking Reassurance

Could you go with me to the store? Do I look like I'm getting sick? Like the whiners and complainers, some folks look to others to fix what ails them. They want constant help and reassurance from their friends, families, and even coworkers. Instead of facing their fears on their own, they lean on others and become dependent.

That's okay when you really need help, but when you continuously ask for reassurance, you're not standing up to your worries. The reassurance works temporarily; it does reduce anxiety at the moment. The problem is that it also reinforces the belief that you can't handle things on your own, which makes you even more anxious.

Hoping for Miracles

How nice life would be if fancy bottles held genies just waiting to grant all wishes. Just rub the bottle and poof — a genie appears to instantly rid you of anxiety, worry, and stress. Nice thought. But miracles rarely happen.

Nothing is wrong with hope. People need hope. Hope combined with dedicated effort can send you on your way to quieting the storm.

Seeking Quick Fixes

Rid Yourself of Anxiety in Three Hours! Listen to these tapes and never feel anxious again, just $29.95. If you take advantage of our special, today only, get free shipping and handling!

Okay, sounds great. Like most quick fixes, if it sounds too good to be true, it likely is. Promised quick fixes do far more to enrich the sellers' bank accounts than help with anxiety. Let solid research and science guide you when choosing your path to de-stressing your life.

Lying on the Couch: Freudian Psychoanalysis

Long-term psychoanalysis may be a worthwhile endeavor for various reasons — we have no complaint about that. But if you have anxiety, long-term therapy seems like cruel and unusual punishment (and expensive, besides). No quick fixes are available for anxiety, but short-term cognitive-behavioral therapy (which most of the techniques in this book come from) can start helping within a matter of weeks or months, not years.

Drinking Your Troubles Away

Many folks turn to alcohol to calm down. And in the short run, let's face it; it works. After work, relaxing with a drink can feel pretty good. In fact, research pretty much confirms that a couple of drinks a day for healthy adults may even have a few health benefits. So what's wrong with drinking to relax?

- ✔ Drinking can become a habit.
- ✔ You may need more and more to feel an effect.
- ✔ Drinking disrupts sleep.
- ✔ Alcohol has many calories.
- ✔ It impairs coordination.
- ✔ It can prevent you from dealing with your problem.

So if a glass of wine at dinner is all you need, don't worry too much if you are in good health. But if that glass becomes three or four, you probably have a problem.

Trying Too Hard

Extreme measures rarely work. Just like wishing without any effort to overcome anxiety doesn't work, trying *too* hard is likely to backfire. Why? Because stressing out about stress can stress you out. Think about it. If you absolutely *must* get rid of your anxiety, you become anxious about doing everything right.

After all, you've had your anxiety for a long time. It takes time to reduce it, and you'll never reach a point when anxiety goes away completely — unless you're dead or in a coma. Be realistic and patient. Make progress; don't expect perfection.

Sipping Herbal Drinks

Have you seen those fancy expensive teas? Some contain Kava Kava or other herbal anxiety remedies — and they cost twice as much as plain teas. They promise relief. Guess what? Most have such small amounts of herbs in them and are so diluted that the only anxiety relief you can expect may come from sitting still and enjoying a moment of quiet. If you want to use an herbal remedy, see Chapter 14 on what works and take herbs in a therapeutic dosage. Don't waste your money on teas with anxiety relief messages plastered on the label.

Taking Medication as a Sole Solution

Chapter 15 covers the medications used in the treatment of anxiety. In this chapter, it appears that we are saying that medications don't work. Well, not really. *Medications work extremely well for some people.* However, many people can't tolerate the side effects; others don't want to take medications. Some worry about the long-term effects of medication. Most importantly, medication doesn't teach people how to cope with their problems.

One class of medications, the benzodiazepines, has been found to interfere with the long-term benefits of exposure therapy. Although benzodiazepines are helpful in selected cases, they can be addictive.

On the other hand, don't get us wrong. Certain medications can provide much needed relief. Pills just aren't the magical cure that many hope for.

Chapter 21

Ten Ways to Deal with Relapse

· ·

· ·

*I*f you're reading this chapter, you've probably made some headway with your anxiety. Maybe, after all your hard work, you've experienced a setback, or perhaps you're worried about one. Not to worry. We have ten ideas for you to use when anxiety pops back.

Expecting Anxiety

Perhaps you've worked hard to overcome your anxiety. And now your hard work has paid off. You've beaten it. Congratulations! But alas, one day you wake up suddenly with anxiety staring you in the face. You turn it into a catastrophe and assume that you failed.

Oh, get real. You'll never totally annihilate anxiety. That is, until you stop breathing. It's bound to show up from time to time. Expect anxiety. Look for its early warning signs. But don't compound matters by getting anxious about your anxiety. If you understand that anxiety happens, you can lessen the impact.

Counting the Swallows

The proverb "One swallow doesn't make a summer" reflects the fact that a single sign doesn't necessarily indicate that something more is inevitable. Anxiety has an ebb and flow. Just because you have an anxious episode or two, doesn't mean that you're back to square one. You figured out how to handle some of your anxiety and that knowledge can still help you. You don't need to start all over again.

You do need to move forward and reapply what you practiced. Catastrophizing about minor setbacks will only increase your anxiety and immobilize your efforts. Regroup, reorganize, and go back at it!

Checking Out Why Anxiety Returned

Minor relapses are a great opportunity to discover what gives you trouble. Figure out what events preceded your latest bout of anxiety:

✔ Have you had some recent difficulties at work — deadlines, promotions, problems with coworkers, and so on?

✔ Have you had recent problems at home?

✔ Have you experienced some major life changes, such as marriage, divorce, the birth of a child, financial setbacks, or a loss of some sort?

If so, understand that an increase in your anxiety is a natural response to events and likely to be temporary. Use the new information about your anxiety triggers to challenge your anxious thinking as described in Chapter 5.

Seeing a Doctor

If you looked high and low for situations or events that may have set off your relapse and can't come up with anything at all, consider making an appointment with your primary care physician. Anxiety can have a number of physical causes:

✔ Prescription medication side effects

✔ Over-the-counter medication side effects

✔ Dietary supplement side effects

✔ Too much caffeine

✔ Physical disorders (see Chapter 2)

Don't try to diagnose yourself. If you experience anxiety with absolutely no discernable cause, please get a complete physical checkup.

Revisiting What Worked Before

If anxiety creeps back into your life, review the strategies that worked for you previously. Some of those techniques may need to become lifelong habits. Keep relaxation (see Chapters 12 and 13) in your life. Exercise on a regular basis (see Chapter 10). Make a long-term habit of writing down at least a few of your anxious thoughts and then challenge them (see Chapter 5). Look at your core beliefs every now and then and dispute them (see Chapter 6). Are you using too many worry words (see Chapter 7)?

Anxiety isn't a disease that you can cure with a one-time injection, pill, or surgery. Some anxiety is a natural part of life. When it mushrooms to a distressing degree, you merely need to reapply your strategies for managing it.

Doing Something Different

We've presented a plethora of strategies for overcoming anxiety. Most likely, you picked a few that felt compatible with your lifestyle. Now consider looking at some ideas you haven't yet attempted. We urge you to do something different. Take a look at the list that follows and choose one of them if you haven't gotten around to trying it yet:

- Rethinking your anxiety (see Chapters 5, 6, and 7)
- Facing fear head on (see Chapter 8)
- Relaxation strategies (see Chapter 12)
- Exercise (see Chapter 10)

And if you simply dabbled at one or more of these techniques, pursue it more aggressively and see if it works better that way. Anything that you haven't tried in this book should be something to consider.

Getting Support

You don't have to face anxiety relapses alone. Talking with others helps you deal with emotional distress. A great source of such support can be found in your local newspaper. Most city newspapers list support groups for just about everything: various health concerns, emotional problems, relational problems, and of course, anxiety.

But what if you live in Pie Town, New Mexico: population 55? Pie Town may not have an anxiety support group. But all is not lost. You can go to an Internet search engine, such as Google (www.google.com) and enter "chat rooms for anxiety." You'll find more than enough interesting sources of support. Try a few out and see if you can find a group that feels compatible. Millions of people suffer from anxiety, and they have great advice and support to offer you. You don't need to suffer alone.

Considering Booster Sessions

If you've seen a professional and later experienced an unexpected increase in your anxiety, think about calling for a few booster sessions. Your therapist isn't going to think you failed. Usually, a second round of therapy helps and doesn't take as long as the first. In addition, some people like to check in every few weeks or months as a kind of prevention. Again, anxiety isn't a disease with a single, one-shot cure.

On the other hand, if you have never seen a professional, and you experience a relapse, you should consider it now. If you've had previous success on your own, you're likely to improve rapidly with a little assistance.

Looking at the Stages of Change

Any kind of change involves a series of steps or stages. These stages don't necessarily occur in a straight, linear fashion. As discussed in greater detail in Chapter 2, these stages include

- **Pre-contemplation:** Not even thinking about change. Obviously, you're not in this stage if you're reading this book.

- **Contemplation:** Thinking about change but not ready to do something about it.

- **Preparation:** Making plans to do something about your problem.

- **Action:** Meeting the problem head-on.

- **Maintenance:** Continued efforts to deal with your problem.

- **Termination:** Only a lucky few reach this point; you no longer even have to think about your problem anymore.

Relapse can occur during any of these stages. For example, you may move back from action to contemplation or even pre-contemplation. Just remember, it's normal. When you step back for a while, it doesn't mean that you can't gather the resources to make another run at the problem. Most who succeed have tried a number of times before they get there.

Accepting Anxiety

With this tip, we've come full circle — back to the top of the list: Anxiety happens. It will return. Welcome it with open arms. It means that you're still alive! Appreciate the positive aspects. Anxiety tells you to pay attention to what's going on around you. Go with the flow.

We're not suggesting that you need to feel horrendous amounts of anxiety. But a little anxiety is unavoidable. And anxiety, when not overwhelming, may help mobilize your resources during difficult challenges.

Chapter 22

Ten Signs That You Need Professional Help

● ●

In This Chapter

▶ Contemplating suicide

▶ Slogging through work troubles

▶ Saying "No" to excessive drug and alcohol use

● ●

Some people find that self-help is all they need. They read about good ways of dealing with their anxiety, and then they apply what they've discovered. Voila! Their anxiety gradually fades to a manageable level.

However, no self-help book is intended to completely replace professional help. And anxiety sometimes requires the assistance of a professional, just like complicated tax matters may call for a certified public accountant or deciding to draw up a will may send you to an attorney. We hope you understand that seeking a mental health professional's assistance is a reasonable choice, not a sign of weakness.

This chapter tells you how to know if you should consider professional assistance for yourself or someone you care about. It's not always an obvious decision, so we give you a list of indicators. And if you still aren't sure, you can always talk with your primary care doctor, who should be able to help you decide.

Having Suicidal Thoughts or Plans

If you find yourself thinking about harming yourself, get help now. Take these thoughts very seriously. Call the national suicide hotline at: **1-800-SUICIDE** (1-800-784-2433). Or call a friend. If your thoughts become overwhelming, call 911 and get to an emergency room. Help is available. And when you do access professional help, be honest about your thoughts; hold nothing back.

Feeling Hopeless

From time to time, everyone feels defeated. But if you begin to feel hopeless about getting better, thinking that the future looks bleak and you can't do much to change it, get professional help. Feelings of hopelessness put you at greater risk for suicide. But you need to know that you *can* feel better. Let others help you.

Handling Anxiety and Depression

You may be experiencing depression mixed with anxiety if you find yourself having some of the following symptoms:

- Feeling sad most of the day
- Losing interest or pleasure in activities
- Change in weight
- Changes in your sleep patterns and habits
- Feeling keyed up or slowed down
- Feeling worthless
- Feeling excessively guilty
- Poor concentration
- Thoughts of death

If you do have anxiety and depression, seek professional help. Depression is a treatable condition. Having the energy to fight both can be hard.

Trying and trying and trying

So you read the book and given your best shot at overcoming anxiety, but for whatever reason, it just hasn't work. That's okay. Don't get more anxious because you didn't get rid of worry and stress. Something else may be going on. Get an experienced mental health professional to help you figure out the next step.

Struggling at Home

You're anxious. The anxiety causes you to be irritable, jumpy, and upset. You hold it together at work and with strangers, but you take it out on the people you care about most, your family. Then you feel guilty, which increases your anxiety. If this sounds like you, a professional may help you decrease the tension at home and ease the pathway to finding peace.

Dealing with Major Problems at Work

Maybe you have no one at home to take your anxiety out on, or home is the haven away from stress. If that's the case, work stress may overwhelm you. If you find your anxiety exploding at work, consider professional help.

First, anxiety sometimes causes irritability and moodiness with co-workers or bosses; such behavior can cause plenty of trouble. Anxiety can also rob you of your short-term memory, make it difficult to focus, or to make decisions. So if anxiety affects your job performance, get help before you hit the unemployment line.

Suffering from Severe Obsessions or Compulsions

Obsessive Compulsive Disorder (OCD) can be serious. See Chapter 2 for more information about OCD. The problem is that people with the disorder often don't seek help until their lives are taken over by unwanted thoughts or repetitive actions. Most people with OCD need professional help. If you or someone you love has more than mild OCD, get professional help.

Understanding Post-Traumatic Stress Disorder

You feel agitated and keyed up. Were you also exposed to a traumatic event, in which

> ✔ You felt helpless and afraid?
>
> ✔ You try not to think about it?
>
> ✔ In spite of your efforts not to think about it, the thoughts and images keep on popping up?

If so, you may have *Post-Traumatic Stress Disorder* (PTSD). See Chapter 2 for a complete description of PTSD. The treatment of PTSD is probably best done by an experienced professional. Many people with PTSD try to tough it out and live life less fully because of their stubbornness.

Going through Sleepless Nights

Is anxiety keeping you awake? That's quite common. If after working on your anxiety awhile, your sleep doesn't improve, be sure to read Chapter 11 about sleep. Too many sleepless nights make it hard to function and make it more difficult to help yourself in the fight against anxiety. If you sleep poorly night after night and awaken tired, check it out with a professional. You may be experiencing depression along with anxiety.

Getting High

Sure, a beer or three can sooth a soul, but excessive drinking or drug abuse is a common problem among those with anxiety disorders. It makes sense; anxious feelings are uncomfortable. What begins as an innocent attempt at feeling better can become another big problem later on. If you find yourself using too much alcohol or another drug to calm your feelings, get professional help before the crutch turns into an addiction.

Finding Help

In the days of managed care, you may not always have as much freedom to consult any professional you want. However, whether you receive a restricted list of professionals from your insurance company or not, it's still a good idea to check out one or more of the following:

> ✔ Ask the insurance company or the state licensing board for the specific profession or license of the referred professional.
>
> ✔ Ask your friends if they know of someone that they had a good experience with.

✔ Ask your primary care doctor. Family physicians usually have a good idea about excellent referrals for various types of problems.

✔ Talk to the professional before making an appointment. Ask about experience with treating anxiety and what approach he takes. Ask about whether you will receive a scientifically verified approach for dealing with anxiety.

✔ Call the psychology department of your local college or university. Sometimes they have referral lists.

✔ Call your state psychological, psychiatric, or counseling association. Or check out national consumer organizations. (See the Appendix in the back of this book for more information.)

Resources for You

∙ ∙

*I*n this Appendix, we provide some additional sources for finding out about and overcoming anxiety as well as other emotional difficulties. These are only a few of the many excellent resources to supplement the information in this book.

Self-Help Books

Antony, Martin & Swinson, Richard. *The Shyness and Social Anxiety Workbook: Proven Techniques for Overcoming Your Fears.* Oakland: New Harbinger Publications, Inc., 2000.

Beckfield, Denise. *Master Your Panic and Take Back Your Life!* Atascadero: Impact Publishers, 2000.

Bien, Thomas & Bien, Beverly. *Mindful Recovery: A Spiritual Path to Healing from Addiction.* New York: John Wiley & Sons, Inc., 2002.

Bourne, Edmund. *The Anxiety and Phobia Workbook.* Oakland: New Harbinger Publications, Inc., 2000.

Burns, David. *The Feeling Good Handbook: Using the New Mood Therapy in Everyday Life.* New York: David Morrow and Company, Inc., 1989.

Carmin, Cheryl; Pollard, Alec; Flynn, Teresa; & Markway, Barbara. *Dying of Embarrassment: Help for Social Anxiety and Phobia.* Oakland: New Harbinger Publications, Inc., 1992.

Craske, Michelle; Barlow, David; & O'Leary, Tracy. *Mastery of Your Anxiety and Worry.* San Antonio: The Psychological Corporation, 1992.

Davis, Martha; Eshelman, Elizabeth; & McKay, Matthew. *The Relaxation and Stress Reduction Workbook.* New York: MJF Books, 1995.

Elliott, Charles & Lassen, Maureen. *Why Can't I Get What I Want? How to Stop Making the Same Old Mistakes and Start Living a Life You Can Love.* Palo Alto: Davies-Black Publishing, 1998.

Ellis, Albert. *Feeling Better, Getting Better, Staying Better: Profound Self-Help Therapy for Your Emotions.* Atascadero: Impact Publishers, 2001.

Greenberger, Dennis & Padesky, Christine. *Mind Over Mood: Change How You Feel by Changing How You Think.* New York: The Guildford Press, 1995.

Kabat-Zinn, Jon. *Full Catastrophe Living: Using the Wisdom of Your Body and Mind to Face Stress, Pain, and Illness.* New York: Bantam Doubleday Dell Publishing Group, Inc., 1990.

Luciani, Joseph. *Self-Coaching: How to Heal Anxiety and Depression.* New York: John Wiley & Sons, 2001.

Prochaska, James; Norcross, John; & DiClemente, Carlo. *Changing For Good: The Revolutionary Program that Explains the Six Stages of Change and Teaches you How to Free Yourself From Bad Habits.* New York: William Morrow & Co., Inc., 1994.

Walker, Eugene. *Learn to Relax: Proven Techniques for Reducing Stress, Tension, and Anxiety — and Promoting Peak Performance.* New York: John Wiley & Sons, Inc., 2000.

Resources to Help Children

Chansky, Tamar. *Freeing Your Child From Obsessive-Compulsive Disorder: A Powerful, Practical Program for Parents of Children and Adolescents.* New York: Three Rivers Press, The Crown Publishing Group, 2001.

Clark, Lynn. *SOS Help for Parents.* Bowling Green: Parents' Press, 1996.

Elliott, Charles & Smith, Laura. *Why Can't I Be the Parent I Want to Be? End Old Patterns and Enjoy Your Children.* Oakland: New Harbinger Publications, Inc., 1999.

Manassis, Katharina. *Keys to Parenting Your Anxious Child.* Hauppauge: Barrans Educational Series, 1996.

Rapee, Ronald (Ed.); Spence, Sue; Cobham, Vannessa; & Wignall, Ann. *Helping Your Anxious Child: A Step-By-Step Guide for Parents.* Oakland: New Harbinger Publications, Inc., 2000.

Schaefer, Charles. *Cats Got Your Tongue? A Story for Children Afraid to Speak.* Washington, D.C.: Magination, American Psychological Association, 1992.

Smith, Laura & Elliott, Charles. *Hollow Kids: Recapturing the Soul of a Generation Lost to the Self-Esteem Myth.* Roseville: Prima Publishing Division of Random House, 2001.

Accessing Web Sites to Discover More About Anxiety

Type the word *anxiety* into a search engine, and literally, thousands of sites pop up. Be careful. The Web is full of unscrupulous sales pitches and misinformation. Be especially cautious about official sounding organizations that promote materials for sale. Don't be fooled by instant cures for anxiety.

Many Web forums host chat rooms for persons with anxiety concerns. Feel free to access them for support. At the same time, realize that you don't know who's sitting on the other end. They may be uneducated about anxiety or, worse, trying to take advantage of a person in distress. Don't believe everything you read.

Here's a list of a variety of legitimate Web sites that don't sell snake oil:

- **The Anxiety Disorders Association of America** Web site (www.adaa.org) lists self-help groups across the United States. They also display a variety of anxiety screening tools for self-assessment. On their site you can find an online newsletter and a message board.

- **Freedom from Fear** (www.freedomfromfear.org) provides screening tools, a message board, and information about anxiety disorders. It also lists professionals who treat anxiety across the United States.

- **WebMD** (www.webmd.com) provides a vast array of information about both physical and mental health issues, including information about psychological treatments, drug therapy, and prevention.

- **The National Alliance for the Mentally Ill** (www.nami.org) is a wonderful organization that serves as an advocate for persons and families affected by mental disorders. Information is available about causes, prevalence, and treatments of disorders of children and adults.

- **The National Institute for Mental Health** (www.nimh.nih.gov) reports on research about a wide variety of mental health issues. They also have an array of educational materials on anxiety. They provide resources for researchers and practitioners in the field.

✔ The **Anxiety Self Help** Web site (www.anxietyselfhelp.com) not only gives basic information about anxiety disorders, but it also has a chat room where people with anxiety concerns can share their stories.

✔ **The American Psychological Association** (www.apa.org/pubinfo) provides information to the public about treatment and interesting facts about anxiety and other emotional disorders.

✔ **The American Psychiatric Association** (www.psych.org/public_info) also has information for the public about anxiety and other mental disorders.

✔ **The Obsessive-Compulsive Foundation** (www.ocfoundation.org) has an annual conference and provides considerable information about the assessment and treatment of Obsessive-Compulsive Disorder. It also has a message board and provides an opportunity to ask experts questions.

✔ **The National Association of School Psychologists** (www.nasponline.org) maintains a site with information or "fact sheets" for parents and teachers.

Index

• *B* •

• F •

• G •

• *Q* •

• *T* •

• **Z** •

Notes

Notes

Notes

Notes

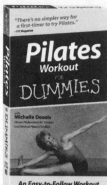

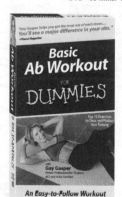

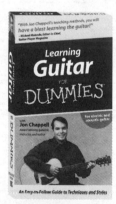

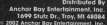

FOR

DUMMIES®

The easy way to get more done and have more fun

PERSONAL FINANCE & BUSINESS

0-7645-2431-3

0-7645-5331-3

0-7645-5307-0

Also available:

Accounting For Dummies
(0-7645-5314-3)

Business Plans Kit For Dummies
(0-7645-5365-8)

Managing For Dummies
(1-5688-4858-7)

Mutual Funds For Dummies
(0-7645-5329-1)

QuickBooks All-in-One Desk Reference For Dummies
(0-7645-1963-8)

Resumes For Dummies
(0-7645-5471-9)

Small Business Kit For Dummies
(0-7645-5093-4)

Starting an eBay Business For Dummies
(0-7645-1547-0)

Taxes For Dummies 2003
(0-7645-5475-1)

HOME, GARDEN, FOOD & WINE

0-7645-5295-3

0-7645-5130-2

0-7645-5250-3

Also available:

Bartending For Dummies
(0-7645-5051-9)

Christmas Cooking For Dummies
(0-7645-5407-7)

Cookies For Dummies
(0-7645-5390-9)

Diabetes Cookbook For Dummies
(0-7645-5230-9)

Grilling For Dummies
(0-7645-5076-4)

Home Maintenance For Dummies
(0-7645-5215-5)

Slow Cookers For Dummies
(0-7645-5240-6)

Wine For Dummies
(0-7645-5114-0)

FITNESS, SPORTS, HOBBIES & PETS

0-7645-5167-1

0-7645-5146-9

0-7645-5106-X

Also available:

Cats For Dummies
(0-7645-5275-9)

Chess For Dummies
(0-7645-5003-9)

Dog Training For Dummies
(0-7645-5286-4)

Labrador Retrievers For Dummies
(0-7645-5281-3)

Martial Arts For Dummies
(0-7645-5358-5)

Piano For Dummies
(0-7645-5105-1)

Pilates For Dummies
(0-7645-5397-6)

Power Yoga For Dummies
(0-7645-5342-9)

Puppies For Dummies
(0-7645-5255-4)

Quilting For Dummies
(0-7645-5118-3)

Rock Guitar For Dummies
(0-7645-5356-9)

Weight Training For Dummies
(0-7645-5168-X)

Available wherever books are sold.
Go to www.dummies.com or call 1-877-762-2974 to order direct

FOR DUMMIES®

A world of resources to help you grow

TRAVEL

0-7645-5453-0

0-7645-5438-7

Walt Disney World & Orlando

0-7645-5444-1

EDUCATION & TEST PREPARATION

0-7645-5194-9

0-7645-5325-9

0-7645-5249-X

HEALTH, SELF-HELP & SPIRITUALITY

0-7645-5154-X

0-7645-5302-X

0-7645-5418-2

FOR DUMMIES®

Helping you expand your horizons and realize your potential

GRAPHICS & WEB SITE DEVELOPMENT

0-7645-1651-5

0-7645-1643-4

0-7645-0895-4

Also available:

Adobe Acrobat 5 PDF For Dummies
(0-7645-1652-3)

ASP.NET For Dummies
(0-7645-0866-0)

ColdFusion MX for Dummies
(0-7645-1672-8)

Dreamweaver MX For Dummies
(0-7645-1630-2)

FrontPage 2002 For Dummies
(0-7645-0821-0)

HTML 4 For Dummies
(0-7645-0723-0)

Illustrator 10 For Dummies
(0-7645-3636-2)

PowerPoint 2002 For Dummies
(0-7645-0817-2)

Web Design For Dummies
(0-7645-0823-7)

PROGRAMMING & DATABASES

0-7645-0746-X

0-7645-1626-4

0-7645-1657-4

Also available:

Access 2002 For Dummies
(0-7645-0818-0)

Beginning Programming For Dummies
(0-7645-0835-0)

Crystal Reports 9 For Dummies
(0-7645-1641-8)

Java & XML For Dummies
(0-7645-1658-2)

Java 2 For Dummies
(0-7645-0765-6)

JavaScript For Dummies
(0-7645-0633-1

Oracle9i For Dummies
(0-7645-0880-6)

Perl For Dummies
(0-7645-0776-1)

PHP and MySQL For Dummies
(0-7645-1650-7)

SQL For Dummies
(0-7645-0737-0)

Visual Basic .NET For Dummies
(0-7645-0867-9)

LINUX, NETWORKING & CERTIFICATION

0-7645-1545-4

0-7645-1760-0

0-7645-0772-9

Also available:

A+ Certification For Dummies
(0-7645-0812-1)

CCNP All-in-One Certification For Dummies
(0-7645-1648-5)

Cisco Networking For Dummies
(0-7645-1668-X)

CISSP For Dummies
(0-7645-1670-1)

CIW Foundations For Dummies
(0-7645-1635-3)

Firewalls For Dummies
(0-7645-0884-9)

Home Networking For Dummies
(0-7645-0857-1)

Red Hat Linux All-in-One Desk Reference For Dummies
(0-7645-2442-9)

UNIX For Dummies
(0-7645-0419-3)

Available wherever books are sold.
Go to www.dummies.com or call 1-877-762-2974 to order direct

WILEY